SHE COULD FLY ™

Volume Two

AN IMPRINT OF
DARK HORSE COMICS

SHE COULD FLY

writer
Christopher Cantwell

artist
Martín Morazzo

Volume Two

THE
LOST
PILOT

colorist
Miroslav Mrva

letterer
Clem Robins

To E, C, and L:
my friends on the Moon
— Christopher Cantwell

To Nico and Pupin,
I miss you both every day.
— Martín Morazzo

Karen Berger
Editor

Richard Bruning
Logo/Book Designer

Rachel Boyadjis
Assistant Editor

Adam Pruett
Digital Art Technician

Mike Richardson
Publisher

First Edition: December 2019
ISBN 978-1-50671-276-5
Digital ISBN 978-1-50671-293-2
Printed in China
10 9 8 7 6 5 4 3 2 1

Published by
Dark Horse Books
A division of
Dark Horse Comics LLC
10956 SE Main Street
Milwaukie, OR 97222

DarkHorse.com
ComicShopLocator.com

SHE COULD FLY Volume Two: The Lost Pilot.

This volume collects issues #1–#5 of SHE COULD FLY: The Lost Pilot.

Library of Congress Cataloging-in-Publication Data
Names: Cantwell, Christopher, writer. | Morazzo, Martin, artist. | Mrva, Miroslav, colourist. | Robins, Clem, 1955- letterer.
Title: The lost pilot / written by Christopher Cantwell ; art by Martin Morazzo ; colored by Miroslav Mrva ; lettered by Clem Robins.
Description: First edition. | Milwaukie, OR : Dark Horse Books/Berger Books, 2019. | Series: She could fly ; Volume two | "This volume collects Issues #1-5 of She Could Fly Volume Two: The Lost Pilot."
Identifiers: LCCN 2019019718 | ISBN 9781506712765 (paperback)
Subjects: LCSH: Comic books, strips, etc. | BISAC: COMICS & GRAPHIC NOVELS / Science Fiction. | COMICS & GRAPHIC NOVELS / Literary.
Classification: LCC PN6728.S464 C36 2019 | DDC 741.5/973--dc23
LC record available at https://lccn.loc.gov/2019019718

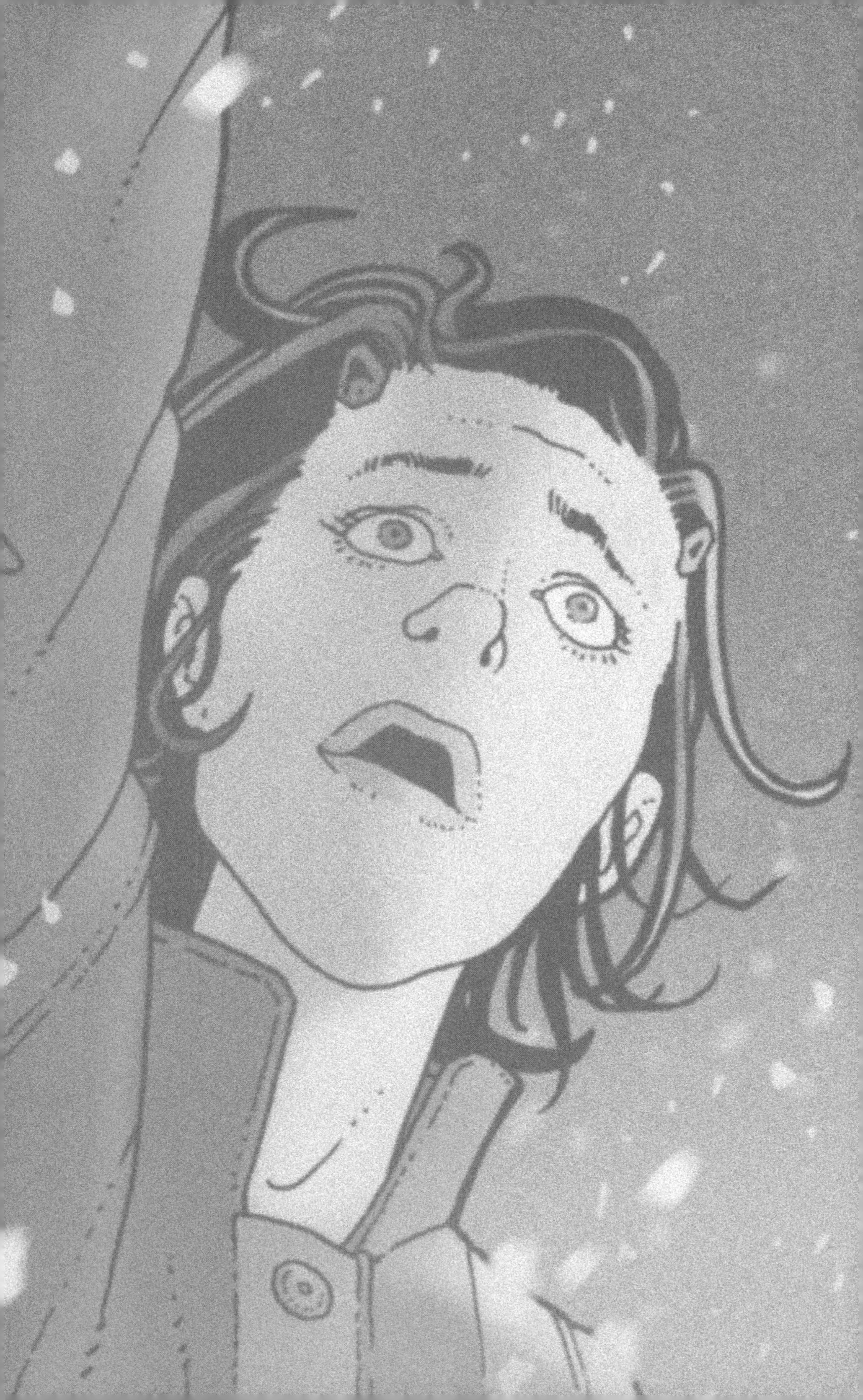

CHAPTER I
"Apple Dumpling"

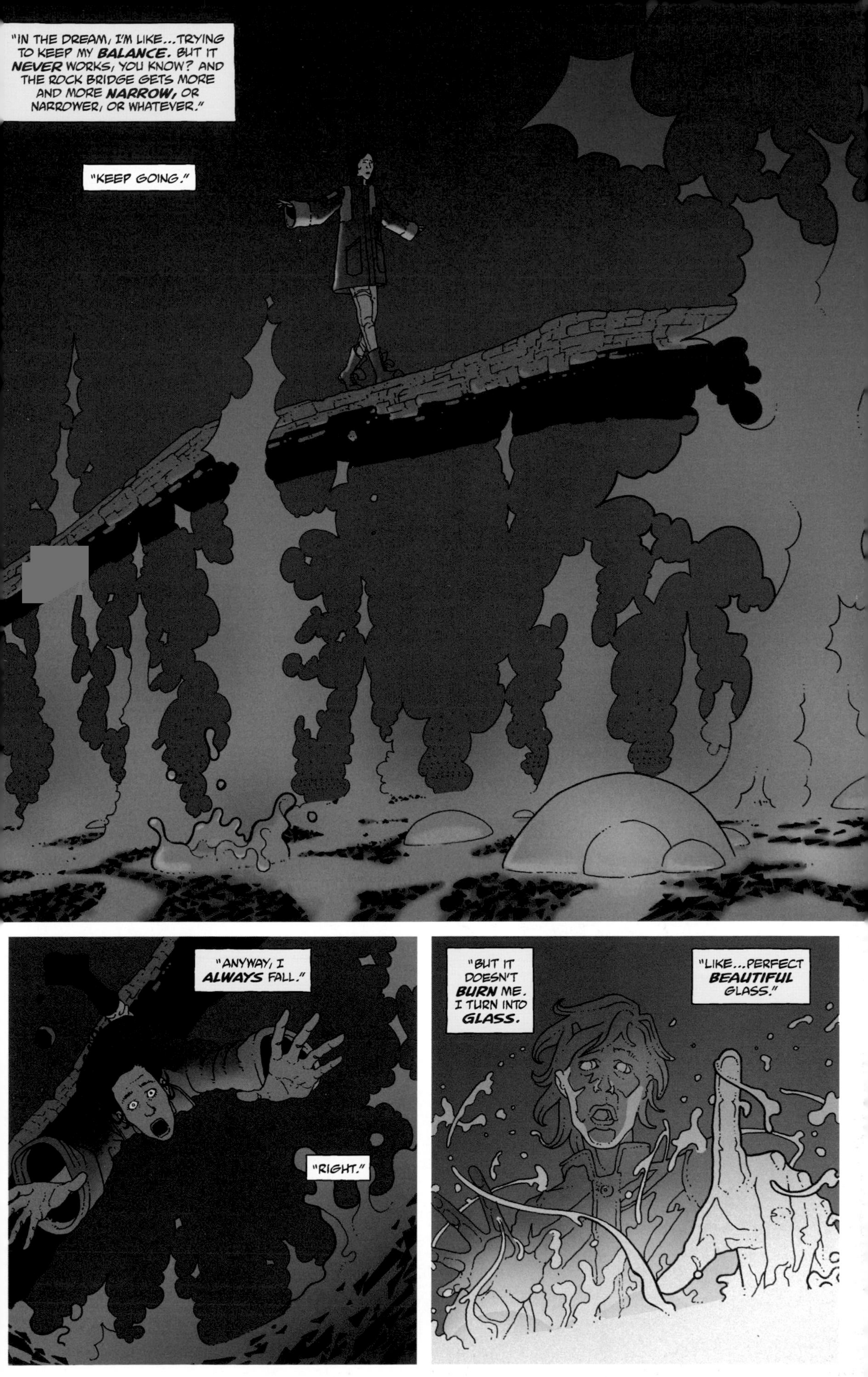
"IN THE DREAM, I'M LIKE...TRYING TO KEEP MY BALANCE. BUT IT NEVER WORKS, YOU KNOW? AND THE ROCK BRIDGE GETS MORE AND MORE NARROW, OR NARROWER, OR WHATEVER."
"KEEP GOING."
"ANYWAY, I ALWAYS FALL."
"RIGHT."
"BUT IT DOESN'T BURN ME. I TURN INTO GLASS.
"LIKE...PERFECT BEAUTIFUL GLASS."

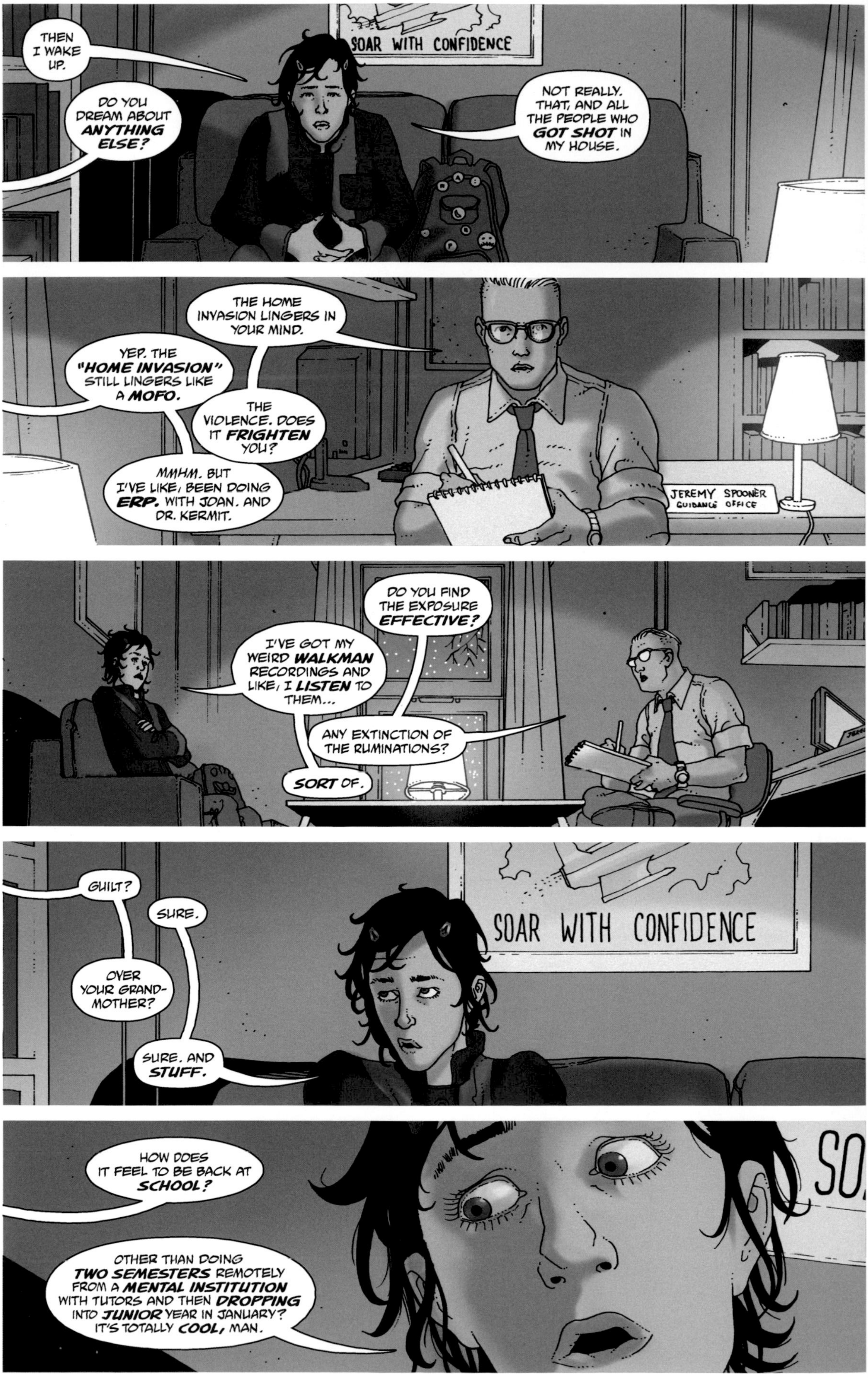
SOAR WITH CONFIDENCE
THEN I WAKE UP.
DO YOU DREAM ABOUT ANYTHING ELSE?
NOT REALLY. THAT, AND ALL THE PEOPLE WHO GOT SHOT IN MY HOUSE.
THE HOME INVASION LINGERS IN YOUR MIND.
YEP. THE "HOME INVASION" STILL LINGERS LIKE A MOFO.
THE VIOLENCE. DOES IT FRIGHTEN YOU?
MMHM. BUT I'VE LIKE, BEEN DOING ERP. WITH JOAN. AND DR. KERMIT.
JEREMY SPOONER
GUIDANCE OFFICE
DO YOU FIND THE EXPOSURE EFFECTIVE?
I'VE GOT MY WEIRD WALKMAN RECORDINGS AND LIKE, I LISTEN TO THEM...
ANY EXTINCTION OF THE RUMINATIONS?
SORT OF.
SOAR WITH CONFIDENCE
GUILT?
SURE.
OVER YOUR GRAND-MOTHER?
SURE. AND STUFF.
HOW DOES IT FEEL TO BE BACK AT SCHOOL?
OTHER THAN DOING TWO SEMESTERS REMOTELY FROM A MENTAL INSTITUTION WITH TUTORS AND THEN DROPPING INTO JUNIOR YEAR IN JANUARY? IT'S TOTALLY COOL, MAN.

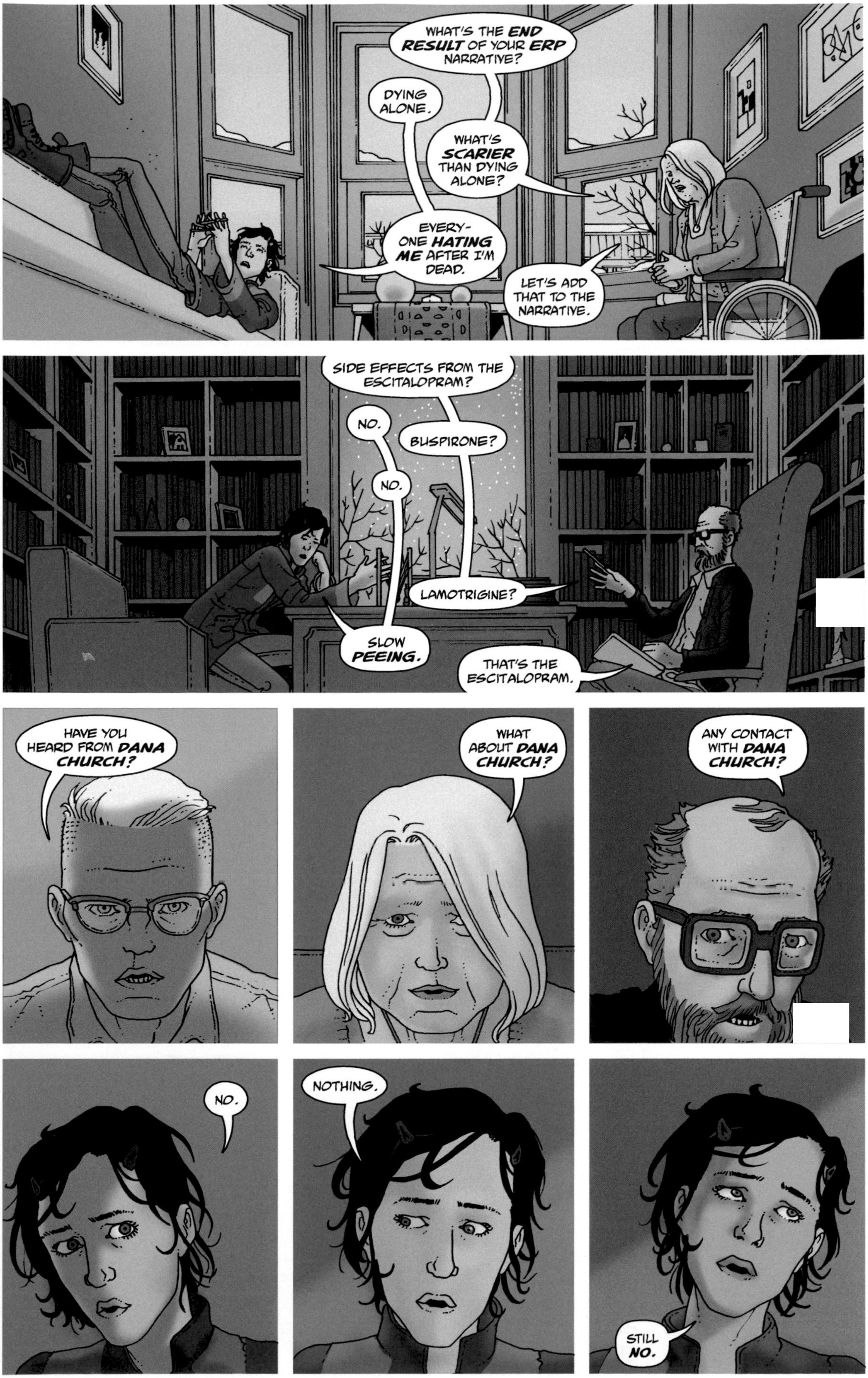
WHAT'S THE END RESULT OF YOUR ERP NARRATIVE?
DYING ALONE.
WHAT'S SCARIER THAN DYING ALONE?
EVERY-ONE HATING ME AFTER I'M DEAD.
LET'S ADD THAT TO THE NARRATIVE.
SIDE EFFECTS FROM THE ESCITALOPRAM?
NO.
BUSPIRONE?
NO.
LAMOTRIGINE?
SLOW PEEING.
THAT'S THE ESCITALOPRAM.
HAVE YOU HEARD FROM DANA CHURCH?
WHAT ABOUT DANA CHURCH?
ANY CONTACT WITH DANA CHURCH?
NO.
NOTHING.
STILL NO.

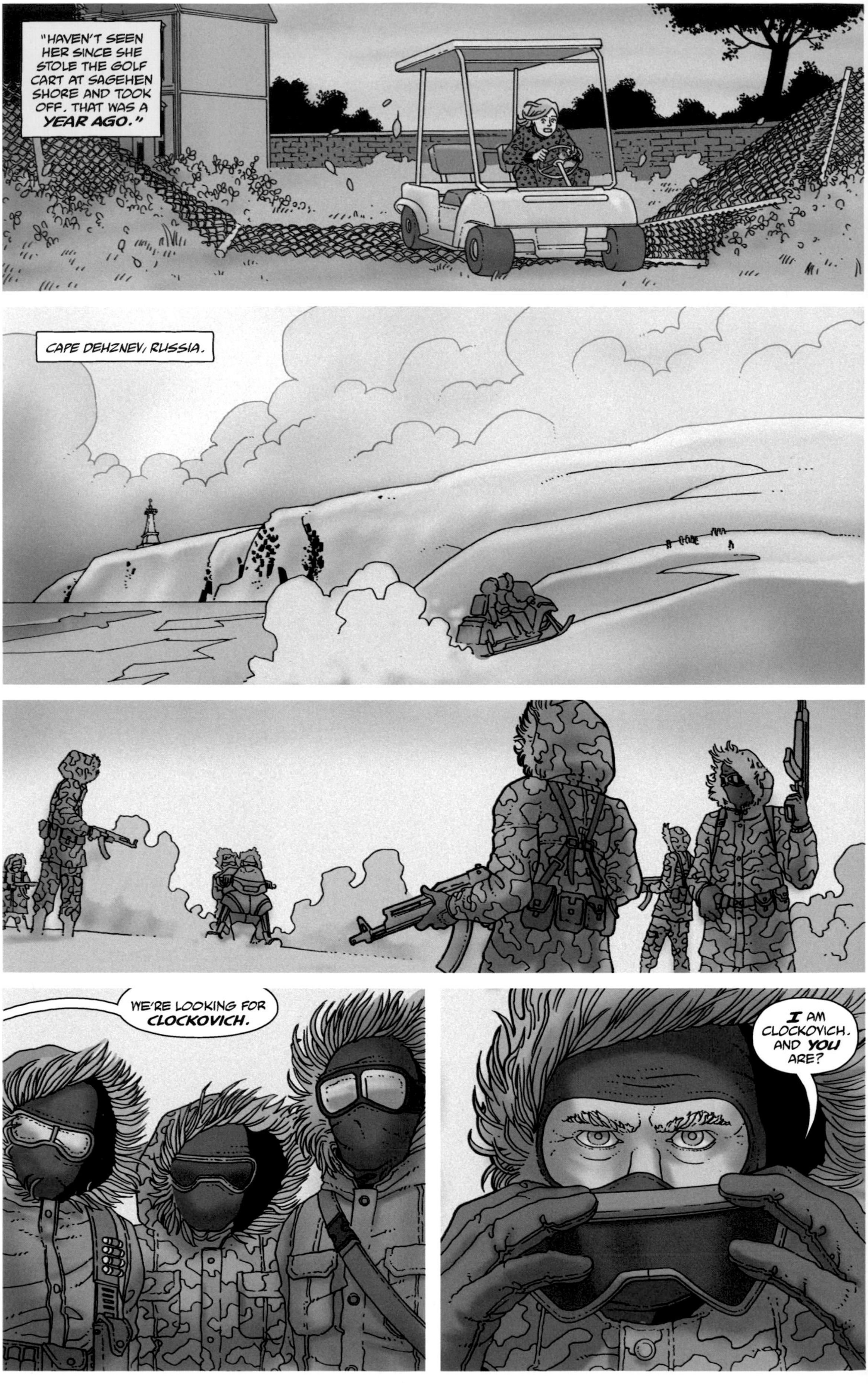
"HAVEN'T SEEN HER SINCE SHE STOLE THE GOLF CART AT SAGEHEN SHORE AND TOOK OFF. THAT WAS A **YEAR AGO.**"
CAPE DEHZNEV, RUSSIA.
WE'RE LOOKING FOR **CLOCKOVICH.**
I AM CLOCKOVICH. AND **YOU** ARE?

DR. NATHAN WONDERBUCK, CALTECH UNIVERSITY.

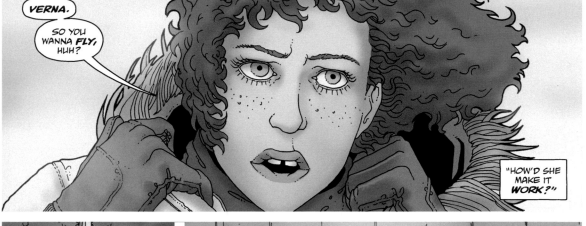

VERNA.

SO YOU WANNA *FLY,* HUH?

"HOW'D SHE MAKE IT *WORK?*"

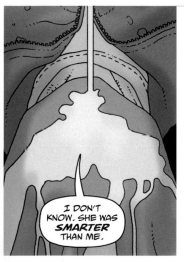

I DON'T KNOW. SHE WAS *SMARTER* THAN ME.

WHO WAS SHE?

GIVE US A *NAME.*

I DON'T *ACK!* KNOW HER *ACK!* NAME...

HOW LONG YOU GOING TO KEEP *LYING* TO US, BILL?

...FOREVER, DICKHEADS.

"THEY LET ME SHELVE BOOKS IN THE LIBRARY."

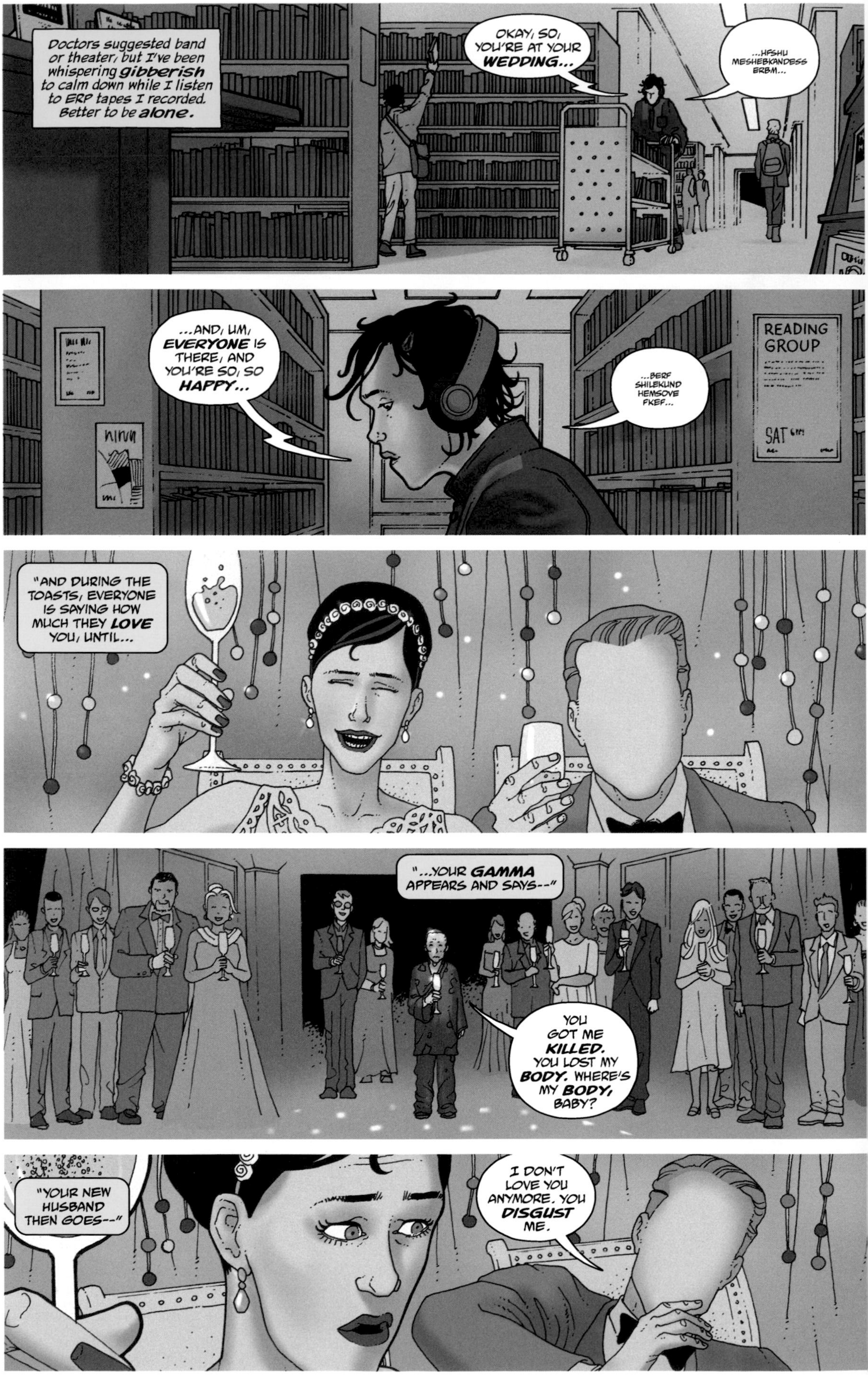
Doctors suggested band or theater, but I've been whispering **gibberish** to calm down while I listen to ERP tapes I recorded. Better to be **alone.**
OKAY, SO, YOU'RE AT YOUR **WEDDING...**
...HFSHU MESHEBKANDESS ERBM...
...AND, UM, **EVERYONE** IS THERE, AND YOU'RE SO, SO **HAPPY...**
...BERF SHILEKUND HEMSOVE FKEF...
READING GROUP
SAT
"AND DURING THE TOASTS, EVERYONE IS SAYING HOW MUCH THEY **LOVE** YOU, UNTIL...
"...YOUR **GAMMA** APPEARS AND SAYS--"
YOU GOT ME **KILLED.** YOU LOST MY **BODY.** WHERE'S MY **BODY,** BABY?
"YOUR NEW HUSBAND THEN GOES--"
I DON'T LOVE YOU ANYMORE. YOU **DISGUST** ME.

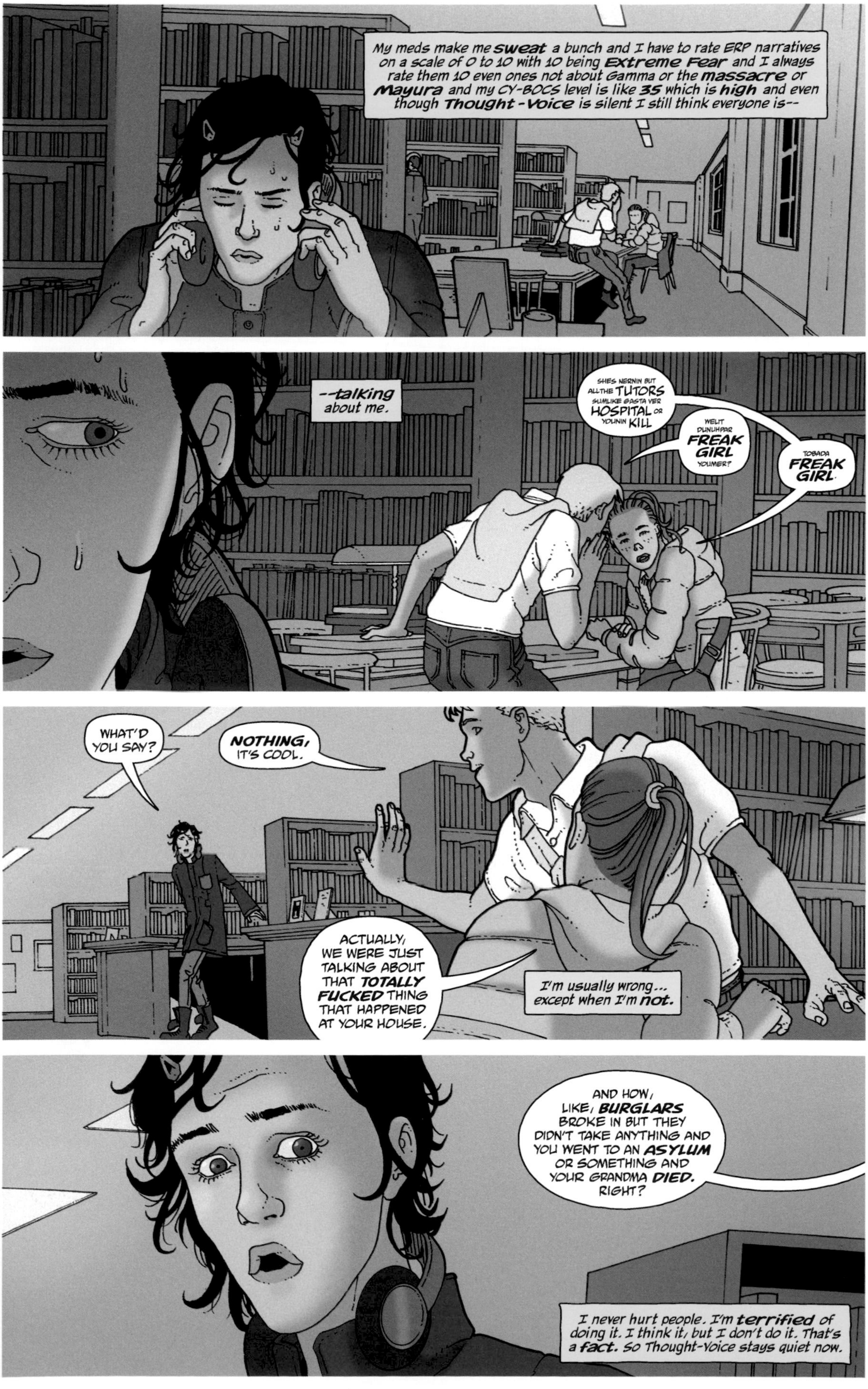
My meds make me sweat a bunch and I have to rate ERP narratives on a scale of 0 to 10 with 10 being Extreme Fear and I always rate them 10 even ones not about Gamma or the massacre or Mayura and my CY-BOCS level is like 35 which is high and even though Thought-Voice is silent I still think everyone is--
--talking about me.
SHES NERNIN BUT ALL THE TUTORS SUMLIKE GASTA VER HOSPITAL OR YOUNIN KILL
WELIT DUNUHPAR FREAK GIRL YOUMER?
TOBADA FREAK GIRL.
WHAT'D YOU SAY?
NOTHING, IT'S COOL.
ACTUALLY, WE WERE JUST TALKING ABOUT THAT TOTALLY FUCKED THING THAT HAPPENED AT YOUR HOUSE.
I'm usually wrong... except when I'm not.
AND HOW, LIKE, BURGLARS BROKE IN BUT THEY DIDN'T TAKE ANYTHING AND YOU WENT TO AN ASYLUM OR SOMETHING AND YOUR GRANDMA DIED. RIGHT?
I never hurt people. I'm terrified of doing it. I think it, but I don't do it. That's a fact. So Thought-Voice stays quiet now.

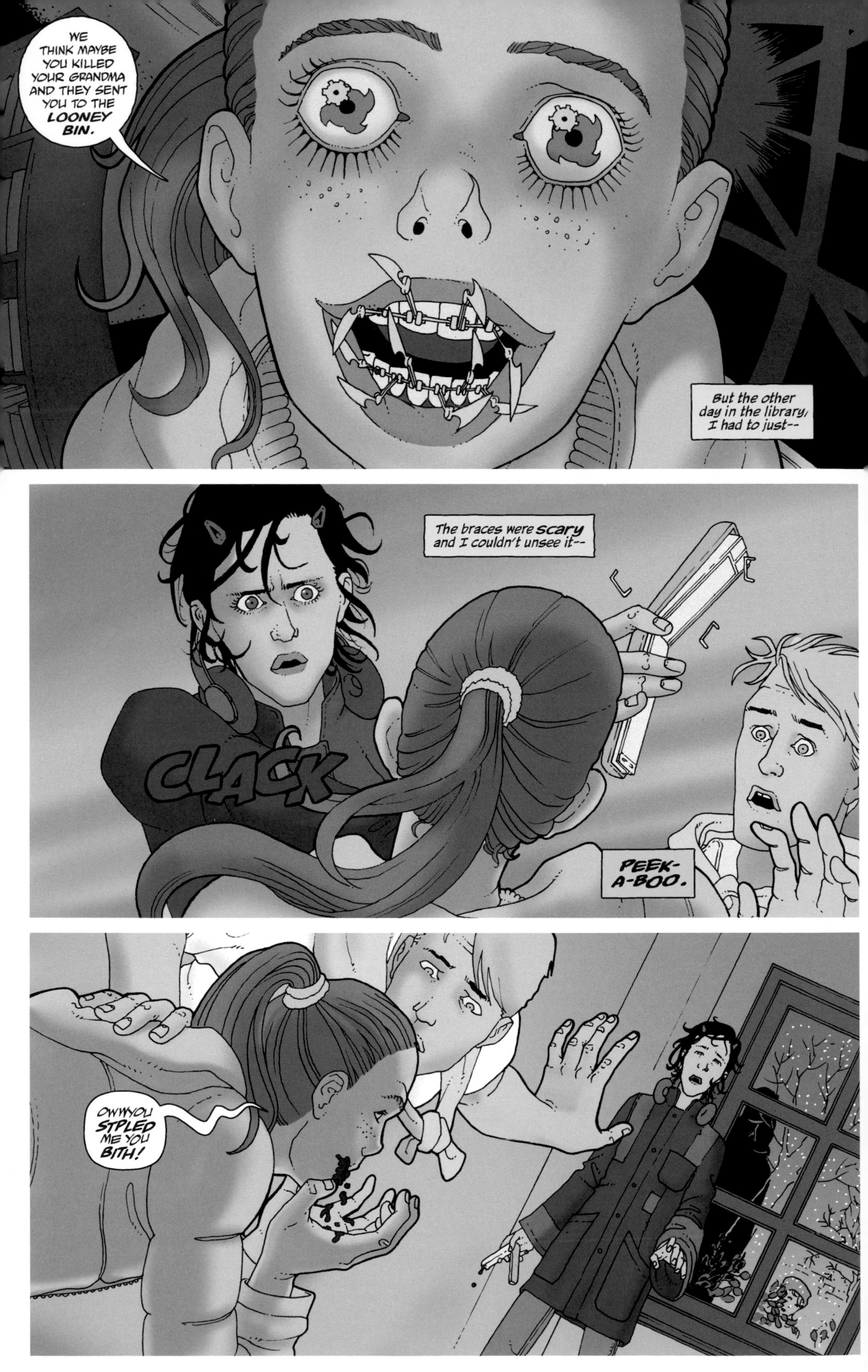
WE THINK MAYBE YOU KILLED YOUR GRANDMA AND THEY SENT YOU TO THE LOONEY BIN.
But the other day in the library, I had to just--
The braces were scary and I couldn't unsee it--
CLACK
PEEK-A-BOO.
OWWYOU STPLED ME YOU BITH!

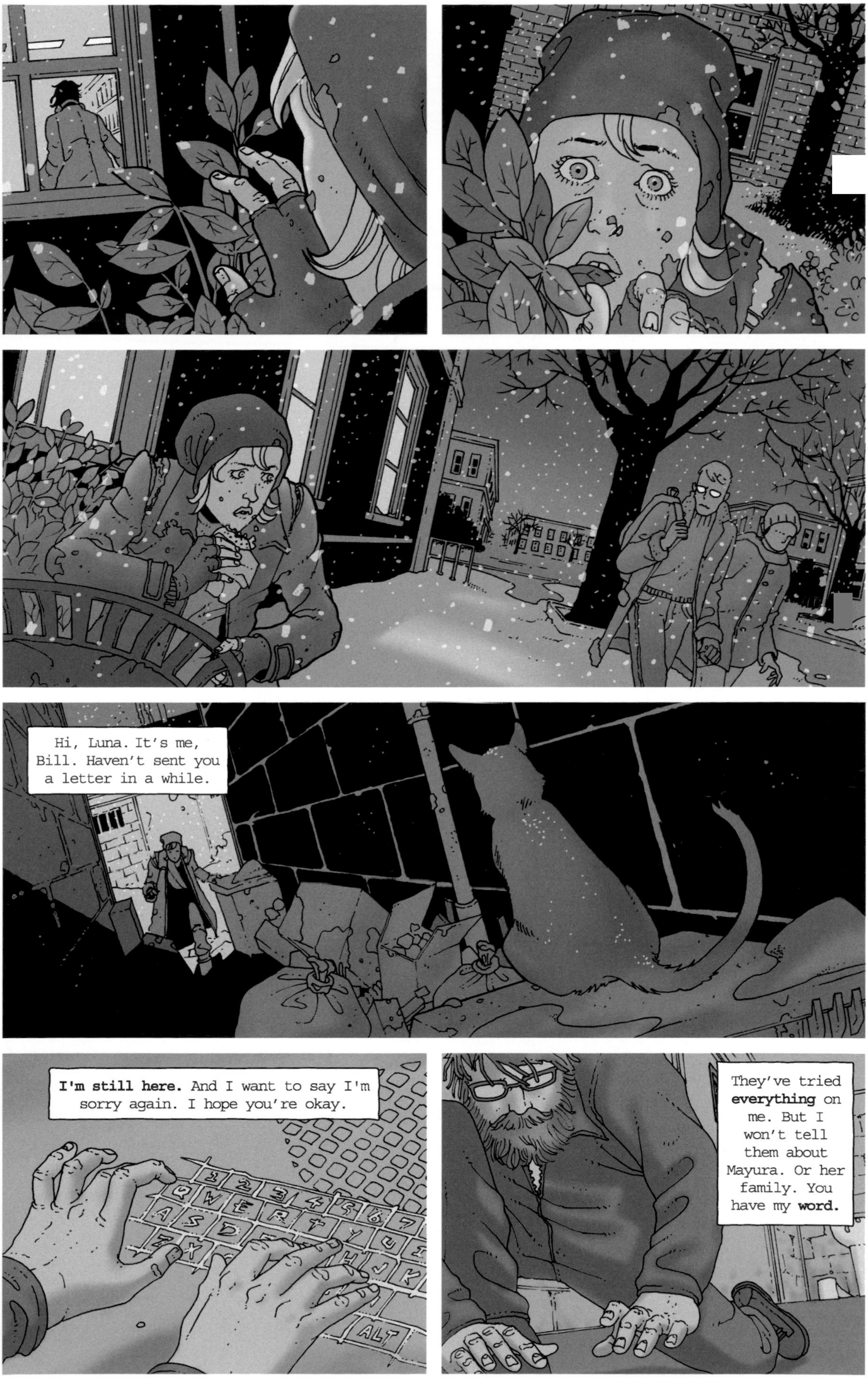
Hi, Luna. It's me, Bill. Haven't sent you a letter in a while.
I'm still here. And I want to say I'm sorry again. I hope you're okay.
They've tried **everything** on me. But I won't tell them about Mayura. Or her family. You have my **word.**

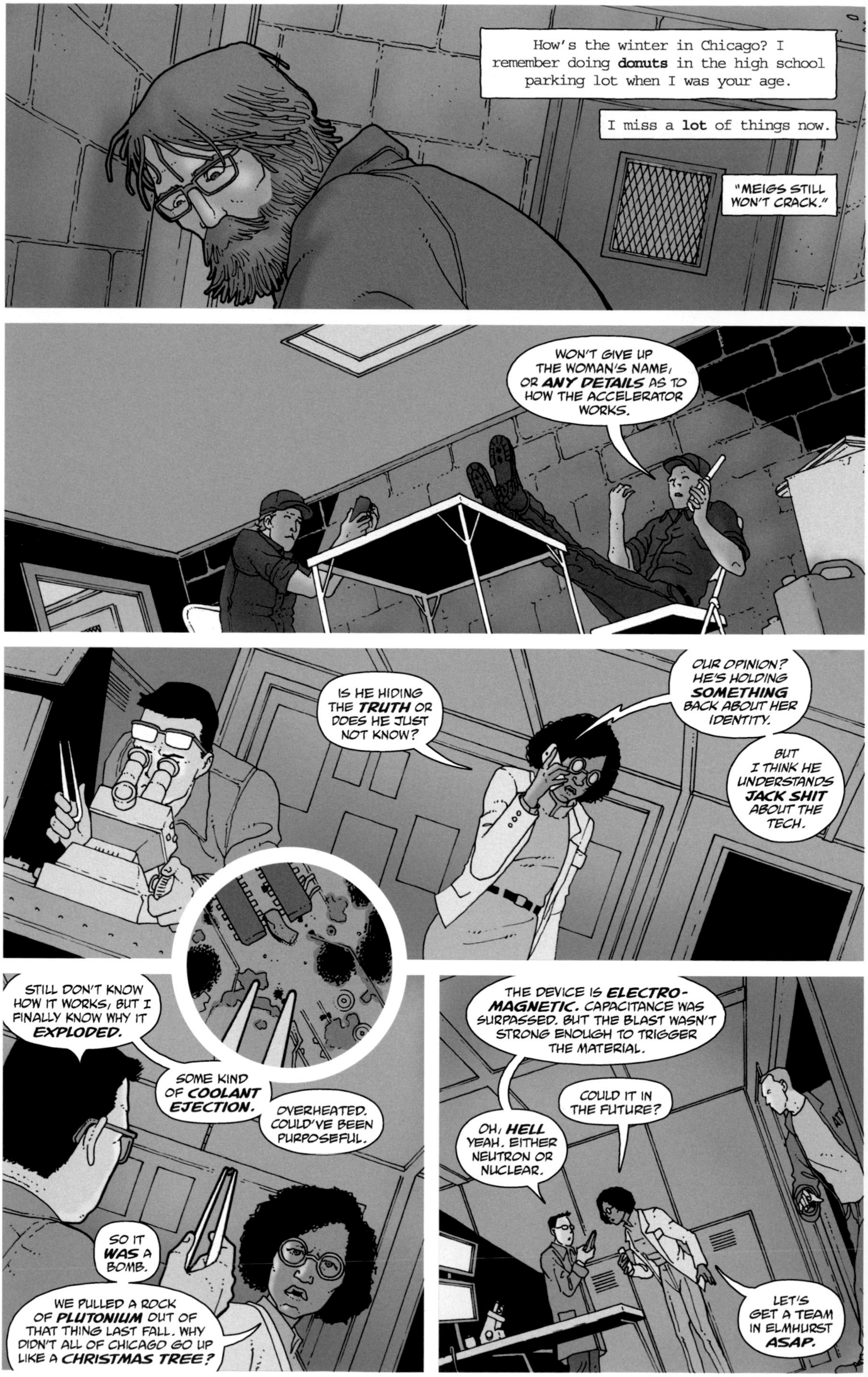
How's the winter in Chicago? I remember doing **donuts** in the high school parking lot when I was your age.
I miss a **lot** of things now.
"MEIGS STILL WON'T CRACK."
WON'T GIVE UP THE WOMAN'S NAME, OR **ANY DETAILS** AS TO HOW THE ACCELERATOR WORKS.
IS HE HIDING THE **TRUTH** OR DOES HE JUST NOT KNOW?
OUR OPINION? HE'S HOLDING **SOMETHING** BACK ABOUT HER IDENTITY.
BUT I THINK HE UNDERSTANDS **JACK SHIT** ABOUT THE TECH.
STILL DON'T KNOW HOW IT WORKS, BUT I FINALLY KNOW WHY IT **EXPLODED.**
SOME KIND OF **COOLANT EJECTION.**
OVERHEATED. COULD'VE BEEN PURPOSEFUL.
SO IT **WAS** A BOMB.
WE PULLED A ROCK OF **PLUTONIUM** OUT OF THAT THING LAST FALL. WHY DIDN'T ALL OF CHICAGO GO UP LIKE A **CHRISTMAS TREE?**
THE DEVICE IS **ELECTRO-MAGNETIC.** CAPACITANCE WAS SURPASSED. BUT THE BLAST WASN'T STRONG ENOUGH TO TRIGGER THE MATERIAL.
COULD IT IN THE FUTURE?
OH, **HELL** YEAH. EITHER NEUTRON OR NUCLEAR.
LET'S GET A TEAM IN ELMHURST **ASAP.**

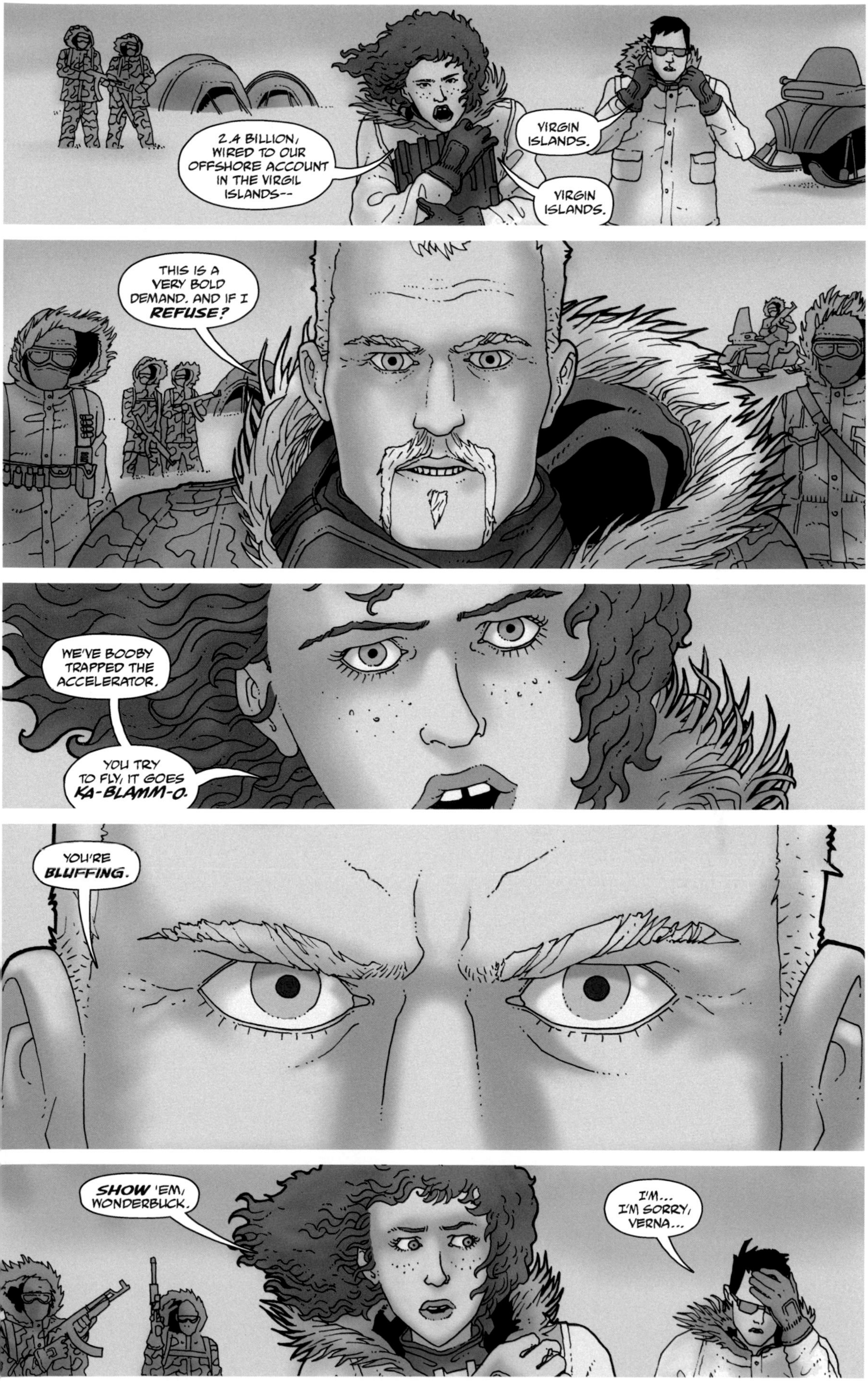
2.4 BILLION, WIRED TO OUR OFFSHORE ACCOUNT IN THE VIRGIL ISLANDS--
VIRGIN ISLANDS.
VIRGIN ISLANDS.
THIS IS A VERY BOLD DEMAND. AND IF I REFUSE?
WE'VE BOOBY TRAPPED THE ACCELERATOR.
YOU TRY TO FLY, IT GOES KA-BLAMM-O.
YOU'RE BLUFFING.
SHOW 'EM, WONDERBUCK.
I'M... I'M SORRY, VERNA...

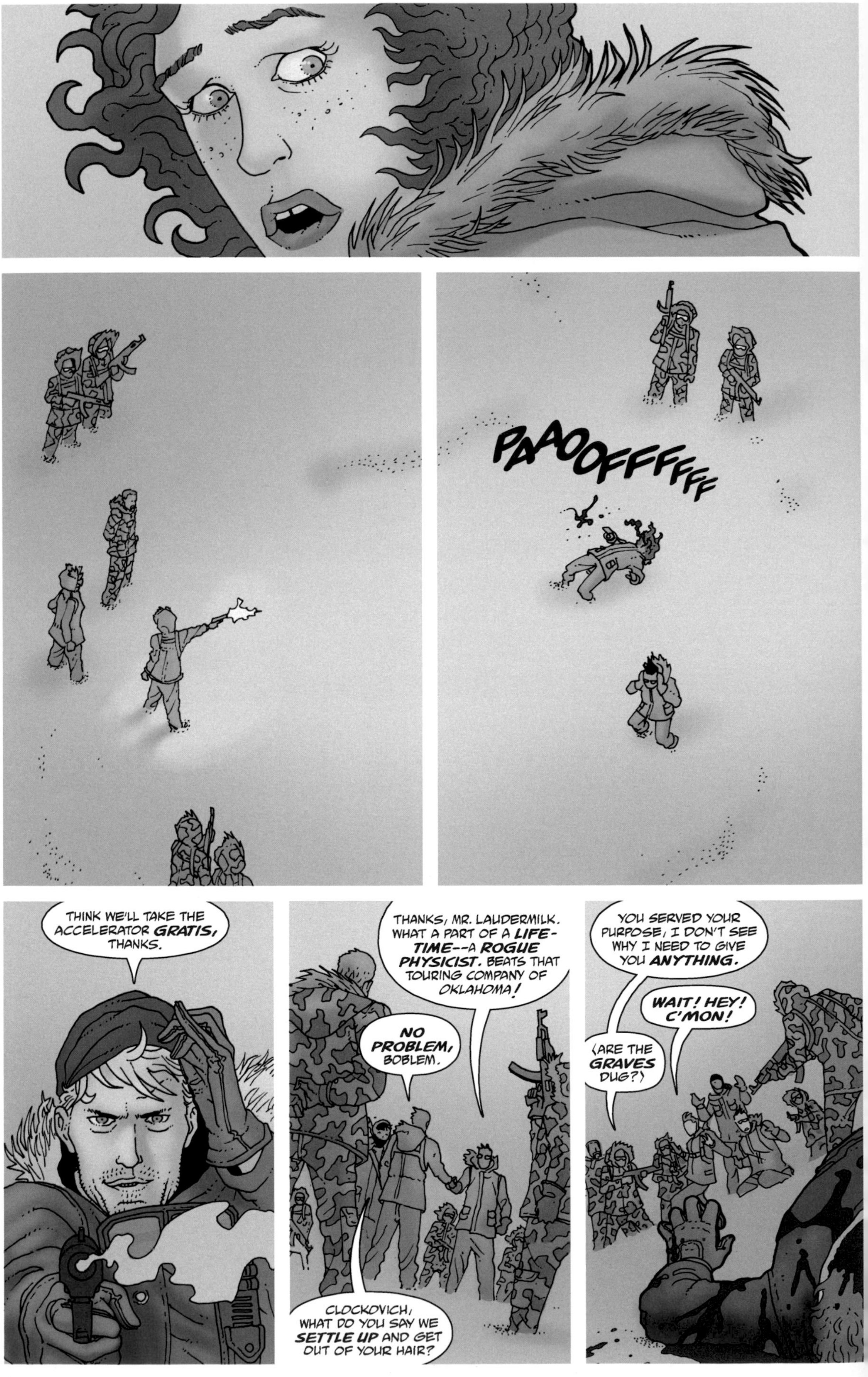
PAAOOFFFFFF
THINK WE'LL TAKE THE ACCELERATOR GRATIS, THANKS.
THANKS, MR. LAUDERMILK. WHAT A PART OF A LIFE-TIME--A ROGUE PHYSICIST. BEATS THAT TOURING COMPANY OF OKLAHOMA!
NO PROBLEM, BOBLEM.
CLOCKOVICH, WHAT DO YOU SAY WE SETTLE UP AND GET OUT OF YOUR HAIR?
YOU SERVED YOUR PURPOSE; I DON'T SEE WHY I NEED TO GIVE YOU ANYTHING.
WAIT! HEY! C'MON!
(ARE THE GRAVES DUG?)

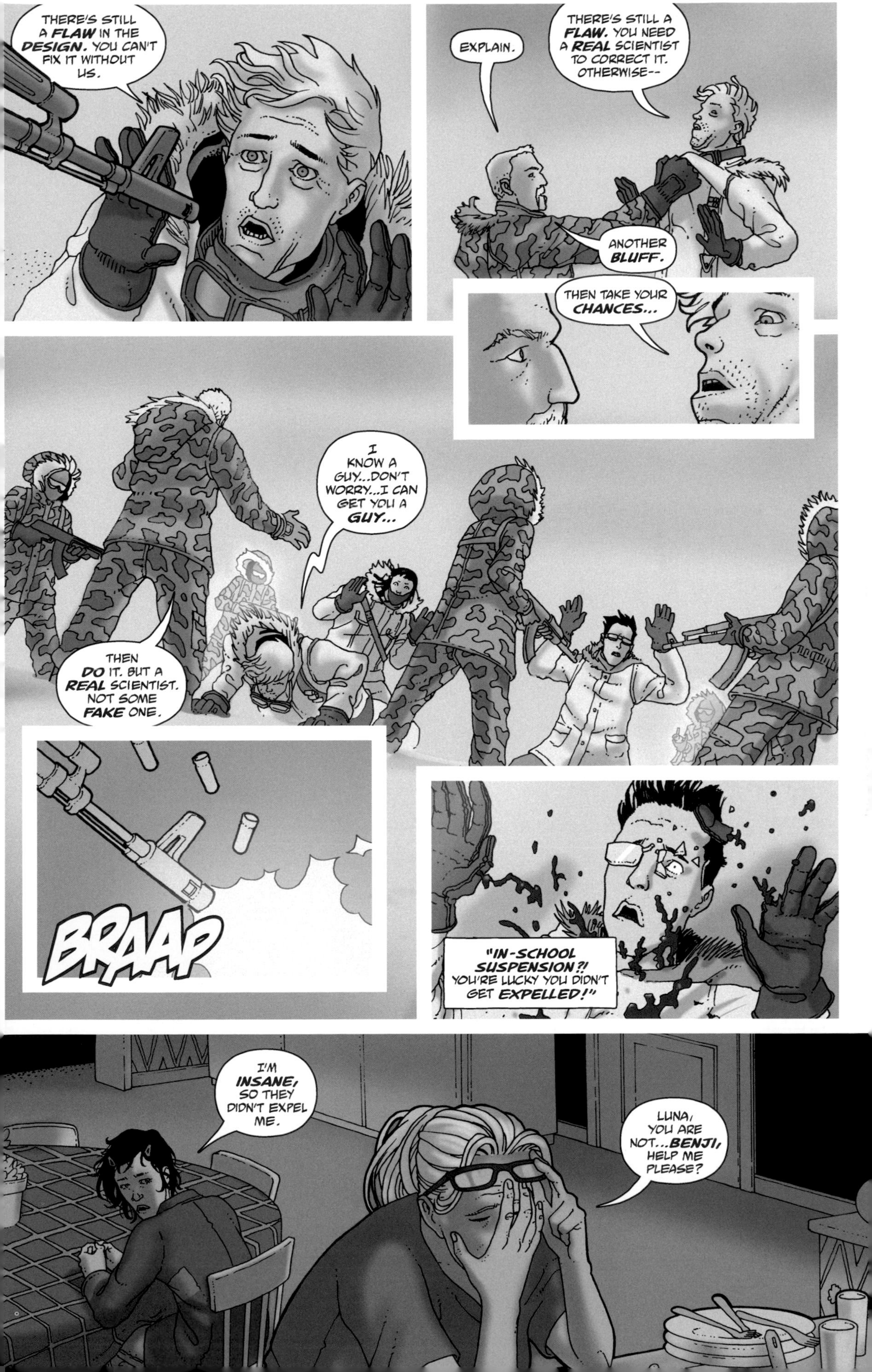
THERE'S STILL A FLAW IN THE DESIGN. YOU CAN'T FIX IT WITHOUT US.
EXPLAIN.
THERE'S STILL A FLAW. YOU NEED A REAL SCIENTIST TO CORRECT IT. OTHERWISE--
ANOTHER BLUFF.
THEN TAKE YOUR CHANCES...
I KNOW A GUY...DON'T WORRY...I CAN GET YOU A GUY...
THEN DO IT. BUT A REAL SCIENTIST. NOT SOME FAKE ONE.
BRAAP
"IN-SCHOOL SUSPENSION?! YOU'RE LUCKY YOU DIDN'T GET EXPELLED!"
I'M INSANE, SO THEY DIDN'T EXPEL ME.
LUNA, YOU ARE NOT...BENJI, HELP ME PLEASE?

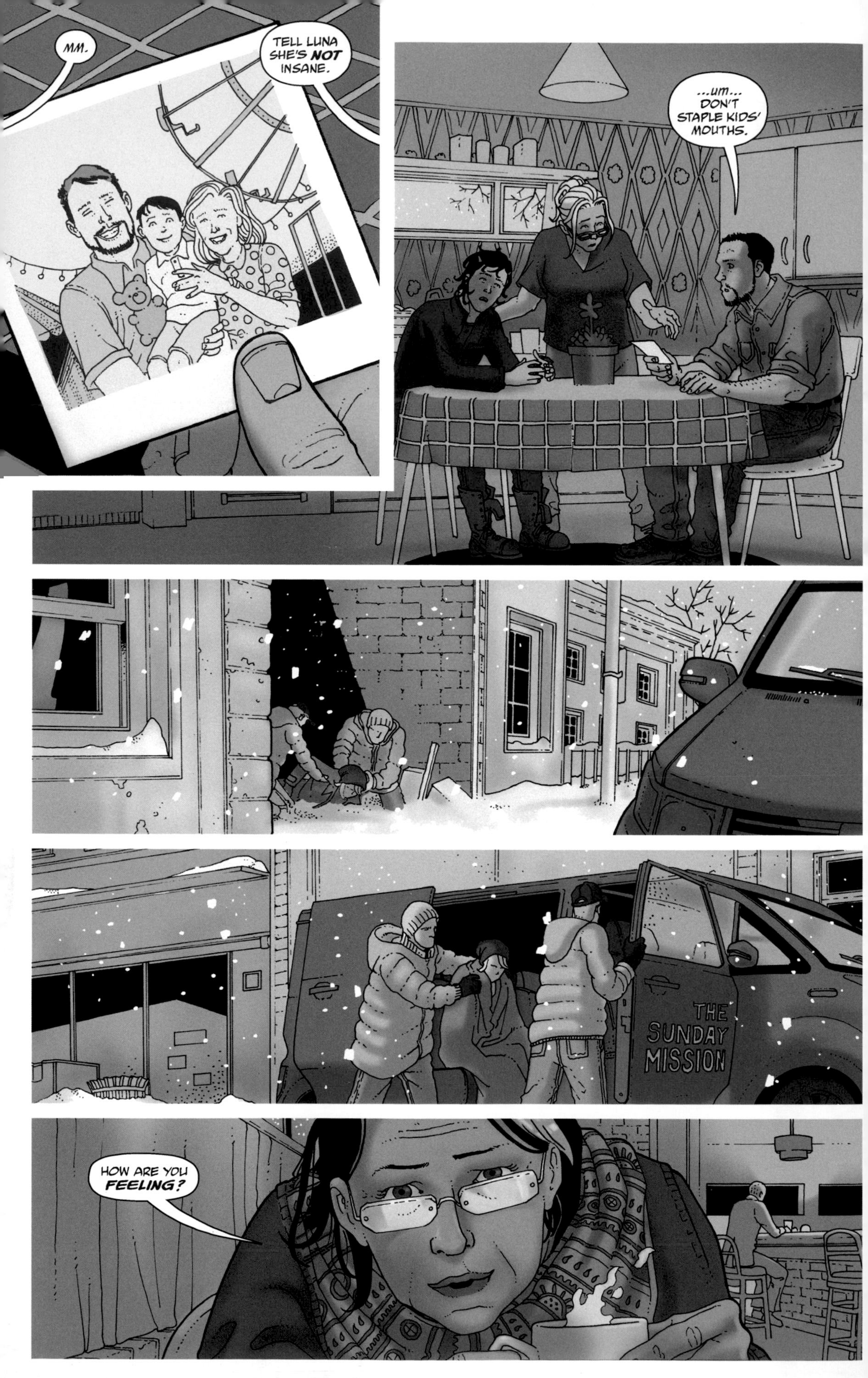
MM.
TELL LUNA SHE'S NOT INSANE.
...um... DON'T STAPLE KIDS' MOUTHS.
THE SUNDAY MISSION
HOW ARE YOU FEELING?

YOU KNOW, I WISH *BETTER.*

HOW'S SCHOOL?

I GOT A THREE DAY IN-SCHOOL SUSPENSION, SO... EASY?

WHAT ABOUT THE *MAYURA* SEARCH?

HONESTLY, I'VE, LIKE...NOT BEEN LOOKING *VERY HARD* RECENTLY...

WELL, SHE GOT SOME *MAIL* AT ARC'S NEW CAMPUS, FORWARDED FROM THE OLD ADDRESS.

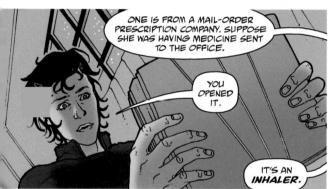

ONE IS FROM A MAIL-ORDER PRESCRIPTION COMPANY. SUPPOSE SHE WAS HAVING MEDICINE SENT TO THE OFFICE.

YOU OPENED IT.

IT'S AN *INHALER.*

I REMEMBER ONE OF HER SONS HAD *ASTHMA.*

I HOPE HE HAS WHAT HE NEEDS.

YOU SEEM *LOST.*

WHAT *IS* THIS PLACE?

THE SUNDAY MISSION FOR THE *HOMELESS.*

DON'T WORRY. *I* DON'T BELONG HERE, EITHER.

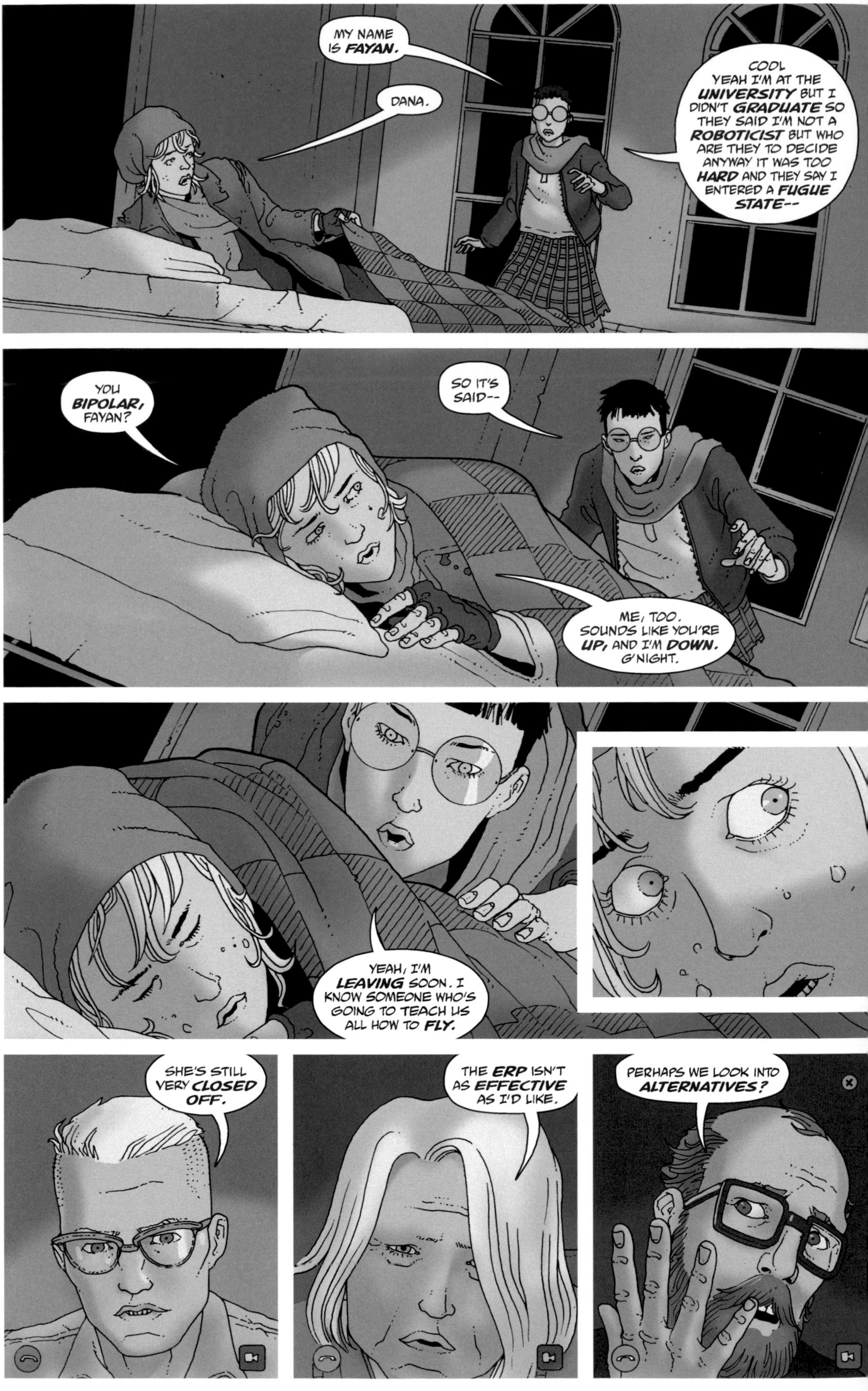

MY NAME IS FAYAN.
DANA.
COOL YEAH I'M AT THE UNIVERSITY BUT I DIDN'T GRADUATE SO THEY SAID I'M NOT A ROBOTICIST BUT WHO ARE THEY TO DECIDE ANYWAY IT WAS TOO HARD AND THEY SAY I ENTERED A FUGUE STATE--
YOU BIPOLAR, FAYAN?
SO IT'S SAID--
ME, TOO. SOUNDS LIKE YOU'RE UP, AND I'M DOWN. G'NIGHT.
YEAH, I'M LEAVING SOON. I KNOW SOMEONE WHO'S GOING TO TEACH US ALL HOW TO FLY.
SHE'S STILL VERY CLOSED OFF.
THE ERP ISN'T AS EFFECTIVE AS I'D LIKE.
PERHAPS WE LOOK INTO ALTERNATIVES?

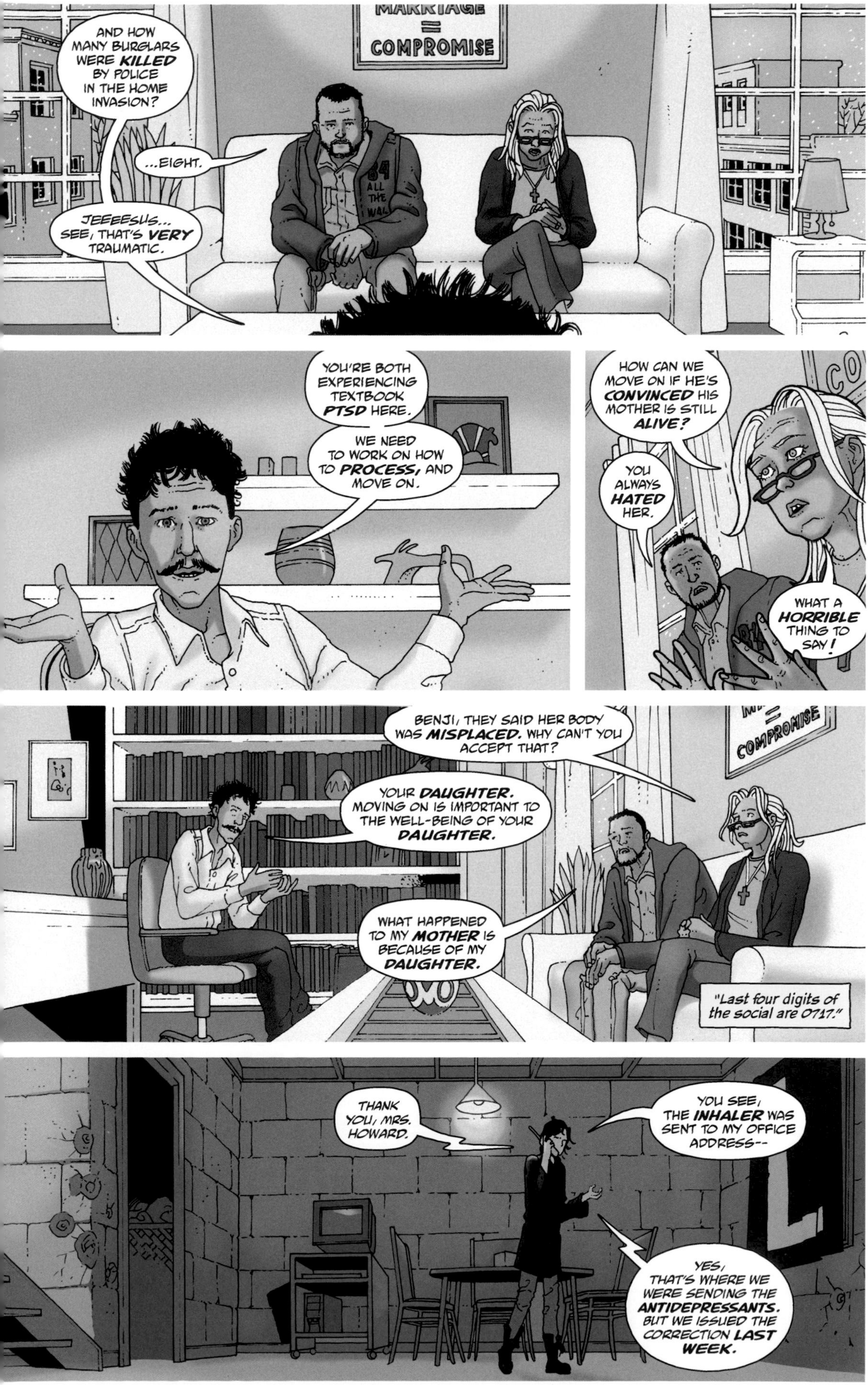
MARRIAGE = COMPROMISE
AND HOW MANY BURGLARS WERE KILLED BY POLICE IN THE HOME INVASION?
...EIGHT.
JEEEESUS... SEE, THAT'S VERY TRAUMATIC.
YOU'RE BOTH EXPERIENCING TEXTBOOK PTSD HERE.
WE NEED TO WORK ON HOW TO PROCESS, AND MOVE ON.
HOW CAN WE MOVE ON IF HE'S CONVINCED HIS MOTHER IS STILL ALIVE?
YOU ALWAYS HATED HER.
WHAT A HORRIBLE THING TO SAY!
BENJI, THEY SAID HER BODY WAS MISPLACED. WHY CAN'T YOU ACCEPT THAT?
YOUR DAUGHTER. MOVING ON IS IMPORTANT TO THE WELL-BEING OF YOUR DAUGHTER.
WHAT HAPPENED TO MY MOTHER IS BECAUSE OF MY DAUGHTER.
"Last four digits of the social are 0717."
THANK YOU, MRS. HOWARD.
YOU SEE, THE INHALER WAS SENT TO MY OFFICE ADDRESS--
YES, THAT'S WHERE WE WERE SENDING THE ANTIDEPRESSANTS. BUT WE ISSUED THE CORRECTION LAST WEEK.

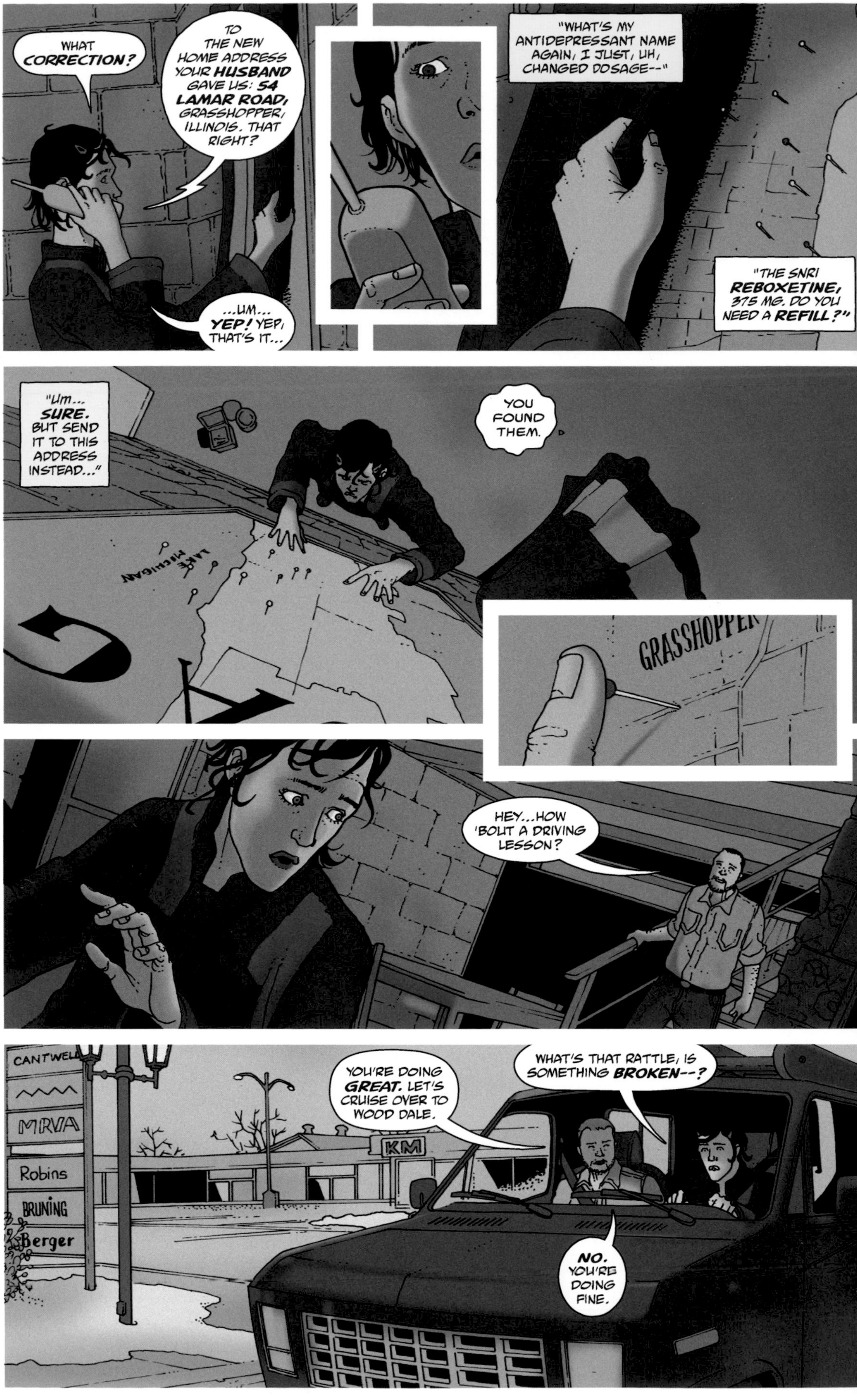
WHAT CORRECTION?
TO THE NEW HOME ADDRESS YOUR HUSBAND GAVE US: 54 LAMAR ROAD, GRASSHOPPER, ILLINOIS. THAT RIGHT?
...UM... YEP! YEP, THAT'S IT...
"WHAT'S MY ANTIDEPRESSANT NAME AGAIN, I JUST, UH, CHANGED DOSAGE--"
"THE SNRI REBOXETINE, 375 MG. DO YOU NEED A REFILL?"
"Um... SURE. BUT SEND IT TO THIS ADDRESS INSTEAD..."
YOU FOUND THEM.
LAKE MICHIGAN
GRASSHOPPER
HEY...HOW 'BOUT A DRIVING LESSON?
CANTWELL
MRVA
Robins
BRUNING
Berger
KM
YOU'RE DOING GREAT. LET'S CRUISE OVER TO WOOD DALE.
WHAT'S THAT RATTLE, IS SOMETHING BROKEN--?
NO. YOU'RE DOING FINE.

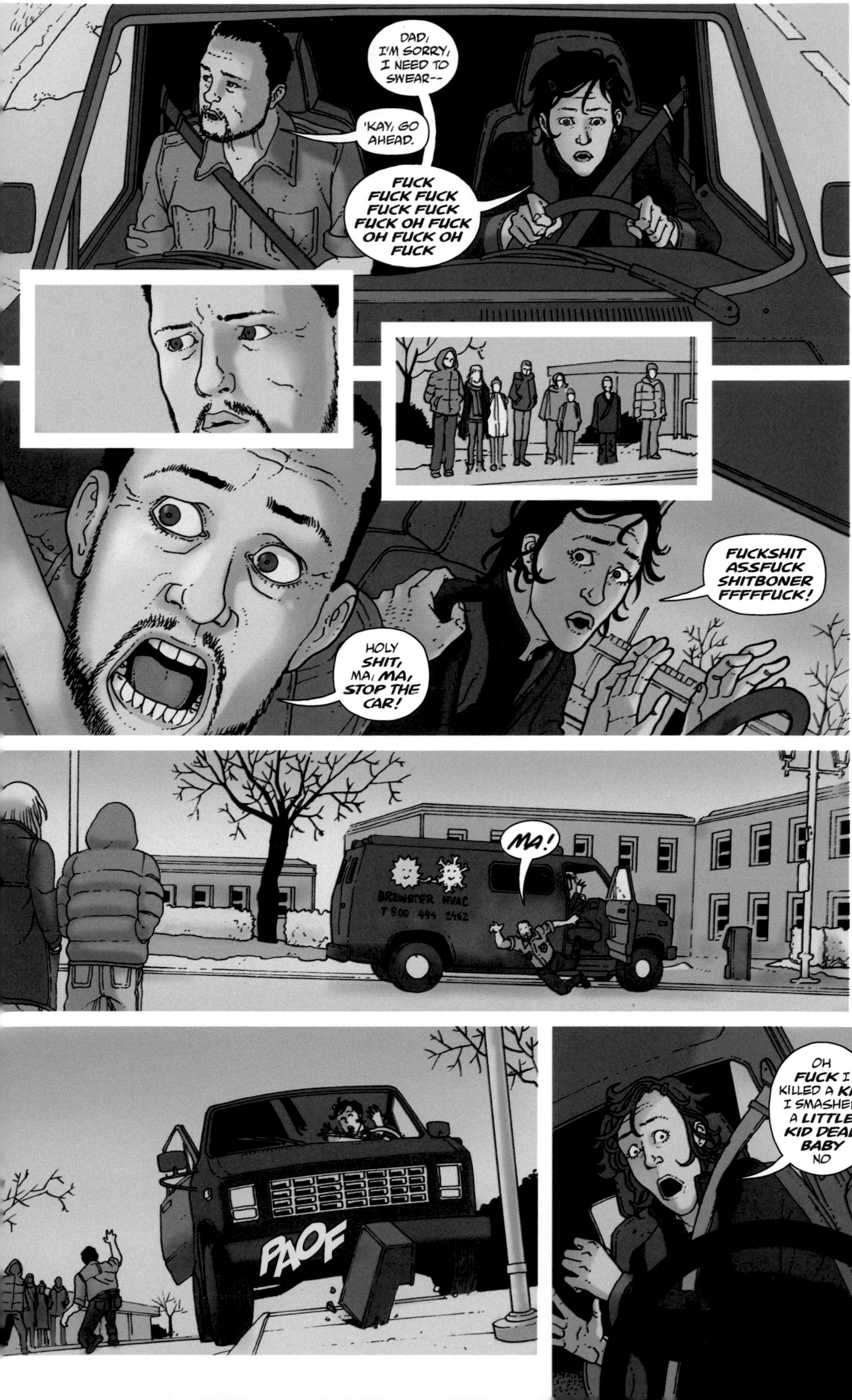
DAD, I'M SORRY, I NEED TO SWEAR--
'KAY, GO AHEAD.
FUCK FUCK FUCK FUCK FUCK FUCK OH FUCK OH FUCK OH FUCK
FUCKSHIT ASSFUCK SHITBONER FFFFFUCK!
HOLY SHIT, MA, MA, STOP THE CAR!
BREWSTER HVAC
T 800 444 2462
MA!
PAOF
OH FUCK I KILLED A KID I SMASHED A LITTLE KID DEAD BABY NO

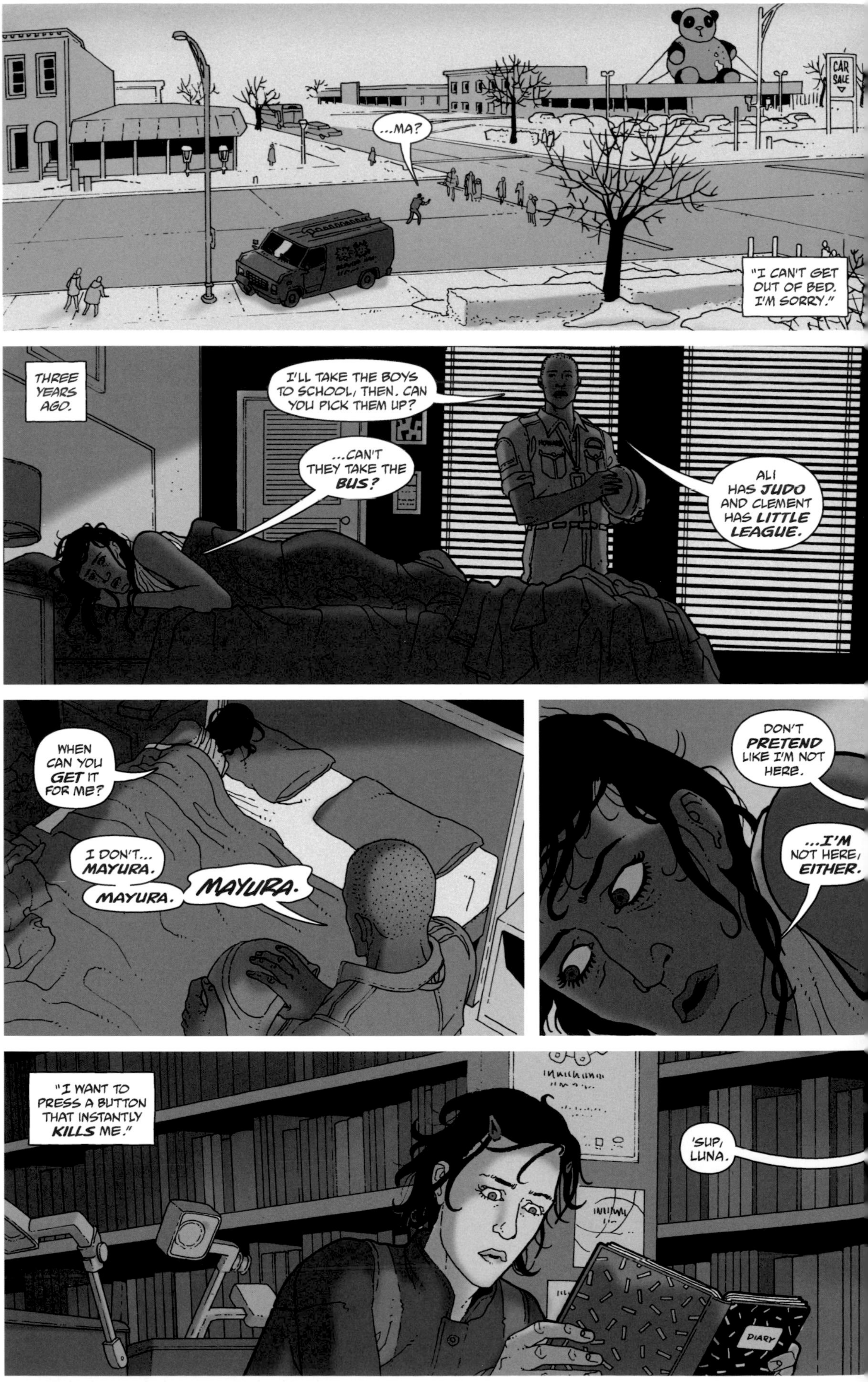
...MA?
"I CAN'T GET OUT OF BED. I'M SORRY."
THREE YEARS AGO.
I'LL TAKE THE BOYS TO SCHOOL, THEN. CAN YOU PICK THEM UP?
...CAN'T THEY TAKE THE BUS?
ALI HAS JUDO AND CLEMENT HAS LITTLE LEAGUE.
WHEN CAN YOU GET IT FOR ME?
I DON'T... MAYURA.
MAYURA.
MAYURA.
DON'T PRETEND LIKE I'M NOT HERE.
...I'M NOT HERE, EITHER.
"I WANT TO PRESS A BUTTON THAT INSTANTLY KILLS ME."
'SUP, LUNA.
DIARY

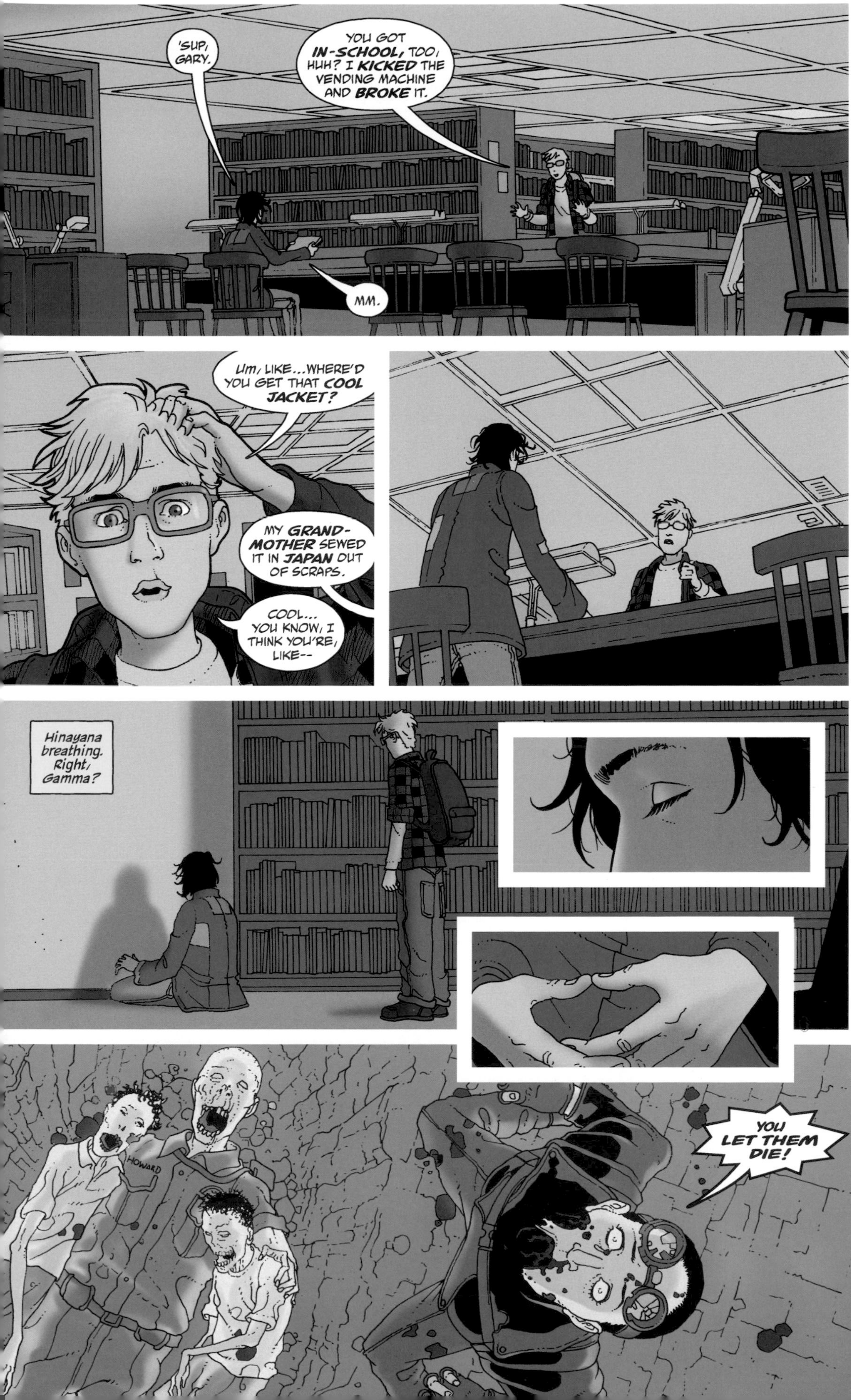
'SUP, GARY.
YOU GOT IN-SCHOOL, TOO, HUH? I KICKED THE VENDING MACHINE AND BROKE IT.
MM.
UM, LIKE...WHERE'D YOU GET THAT COOL JACKET?
MY GRAND-MOTHER SEWED IT IN JAPAN OUT OF SCRAPS.
COOL... YOU KNOW, I THINK YOU'RE, LIKE--
Hinayana breathing. Right, Gamma?
HOWARD
YOU LET THEM DIE!

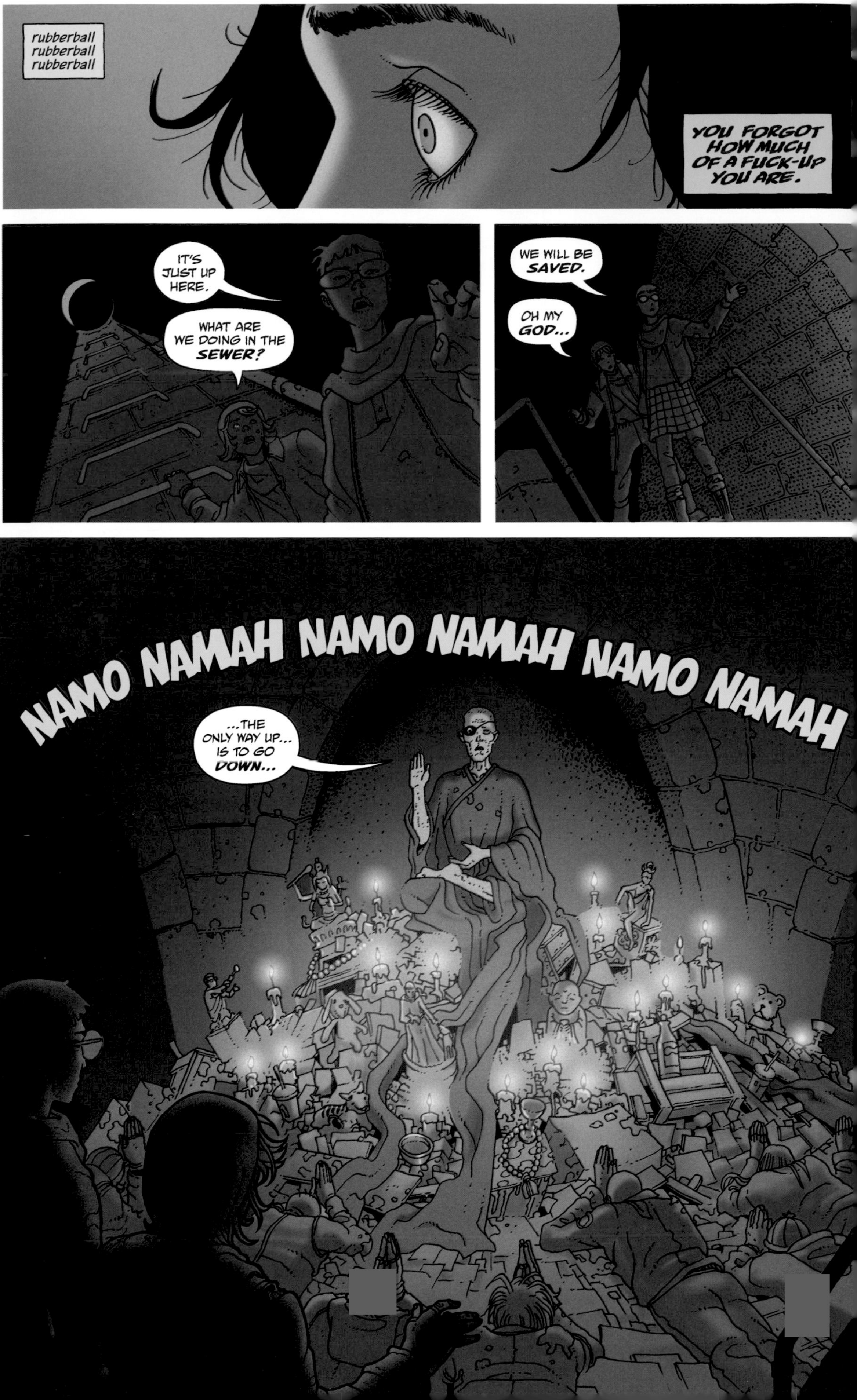
rubberball
rubberball
rubberball
YOU FORGOT HOW MUCH OF A FUCK-UP YOU ARE.
IT'S JUST UP HERE.
WHAT ARE WE DOING IN THE SEWER?
WE WILL BE SAVED.
OH MY GOD...
NAMO NAMAH NAMO NAMAH NAMO NAMAH
...THE ONLY WAY UP... IS TO GO DOWN...

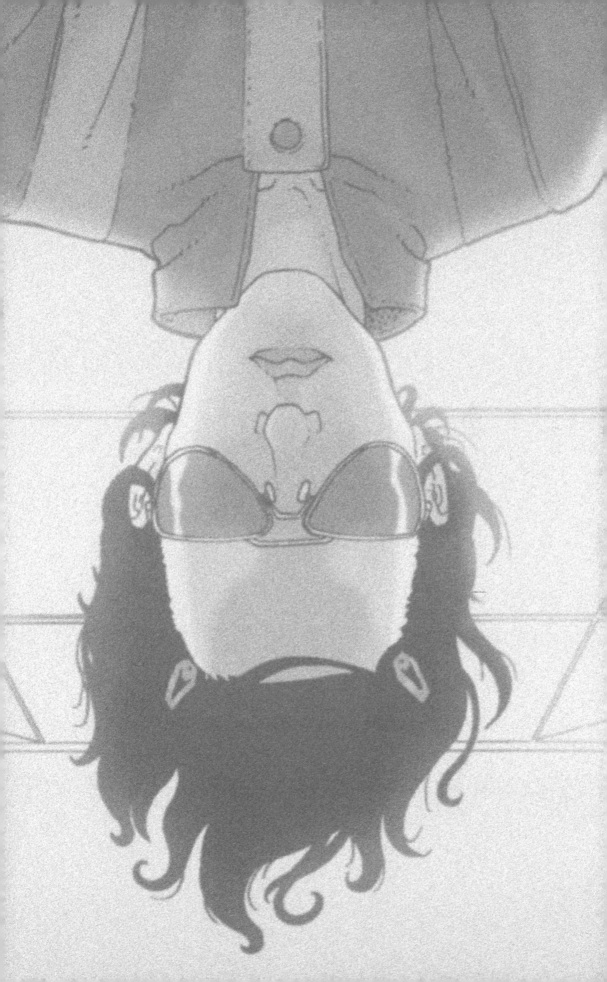

CHAPTER II
"Animal"

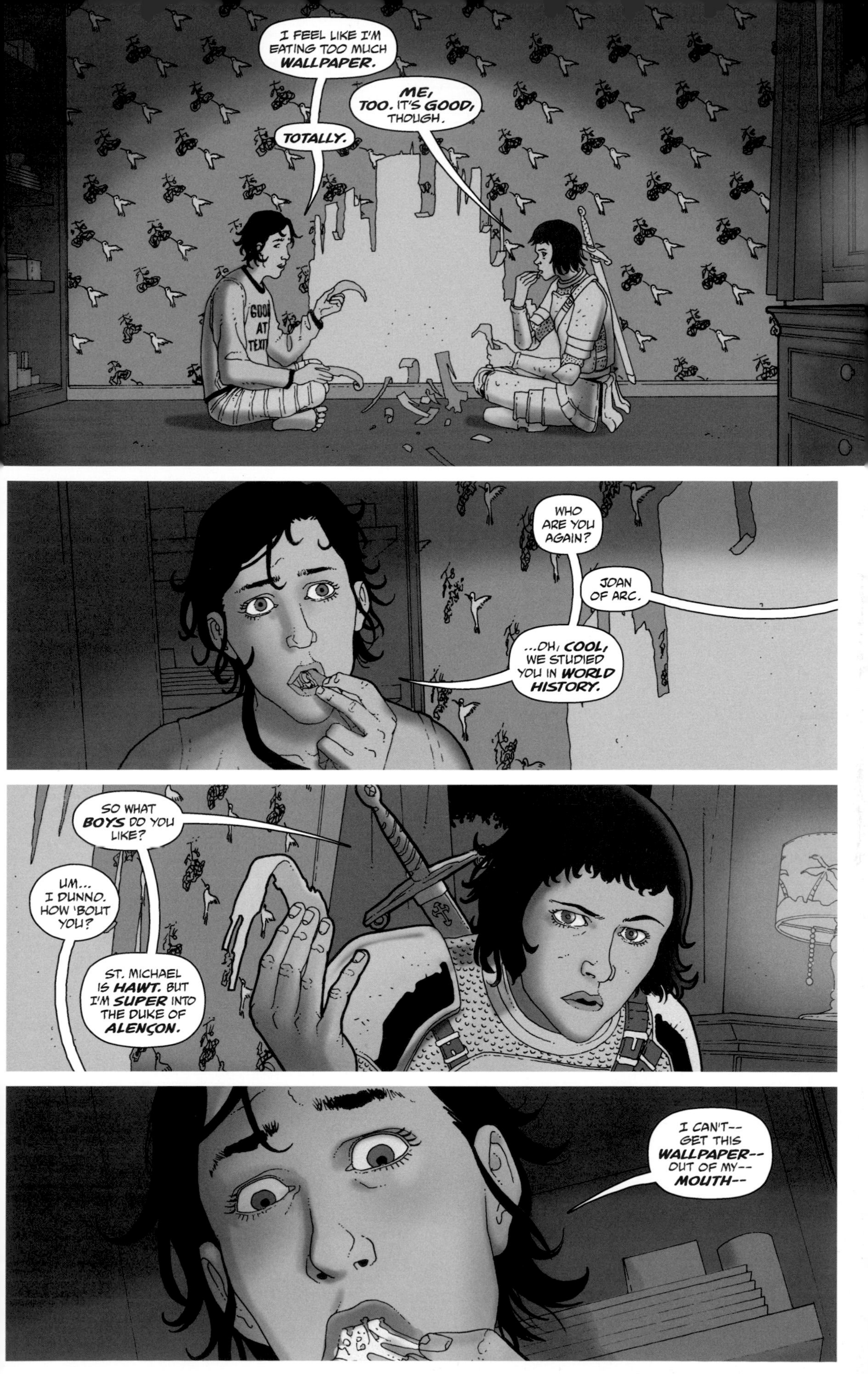
I FEEL LIKE I'M EATING TOO MUCH WALLPAPER.
TOTALLY.
ME, TOO. IT'S GOOD, THOUGH.
GOOD AT TEXT
WHO ARE YOU AGAIN?
JOAN OF ARC.
...OH, COOL, WE STUDIED YOU IN WORLD HISTORY.
SO WHAT BOYS DO YOU LIKE?
UM... I DUNNO. HOW 'BOUT YOU?
ST. MICHAEL IS HAWT. BUT I'M SUPER INTO THE DUKE OF ALENÇON.
I CAN'T-- GET THIS WALLPAPER-- OUT OF MY-- MOUTH--

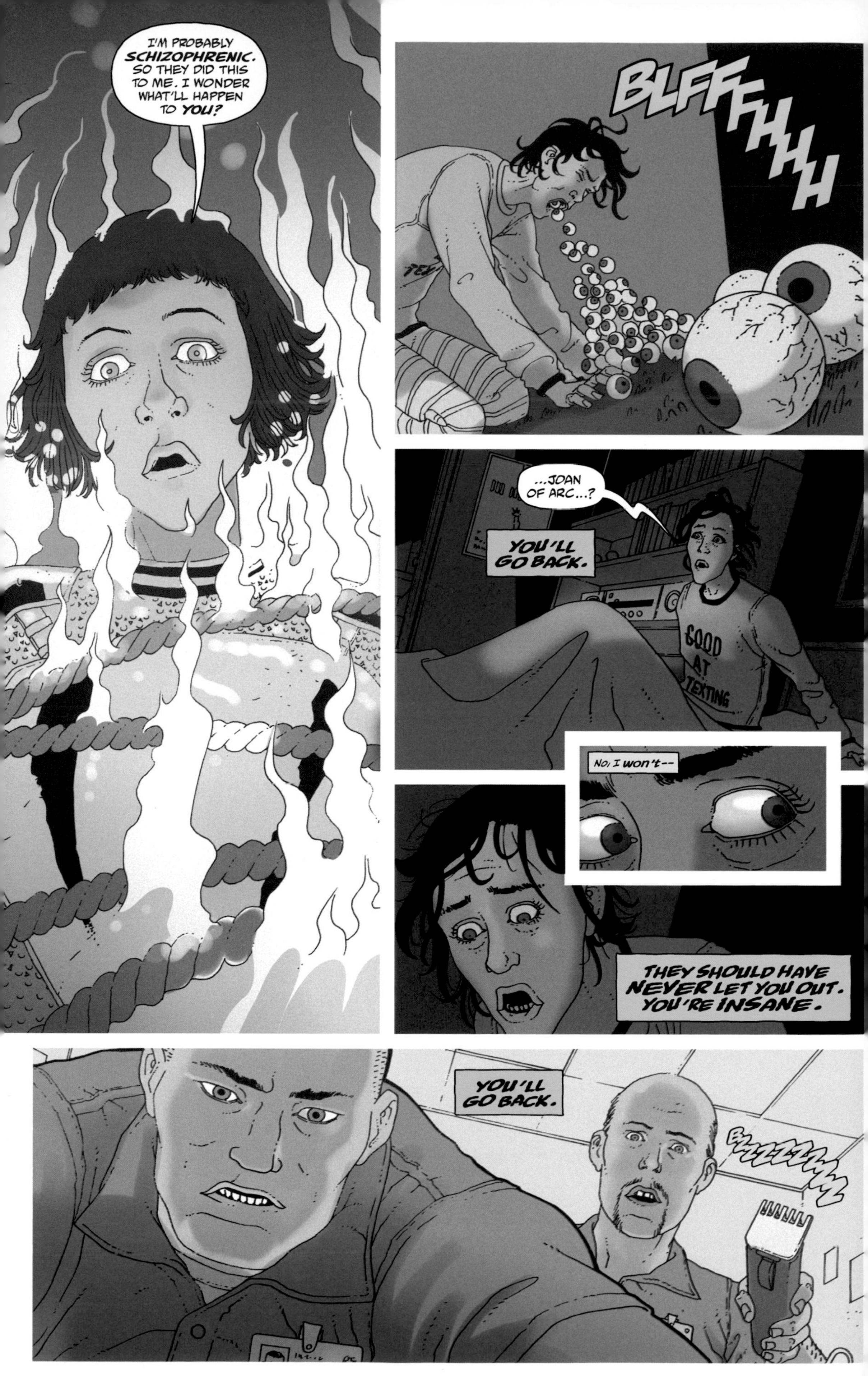
I'M PROBABLY SCHIZOPHRENIC. SO THEY DID THIS TO ME. I WONDER WHAT'LL HAPPEN TO YOU?
BLFFFHHH
...JOAN OF ARC...?
YOU'LL GO BACK.
GOOD AT TEXTING
No, I won't--
THEY SHOULD HAVE NEVER LET YOU OUT. YOU'RE INSANE.
YOU'LL GO BACK.

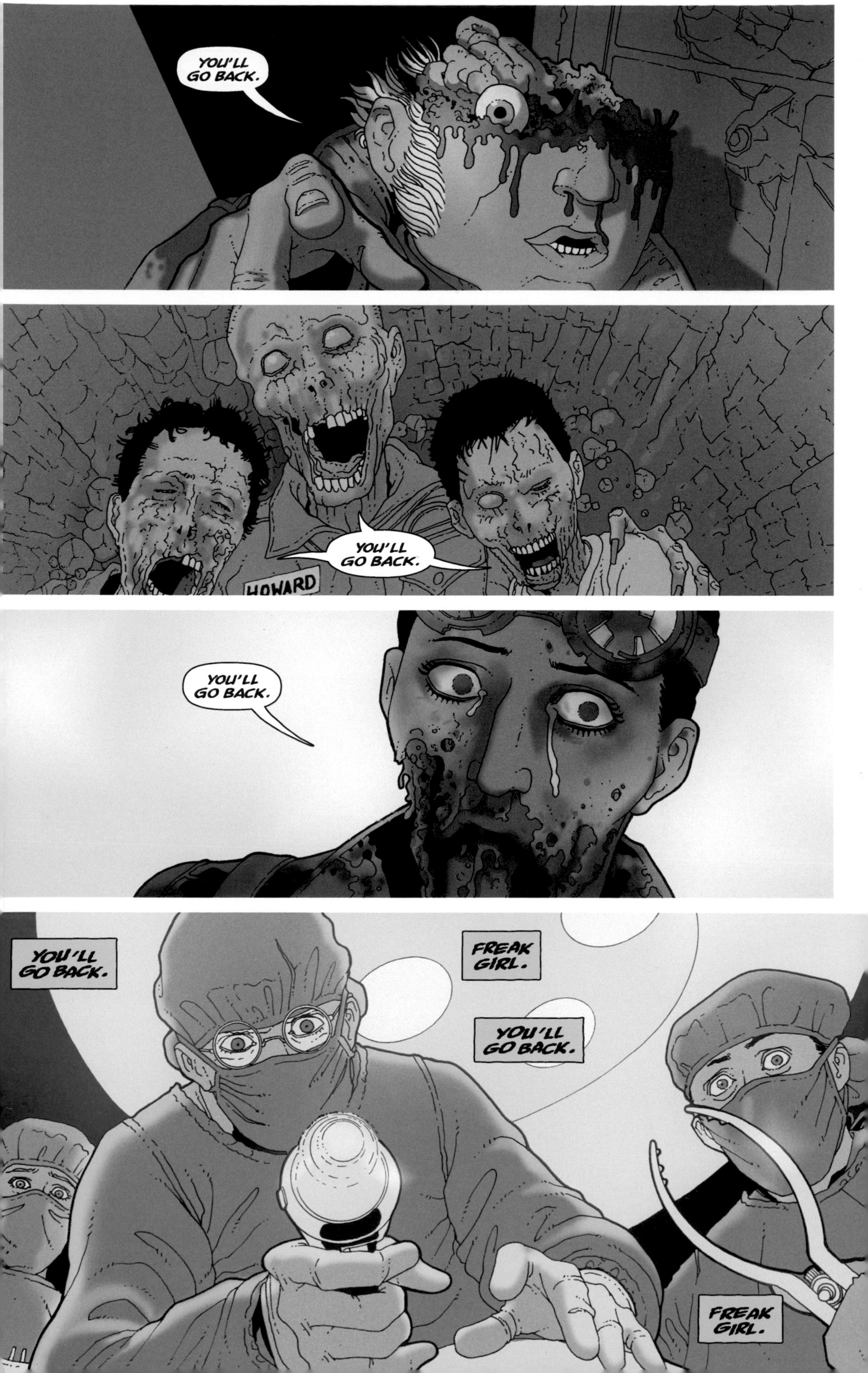
YOU'LL GO BACK.
YOU'LL GO BACK.
HOWARD
YOU'LL GO BACK.
YOU'LL GO BACK.
FREAK GIRL.
YOU'LL GO BACK.
FREAK GIRL.

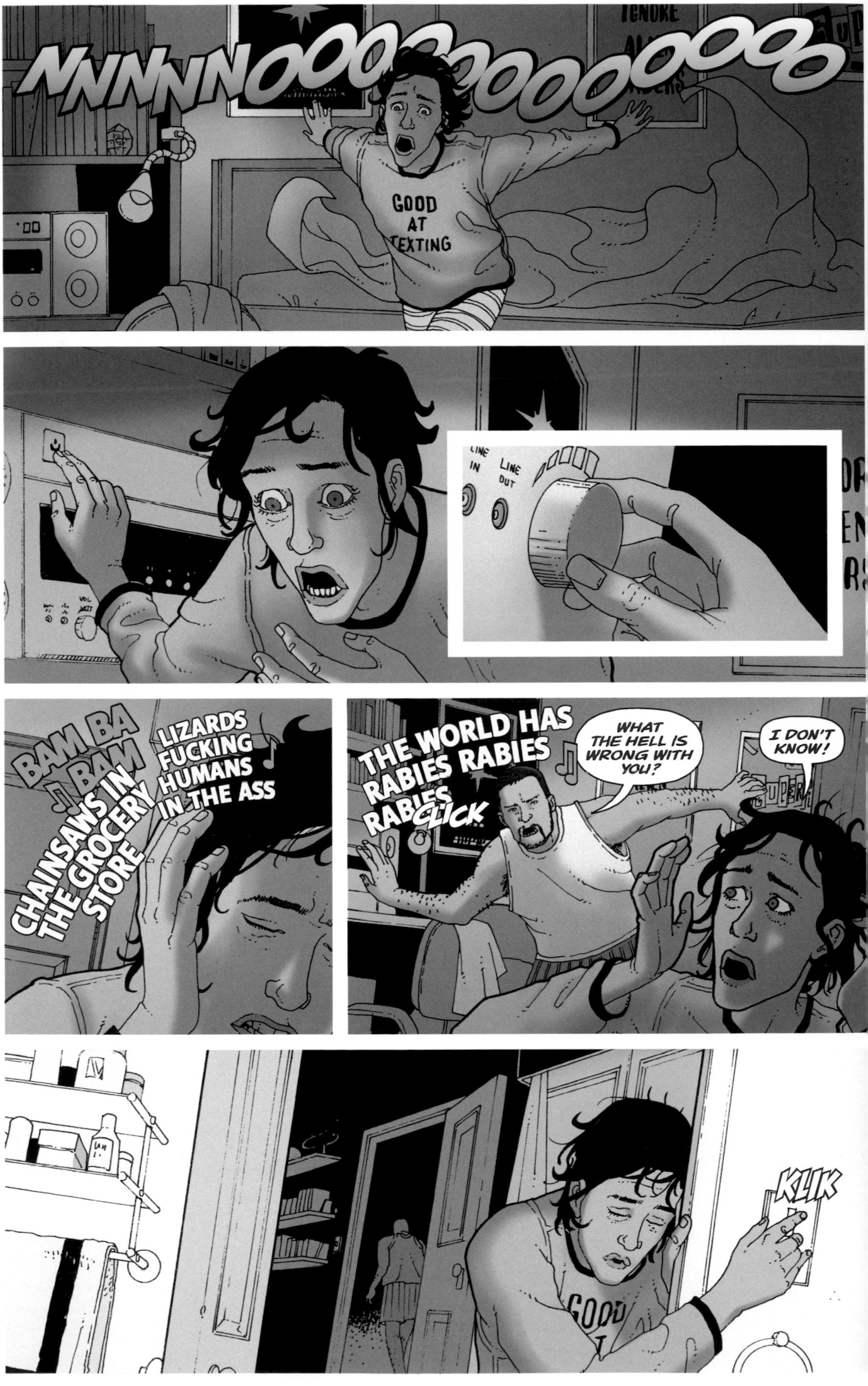
NNNNNOOOOOOOOOOOOOOO
GOOD AT TEXTING
LINE IN
LINE OUT
BAM BA BAM
CHAINSAWS IN THE GROCERY STORE
LIZARDS FUCKING HUMANS IN THE ASS
THE WORLD HAS RABIES RABIES RABIES
CLICK
WHAT THE HELL IS WRONG WITH YOU?
I DON'T KNOW!
KLIK

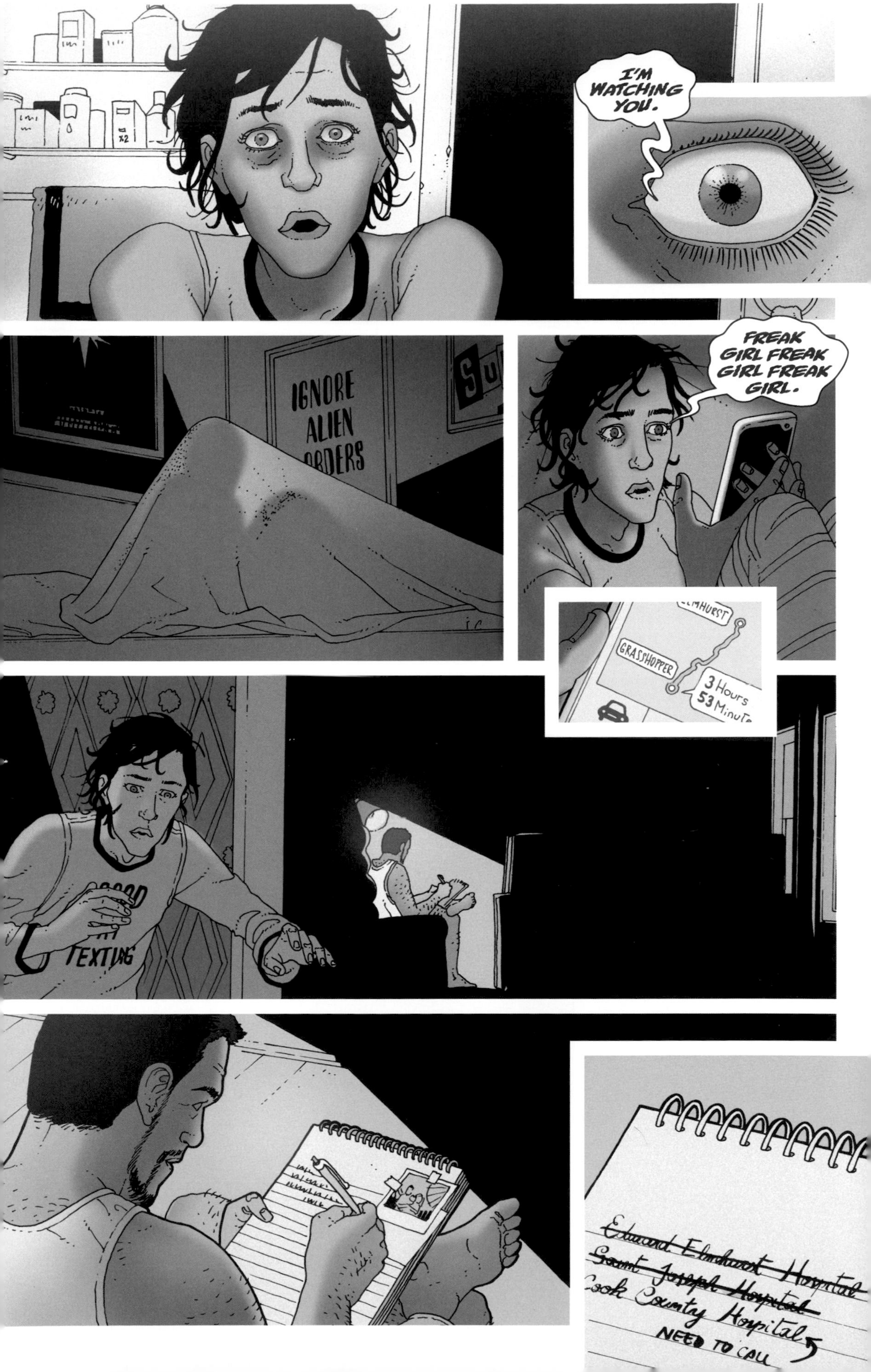
I'M WATCHING YOU.
IGNORE ALIEN ORDERS
FREAK GIRL FREAK GIRL FREAK GIRL.
GRASSHOPPER
3 Hours 53 Minute
TEXTING
Edward Elmhurst Hospital
Saint Joseph Hospital
Cook County Hospital
NEED TO CALL

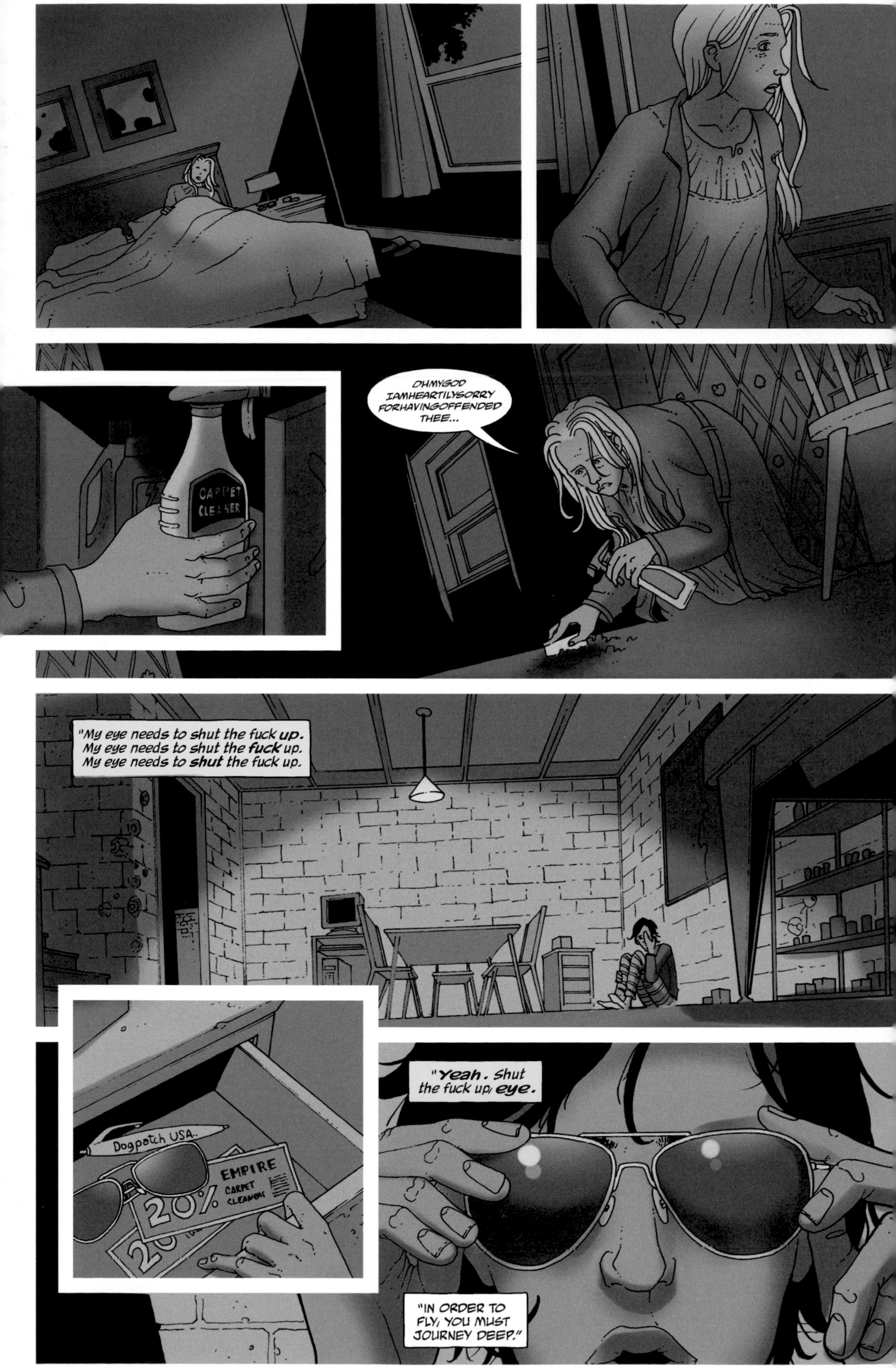
OHMYGOD
IAMHEARTILYSORRY
FORHAVINGOFFENDED
THEE...
CARPET
CLEANER
"My eye needs to shut the fuck up.
My eye needs to shut the fuck up.
My eye needs to shut the fuck up.
Dogpatch USA
EMPIRE
CARPET
CLEANERS
20%
"Yeah. Shut
the fuck up, eye.
"IN ORDER TO
FLY, YOU MUST
JOURNEY DEEP."

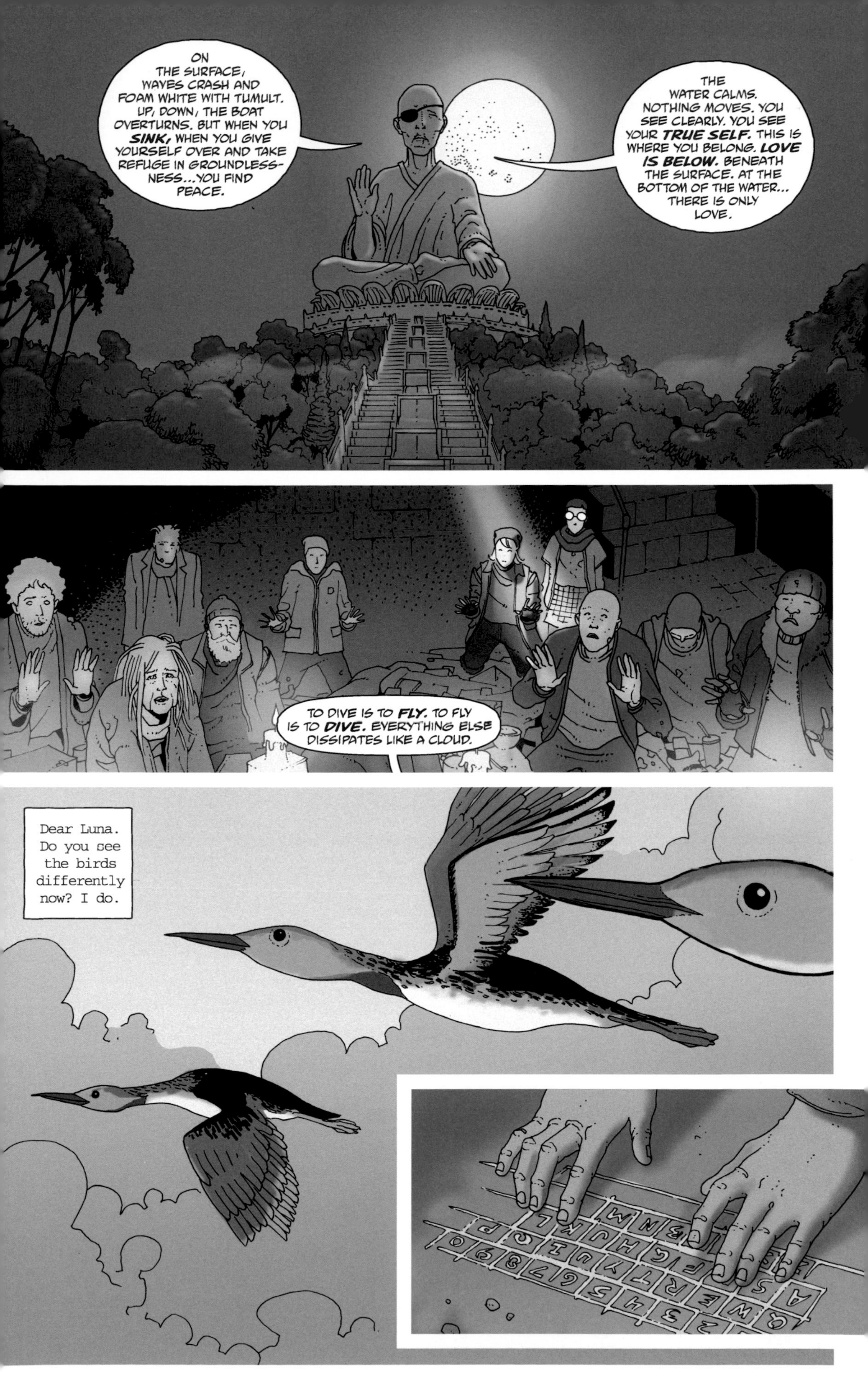
ON THE SURFACE, WAVES CRASH AND FOAM WHITE WITH TUMULT. UP, DOWN, THE BOAT OVERTURNS. BUT WHEN YOU **SINK,** WHEN YOU GIVE YOURSELF OVER AND TAKE REFUGE IN GROUNDLESS-NESS...YOU FIND PEACE.
THE WATER CALMS. NOTHING MOVES. YOU SEE CLEARLY. YOU SEE YOUR **TRUE SELF.** THIS IS WHERE YOU BELONG. **LOVE IS BELOW.** BENEATH THE SURFACE. AT THE BOTTOM OF THE WATER... THERE IS ONLY LOVE.
TO DIVE IS TO **FLY.** TO FLY IS TO **DIVE.** EVERYTHING ELSE DISSIPATES LIKE A CLOUD.
Dear Luna. Do you see the birds differently now? I do.

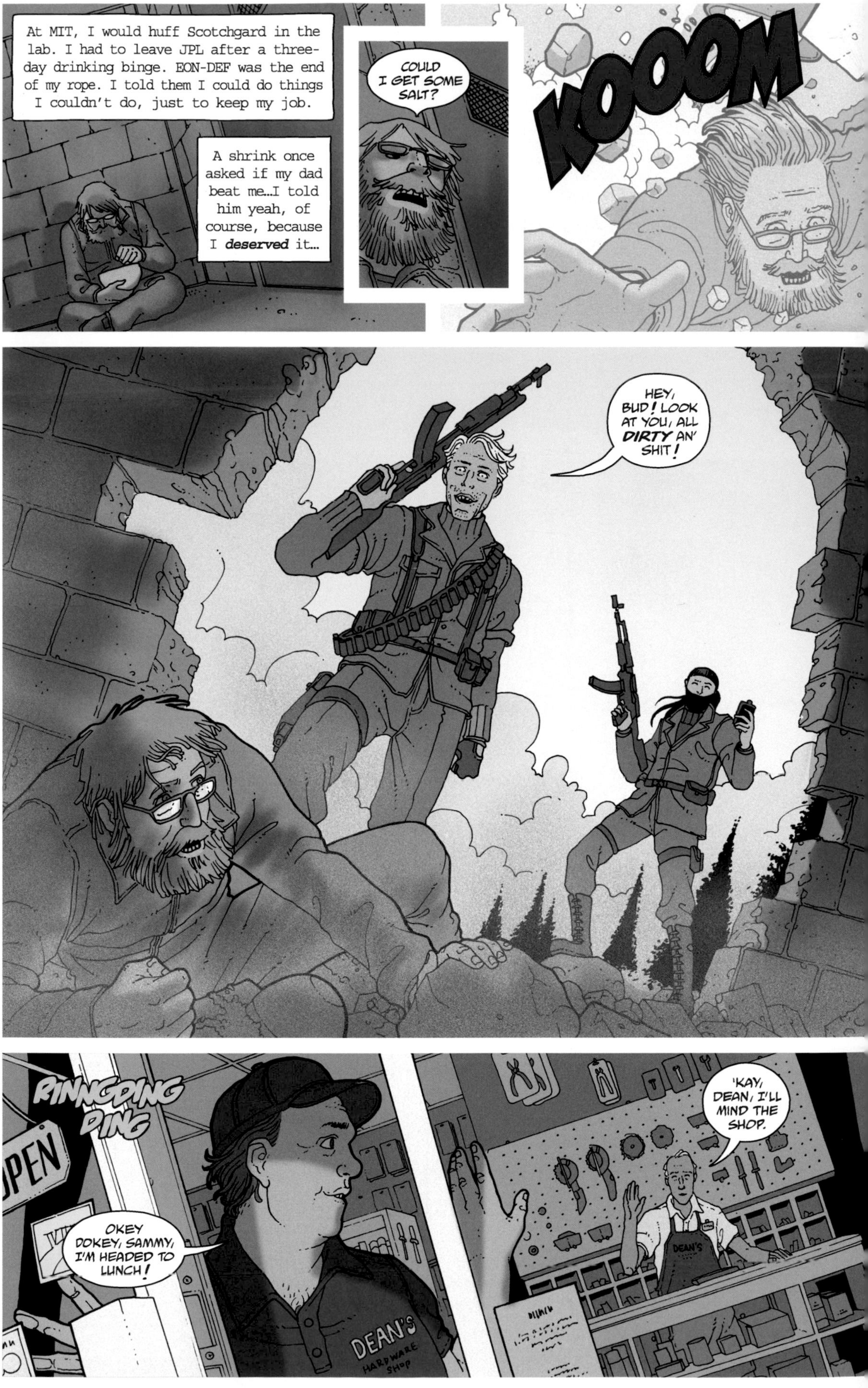
At MIT, I would huff Scotchgard in the lab. I had to leave JPL after a three-day drinking binge. EON-DEF was the end of my rope. I told them I could do things I couldn't do, just to keep my job.
A shrink once asked if my dad beat me...I told him yeah, of course, because I ***deserved*** it...
COULD I GET SOME SALT?
KOOOM
HEY, BUD! LOOK AT YOU, ALL ***DIRTY*** AN' SHIT!
RINNGDING DING
OPEN
OKEY DOKEY, SAMMY, I'M HEADED TO LUNCH!
DEAN'S HARDWARE SHOP
'KAY, DEAN, I'LL MIND THE SHOP.
DEAN'S

"SAMMY," HUH?

BEEN HARD TO TRACK YOU DOWN, DICK. THOUGHT YOU'D GONE OVERSEAS. WOULDN'T HAVE GUESSED A *HARDWARE* STORE IN POUGHKEEPSIE.

YEAH, WELL...I'M OLD FASHIONED.

I KNOW YOU CONNECTED BILL AND CHINESE INTEL. BUT WHO INTERCEPTED BILL'S WORK BEFORE THAT? WHO WAS THE *FLYING WOMAN?*

ASK FUNK. HE RAN *EON-DEF,* AND DAN LAUDERMILK.

YOU DIDN'T HEAR? FUNK OFFED HIM-SELF IN PRISON. BED SHEET THING.

WHO WAS SHE, DICK?

AN UNSECURED FAX...SOMEONE AT AN ELECTRICAL ENGINEERING FIRM...LOOK, AM I GOING TO *PRISON?*

I NEED A *NAME.*

I DON'T WANNA GO TO PRISON...

I CAN'T PROMISE ANY--

THEN *FUCK-A-DOODLE-DO,* YOU CAN KISS MY ASS--

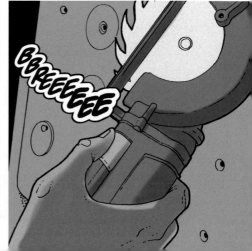

BBREEEEEE

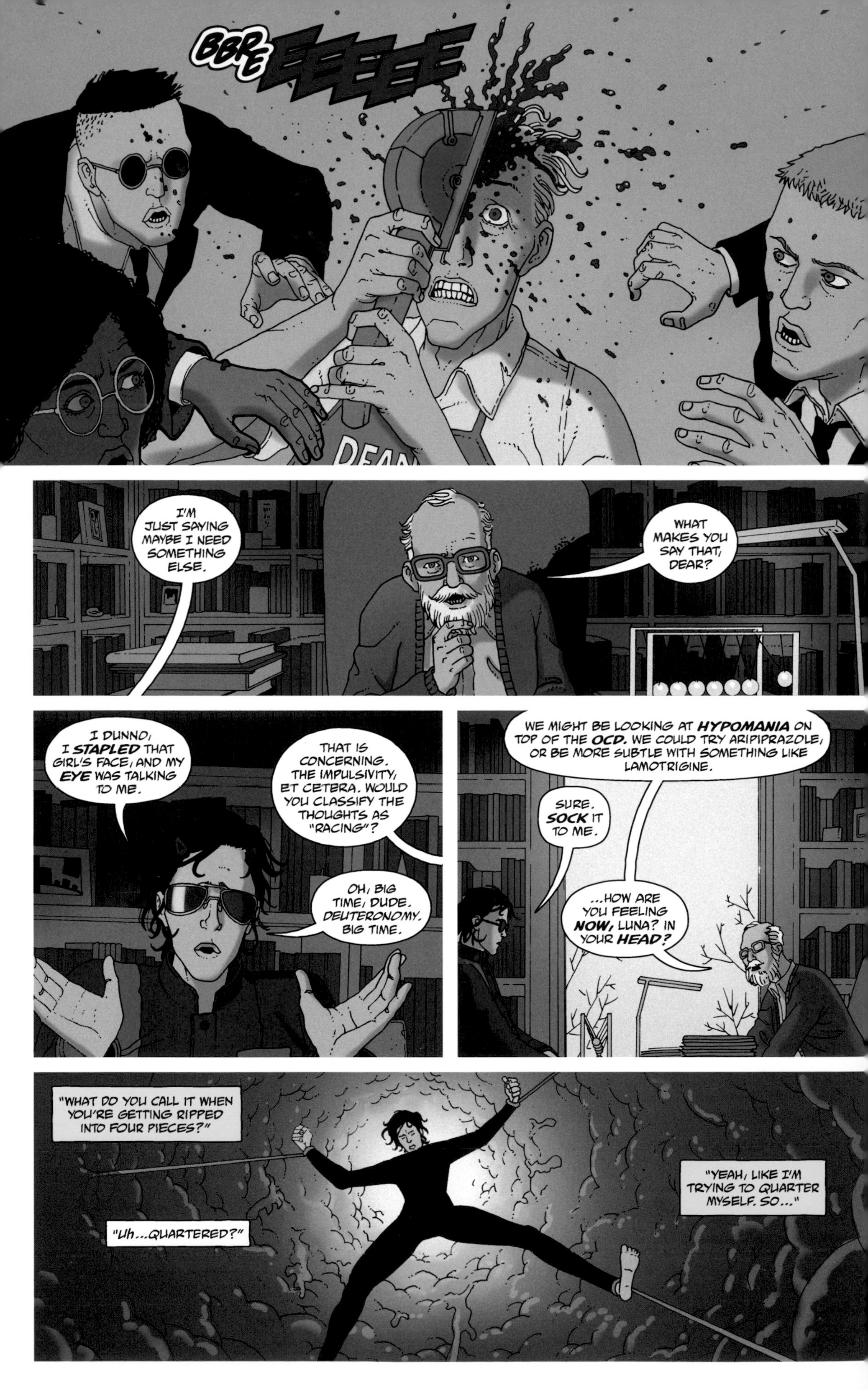
BBRREEEEEEE
DEAN
I'M JUST SAYING MAYBE I NEED SOMETHING ELSE.
WHAT MAKES YOU SAY THAT, DEAR?
I DUNNO, I STAPLED THAT GIRL'S FACE, AND MY EYE WAS TALKING TO ME.
THAT IS CONCERNING. THE IMPULSIVITY, ET CETERA. WOULD YOU CLASSIFY THE THOUGHTS AS "RACING"?
OH, BIG TIME, DUDE. DEUTERONOMY. BIG TIME.
WE MIGHT BE LOOKING AT HYPOMANIA ON TOP OF THE OCD. WE COULD TRY ARIPIPRAZOLE, OR BE MORE SUBTLE WITH SOMETHING LIKE LAMOTRIGINE.
SURE. SOCK IT TO ME.
...HOW ARE YOU FEELING NOW, LUNA? IN YOUR HEAD?
"WHAT DO YOU CALL IT WHEN YOU'RE GETTING RIPPED INTO FOUR PIECES?"
"Uh...QUARTERED?"
"YEAH, LIKE I'M TRYING TO QUARTER MYSELF. SO..."

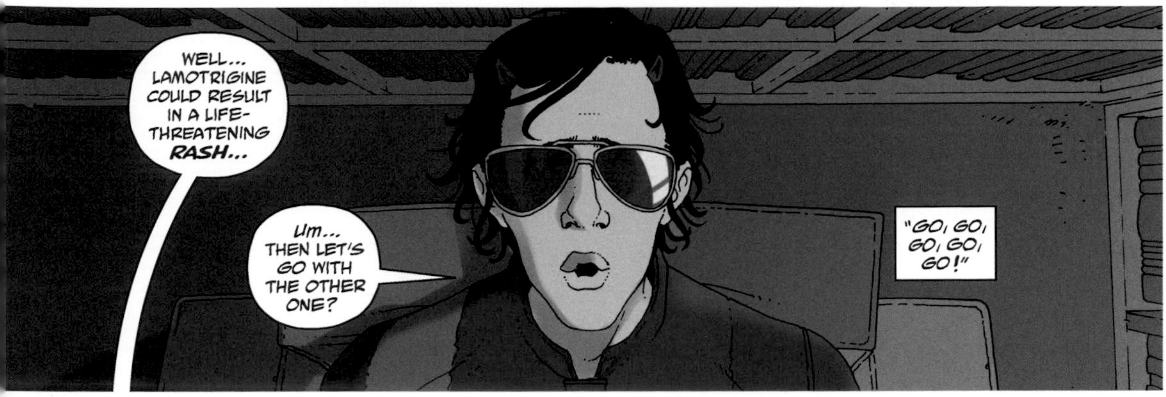
WELL... LAMOTRIGINE COULD RESULT IN A LIFE-THREATENING RASH...
UM... THEN LET'S GO WITH THE OTHER ONE?
"GO, GO, GO, GO, GO!"

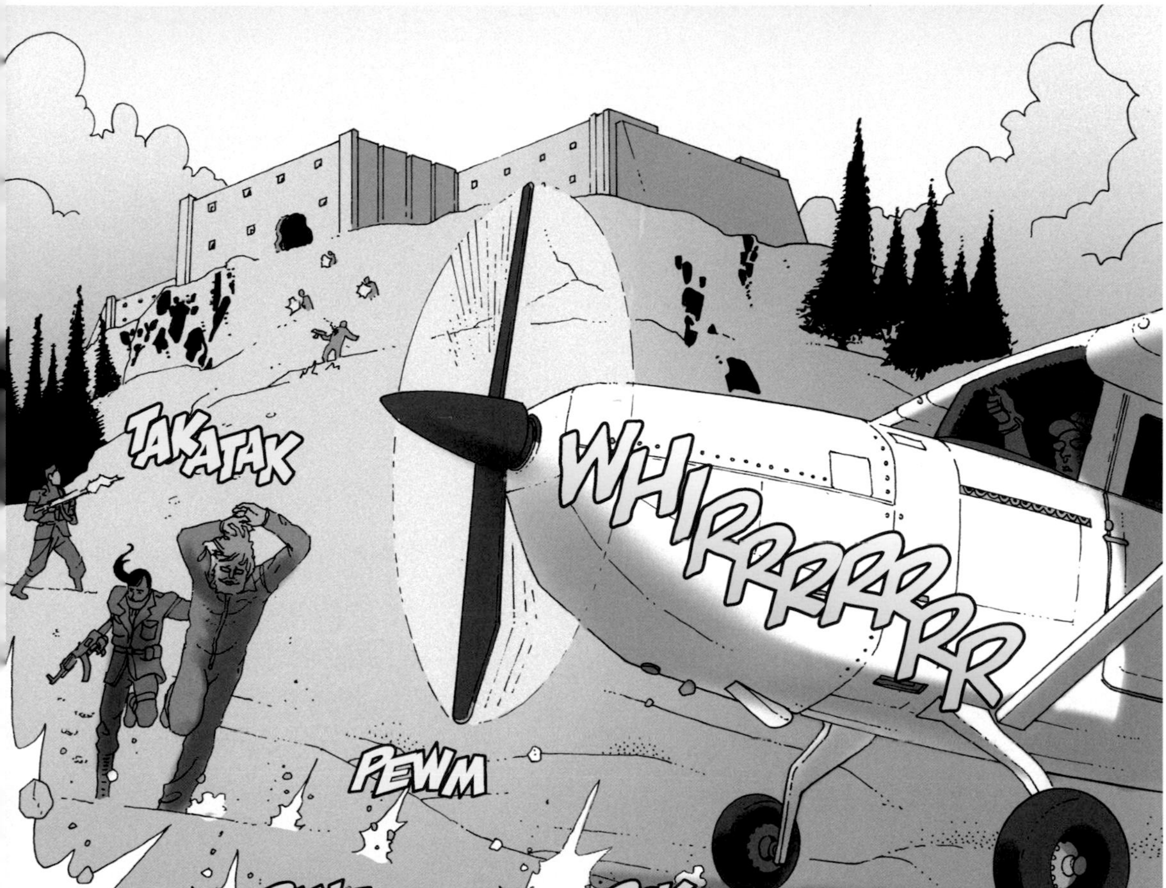
TAKATAK
WHIRRRRRRR
PEWM
PANG
POK

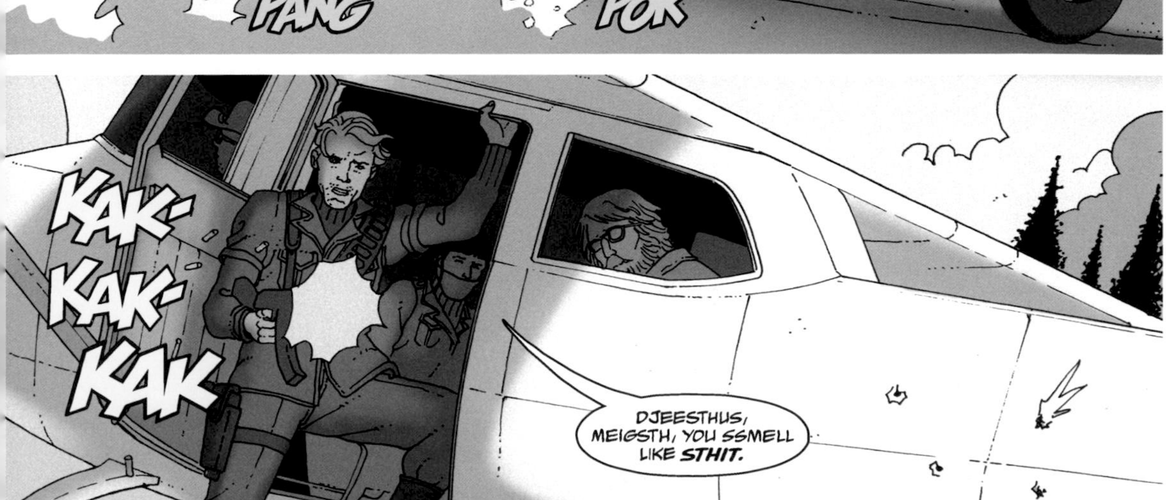
KAK-KAK-KAK
DJEESTHUS, MEIGSTH, YOU SSMELL LIKE STHIT.

"OKAY, BILLY BOY. LET'S TALK SHOP."

THE ACCELERATOR. ELECTRO-MAGNETIC PROPULSION. *PLUTONIUM* CORE. SYSTEM IS SUPER-COOLED BY HELIUM 4. RIGHT?

ACCORDING TO MAYURA HOWARD, YES.

WHERE'D SHE GO RIGHT WHERE YOU WENT WRONG? BEFORE SHE WENT WRONG HERSELF?

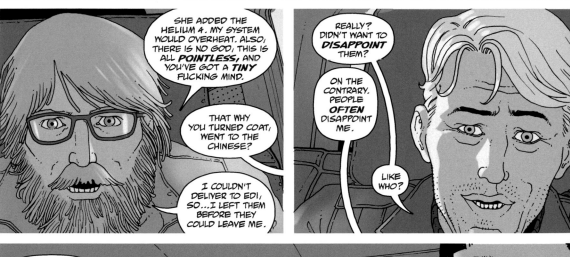

SHE ADDED THE HELIUM 4. MY SYSTEM WOULD OVERHEAT. ALSO, THERE IS NO GOD, THIS IS ALL *POINTLESS,* AND YOU'VE GOT A *TINY* FUCKING MIND.

THAT WHY YOU TURNED COAT, WENT TO THE CHINESE?

I COULDN'T DELIVER TO EDI, SO...I LEFT THEM BEFORE THEY COULD LEAVE ME.

REALLY? DIDN'T WANT TO *DISAPPOINT* THEM?

ON THE CONTRARY, PEOPLE *OFTEN* DISAPPOINT ME.

LIKE WHO?

EVERYONE.

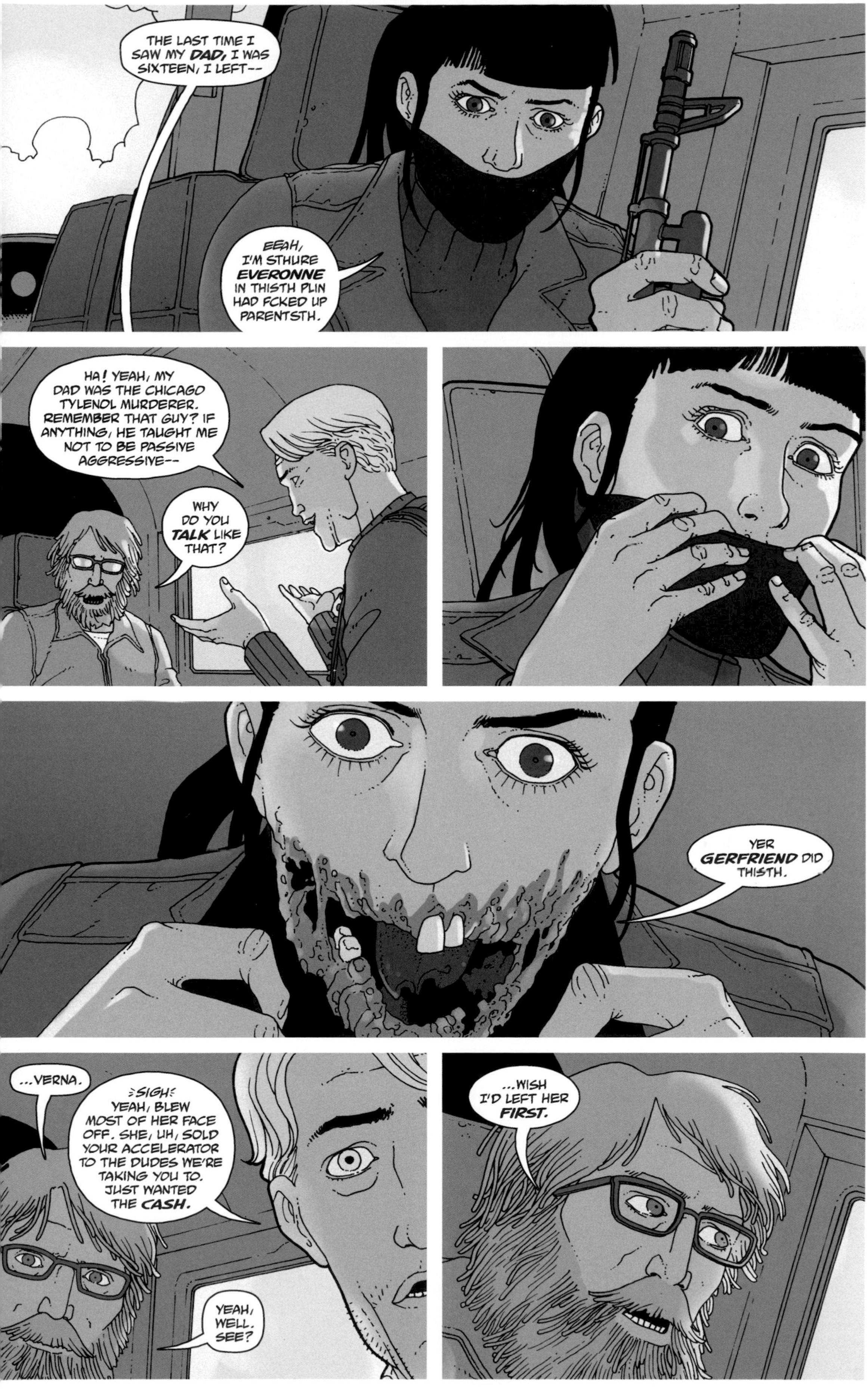
THE LAST TIME I SAW MY DAD, I WAS SIXTEEN, I LEFT--
EEAH, I'M STHURE EVERONNE IN THISTH PLIN HAD FCKED UP PARENTSTH.
HA! YEAH, MY DAD WAS THE CHICAGO TYLENOL MURDERER. REMEMBER THAT GUY? IF ANYTHING, HE TAUGHT ME NOT TO BE PASSIVE AGGRESSIVE--
WHY DO YOU TALK LIKE THAT?
YER GERFRIEND DID THISTH.
...VERNA.
≶SIGH≷ YEAH, BLEW MOST OF HER FACE OFF. SHE, UH, SOLD YOUR ACCELERATOR TO THE DUDES WE'RE TAKING YOU TO. JUST WANTED THE CASH.
YEAH, WELL. SEE?
...WISH I'D LEFT HER FIRST.

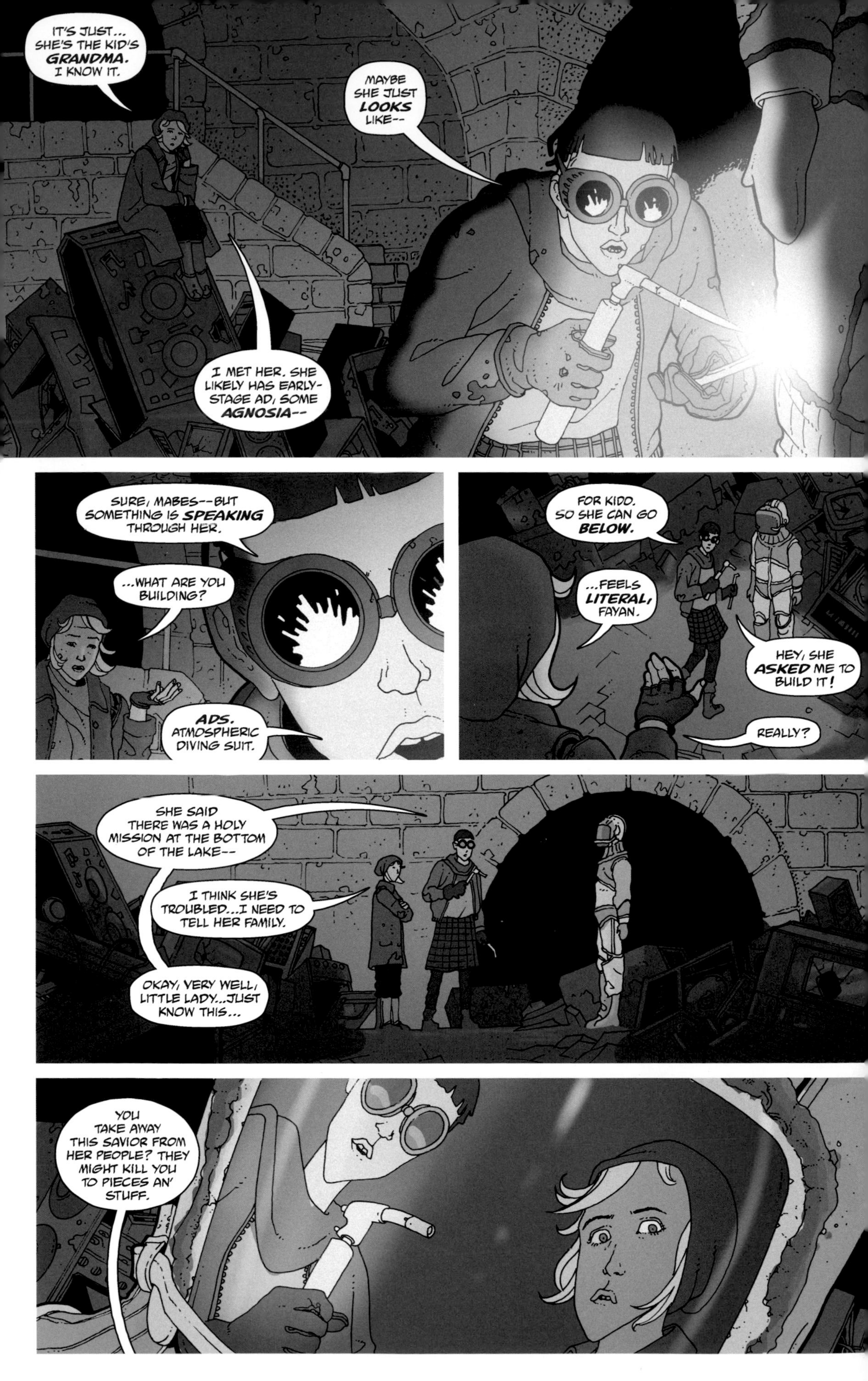
IT'S JUST... SHE'S THE KID'S GRANDMA. I KNOW IT.
MAYBE SHE JUST LOOKS LIKE--
I MET HER. SHE LIKELY HAS EARLY-STAGE AD, SOME AGNOSIA--
SURE, MABES--BUT SOMETHING IS SPEAKING THROUGH HER.
...WHAT ARE YOU BUILDING?
ADS. ATMOSPHERIC DIVING SUIT.
FOR KIDD. SO SHE CAN GO BELOW.
...FEELS LITERAL, FAYAN.
HEY, SHE ASKED ME TO BUILD IT!
REALLY?
SHE SAID THERE WAS A HOLY MISSION AT THE BOTTOM OF THE LAKE--
I THINK SHE'S TROUBLED...I NEED TO TELL HER FAMILY.
OKAY, VERY WELL, LITTLE LADY...JUST KNOW THIS...
YOU TAKE AWAY THIS SAVIOR FROM HER PEOPLE? THEY MIGHT KILL YOU TO PIECES AN' STUFF.

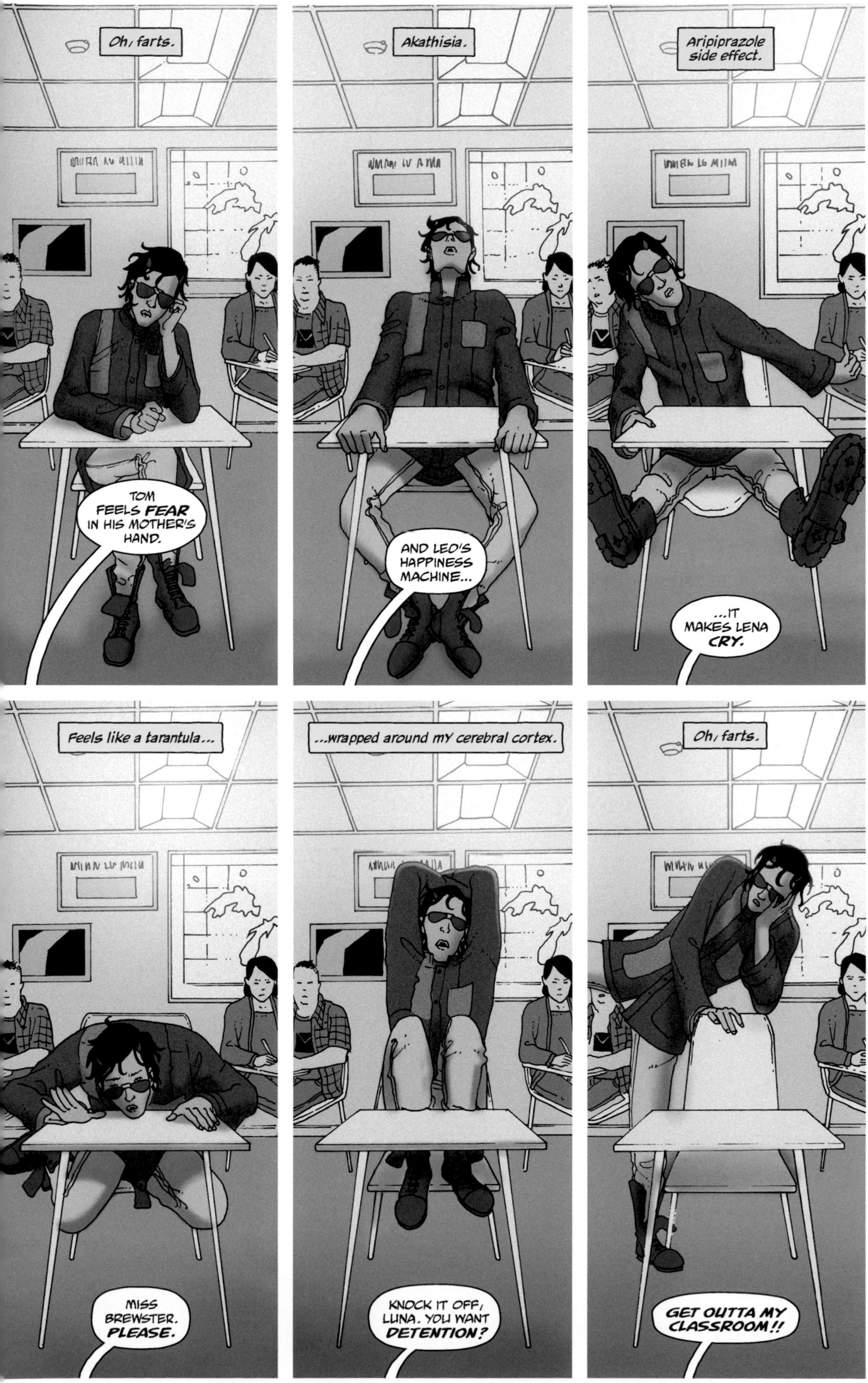
Oh, farts.
TOM FEELS FEAR IN HIS MOTHER'S HAND.
Akathisia.
AND LEO'S HAPPINESS MACHINE...
Aripiprazole side effect.
...IT MAKES LENA CRY.
Feels like a tarantula...
MISS BREWSTER. PLEASE.
...wrapped around my cerebral cortex.
KNOCK IT OFF, LUNA. YOU WANT DETENTION?
Oh, farts.
GET OUTTA MY CLASSROOM!!

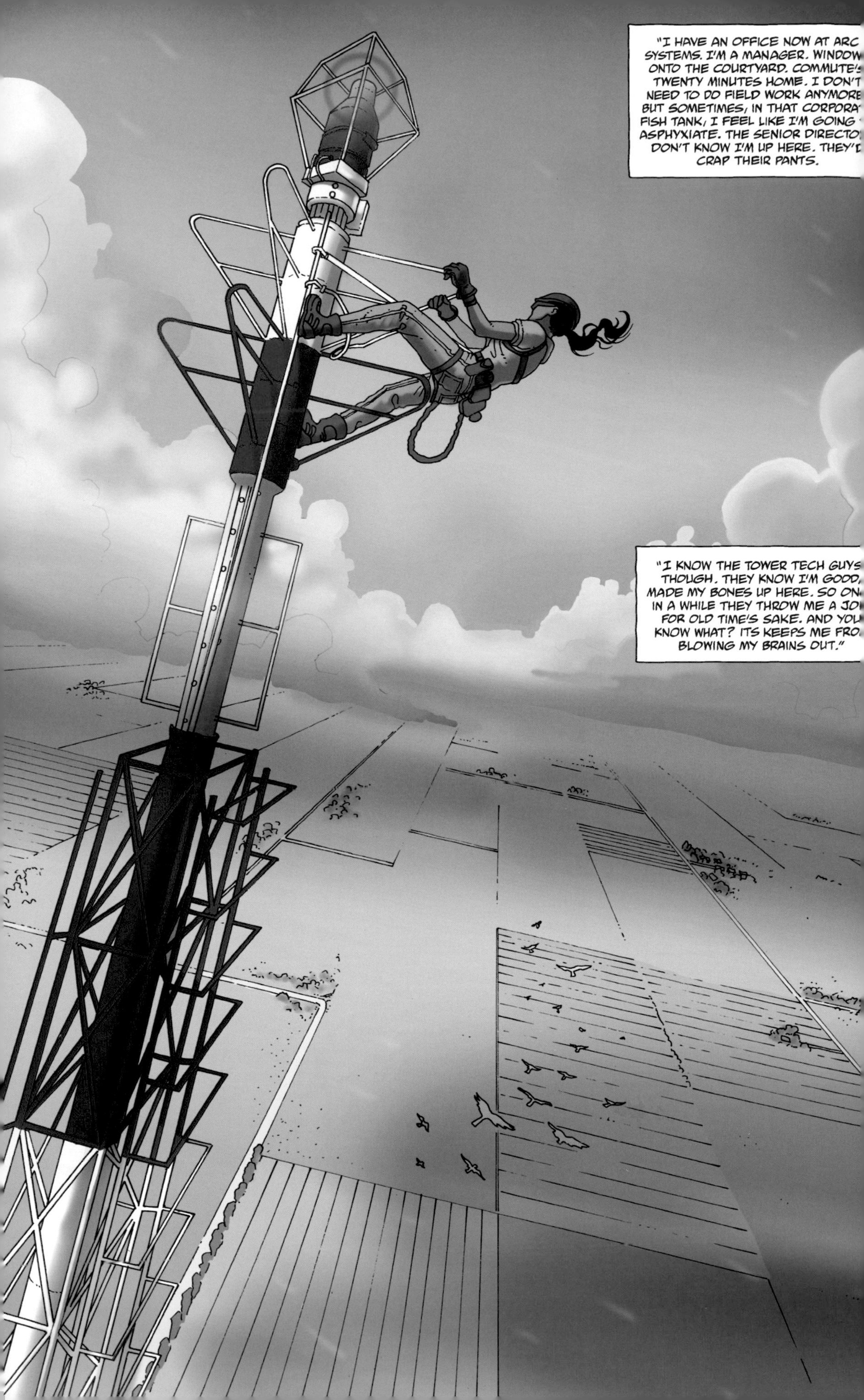
"I HAVE AN OFFICE NOW AT ARC SYSTEMS. I'M A MANAGER. WINDOW ONTO THE COURTYARD. COMMUTE'S TWENTY MINUTES HOME. I DON'T NEED TO DO FIELD WORK ANYMORE BUT SOMETIMES, IN THAT CORPORA FISH TANK, I FEEL LIKE I'M GOING ASPHYXIATE. THE SENIOR DIRECTO DON'T KNOW I'M UP HERE. THEY' CRAP THEIR PANTS.
"I KNOW THE TOWER TECH GUYS THOUGH. THEY KNOW I'M GOOD, MADE MY BONES UP HERE. SO ON IN A WHILE THEY THROW ME A JO FOR OLD TIME'S SAKE. AND YOU KNOW WHAT? ITS KEEPS ME FRO BLOWING MY BRAINS OUT."

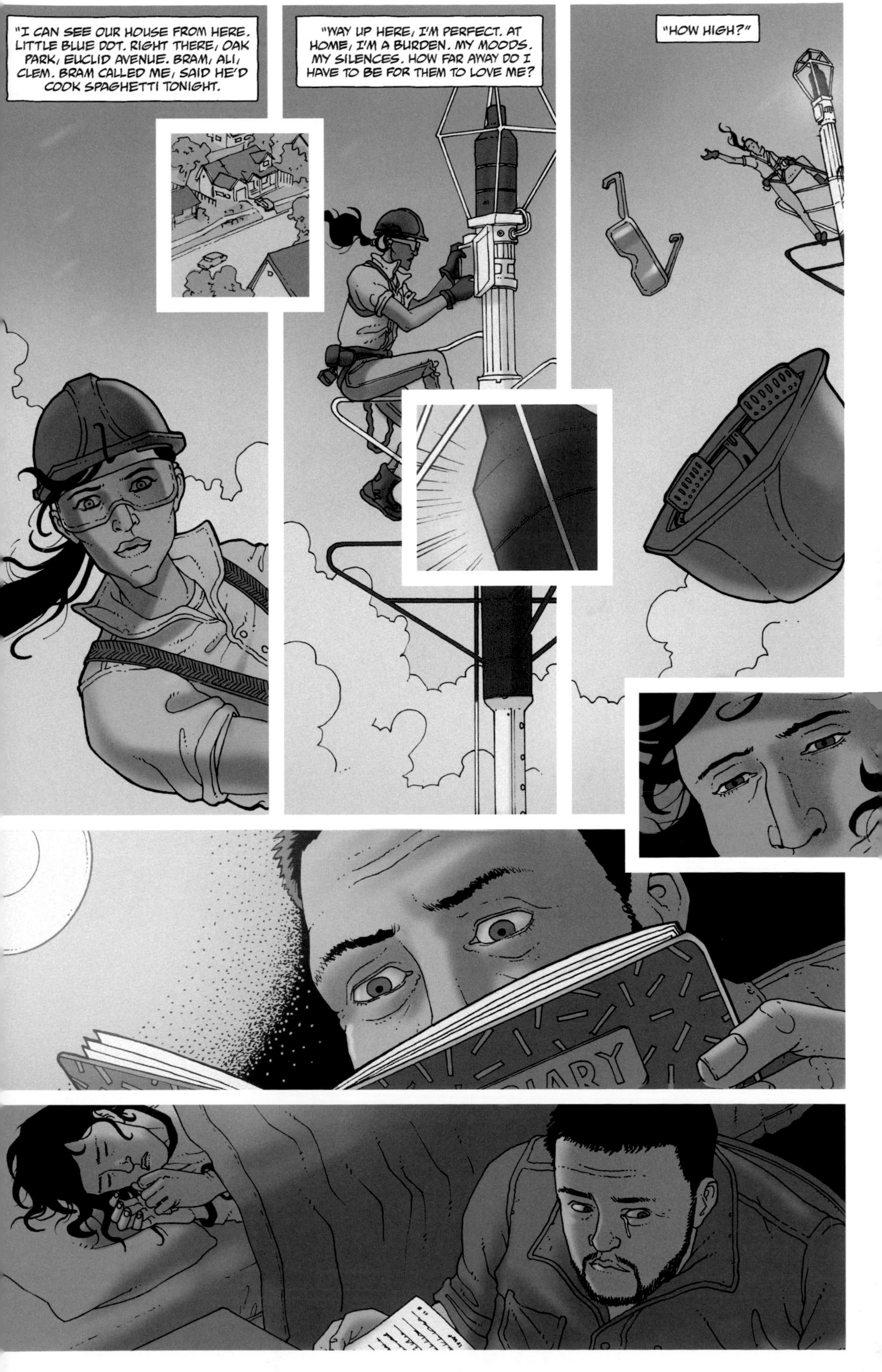
"I CAN SEE OUR HOUSE FROM HERE. LITTLE BLUE DOT. RIGHT THERE, OAK PARK, EUCLID AVENUE. BRAM, ALI, CLEM. BRAM CALLED ME, SAID HE'D COOK SPAGHETTI TONIGHT.
"WAY UP HERE, I'M PERFECT. AT HOME, I'M A BURDEN. MY MOODS. MY SILENCES. HOW FAR AWAY DO I HAVE TO BE FOR THEM TO LOVE ME?
"HOW HIGH?"
DIARY

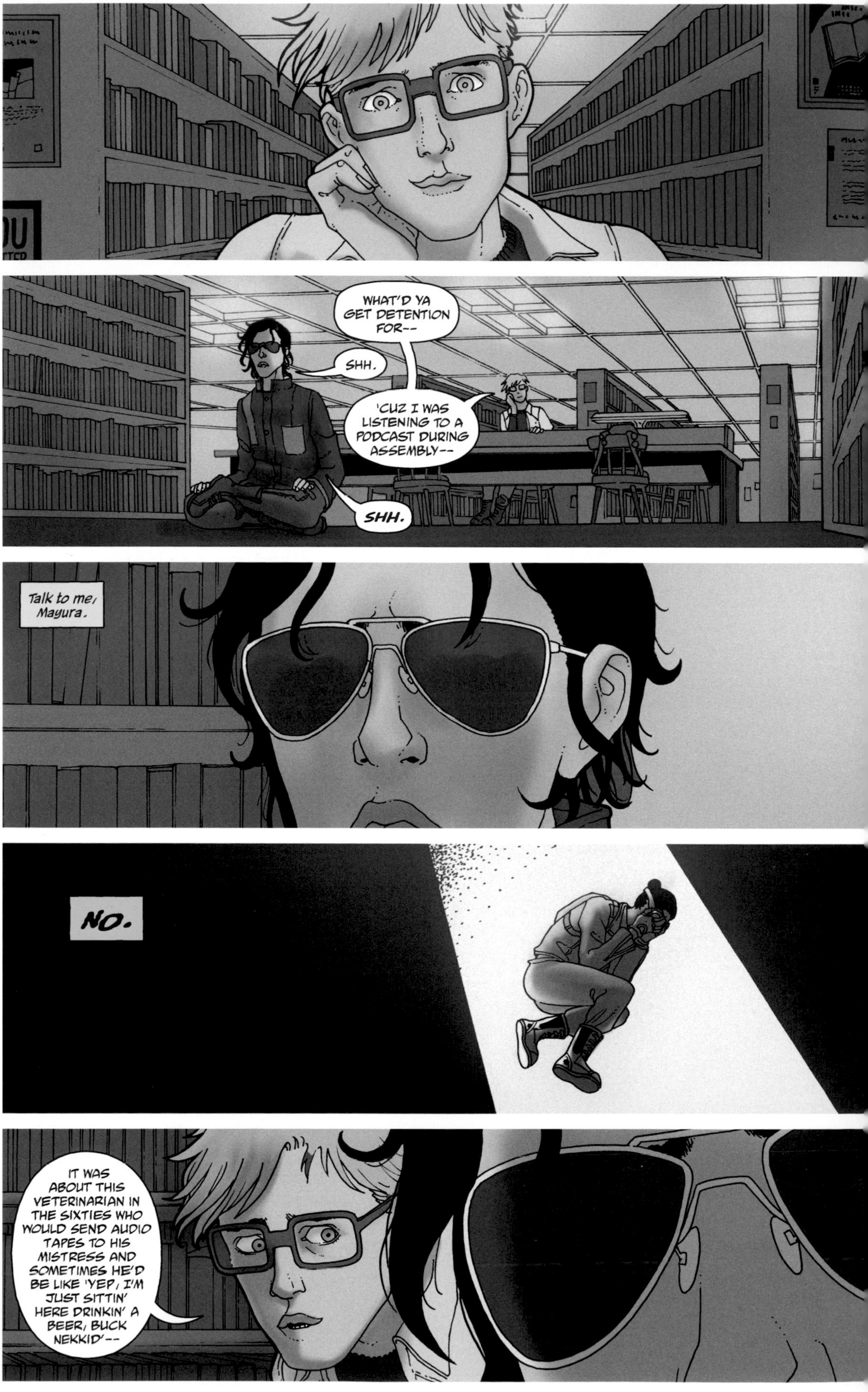
WHAT'D YA GET DETENTION FOR--
SHH.
'CUZ I WAS LISTENING TO A PODCAST DURING ASSEMBLY--
SHH.
Talk to me, Mayura.
NO.
IT WAS ABOUT THIS VETERINARIAN IN THE SIXTIES WHO WOULD SEND AUDIO TAPES TO HIS MISTRESS AND SOMETIMES HE'D BE LIKE 'YEP, I'M JUST SITTIN' HERE DRINKIN' A BEER, BUCK NEKKID'--

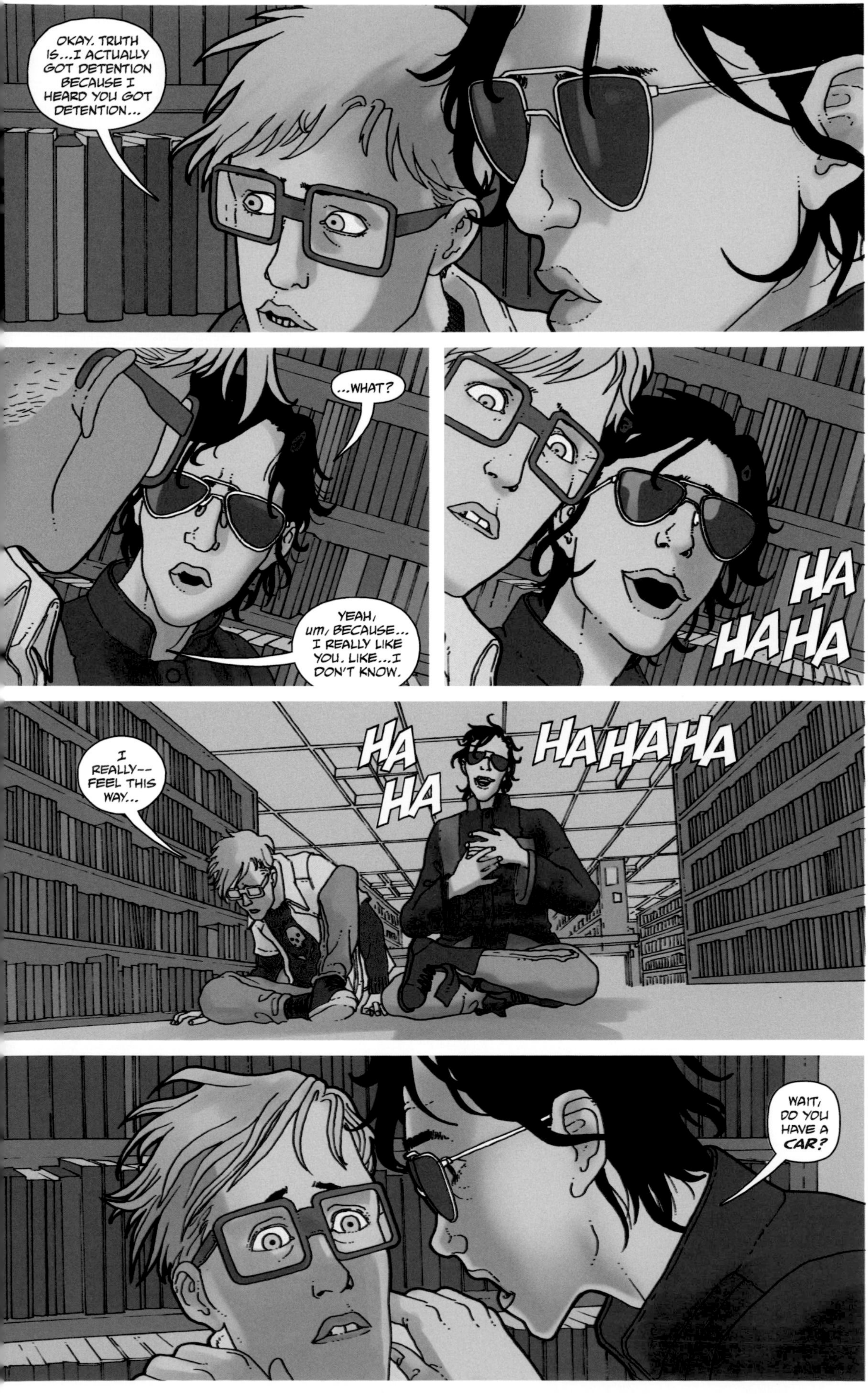
OKAY. TRUTH IS...I ACTUALLY GOT DETENTION BECAUSE I HEARD YOU GOT DETENTION...
...WHAT?
YEAH, UM, BECAUSE... I REALLY LIKE YOU. LIKE...I DON'T KNOW.
HA HAHA
I REALLY-- FEEL THIS WAY...
HA HA
HAHAHA
WAIT, DO YOU HAVE A CAR?

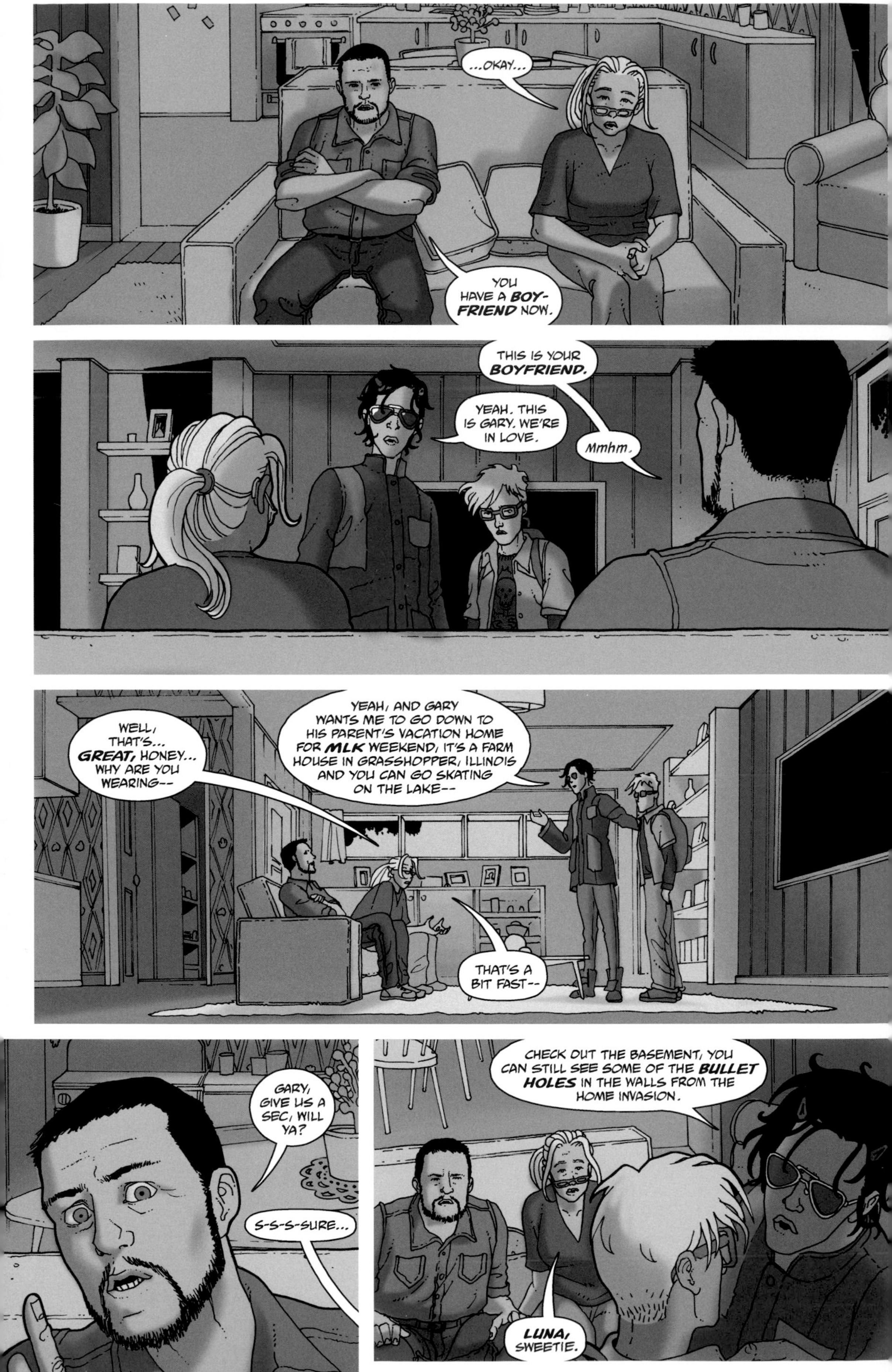
...OKAY...
YOU HAVE A BOY-FRIEND NOW.
THIS IS YOUR BOYFRIEND.
YEAH. THIS IS GARY. WE'RE IN LOVE.
Mmhm.
WELL, THAT'S... GREAT, HONEY... WHY ARE YOU WEARING--
YEAH, AND GARY WANTS ME TO GO DOWN TO HIS PARENT'S VACATION HOME FOR MLK WEEKEND, IT'S A FARM HOUSE IN GRASSHOPPER, ILLINOIS AND YOU CAN GO SKATING ON THE LAKE--
THAT'S A BIT FAST--
GARY, GIVE US A SEC, WILL YA?
S-S-S-SURE...
CHECK OUT THE BASEMENT, YOU CAN STILL SEE SOME OF THE BULLET HOLES IN THE WALLS FROM THE HOME INVASION.
LUNA, SWEETIE.

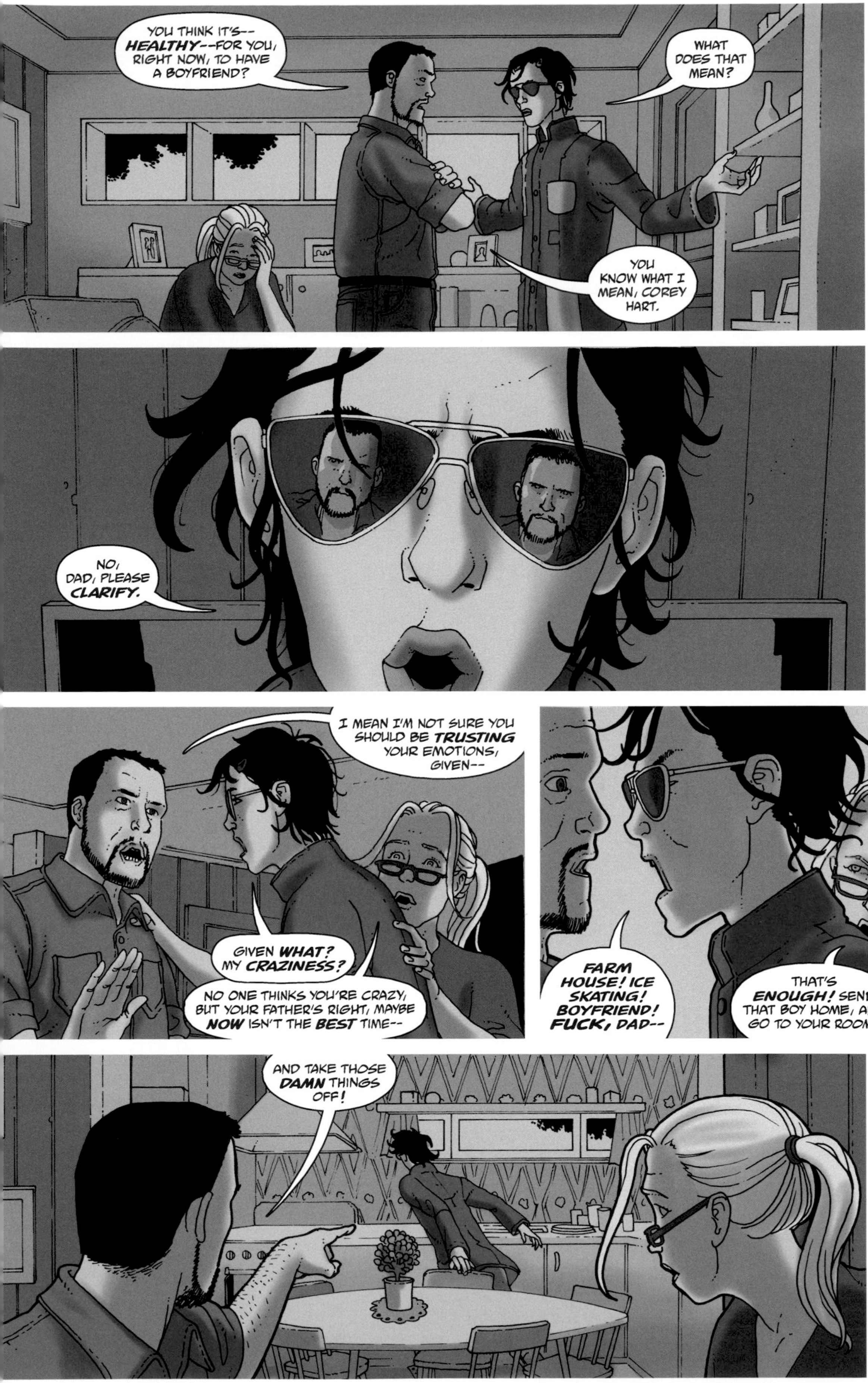
YOU THINK IT'S--
HEALTHY--FOR YOU, RIGHT NOW, TO HAVE A BOYFRIEND?
WHAT DOES THAT MEAN?
YOU KNOW WHAT I MEAN, COREY HART.
NO, DAD, PLEASE CLARIFY.
I MEAN I'M NOT SURE YOU SHOULD BE TRUSTING YOUR EMOTIONS, GIVEN--
GIVEN WHAT? MY CRAZINESS?
NO ONE THINKS YOU'RE CRAZY, BUT YOUR FATHER'S RIGHT, MAYBE NOW ISN'T THE BEST TIME--
FARM HOUSE! ICE SKATING! BOYFRIEND! FUCK, DAD--
THAT'S ENOUGH! SEND THAT BOY HOME, AND GO TO YOUR ROOM!
AND TAKE THOSE DAMN THINGS OFF!

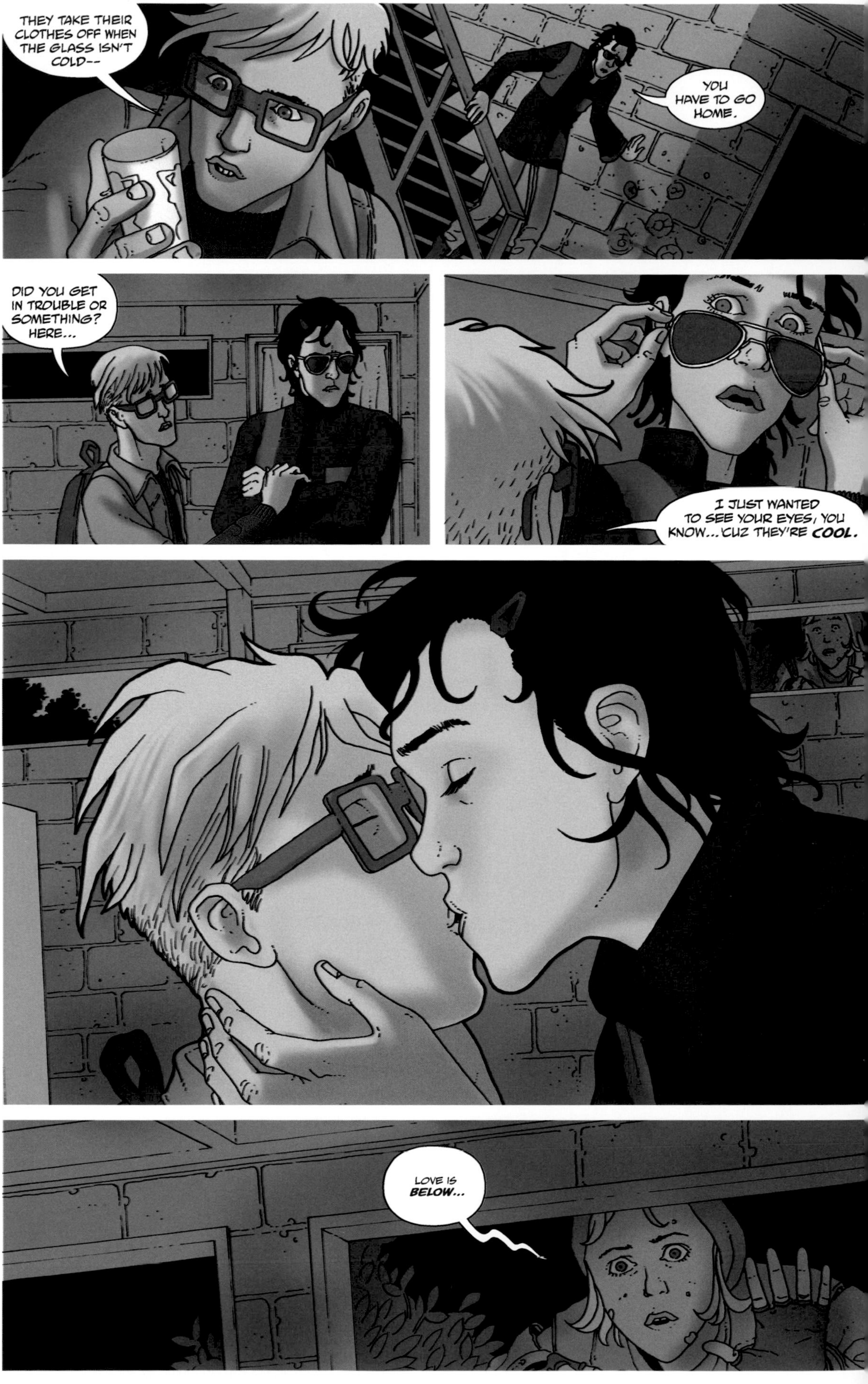
THEY TAKE THEIR CLOTHES OFF WHEN THE GLASS ISN'T COLD--
YOU HAVE TO GO HOME.
DID YOU GET IN TROUBLE OR SOMETHING? HERE...
I JUST WANTED TO SEE YOUR EYES, YOU KNOW...'CUZ THEY'RE COOL.
LOVE IS BELOW...

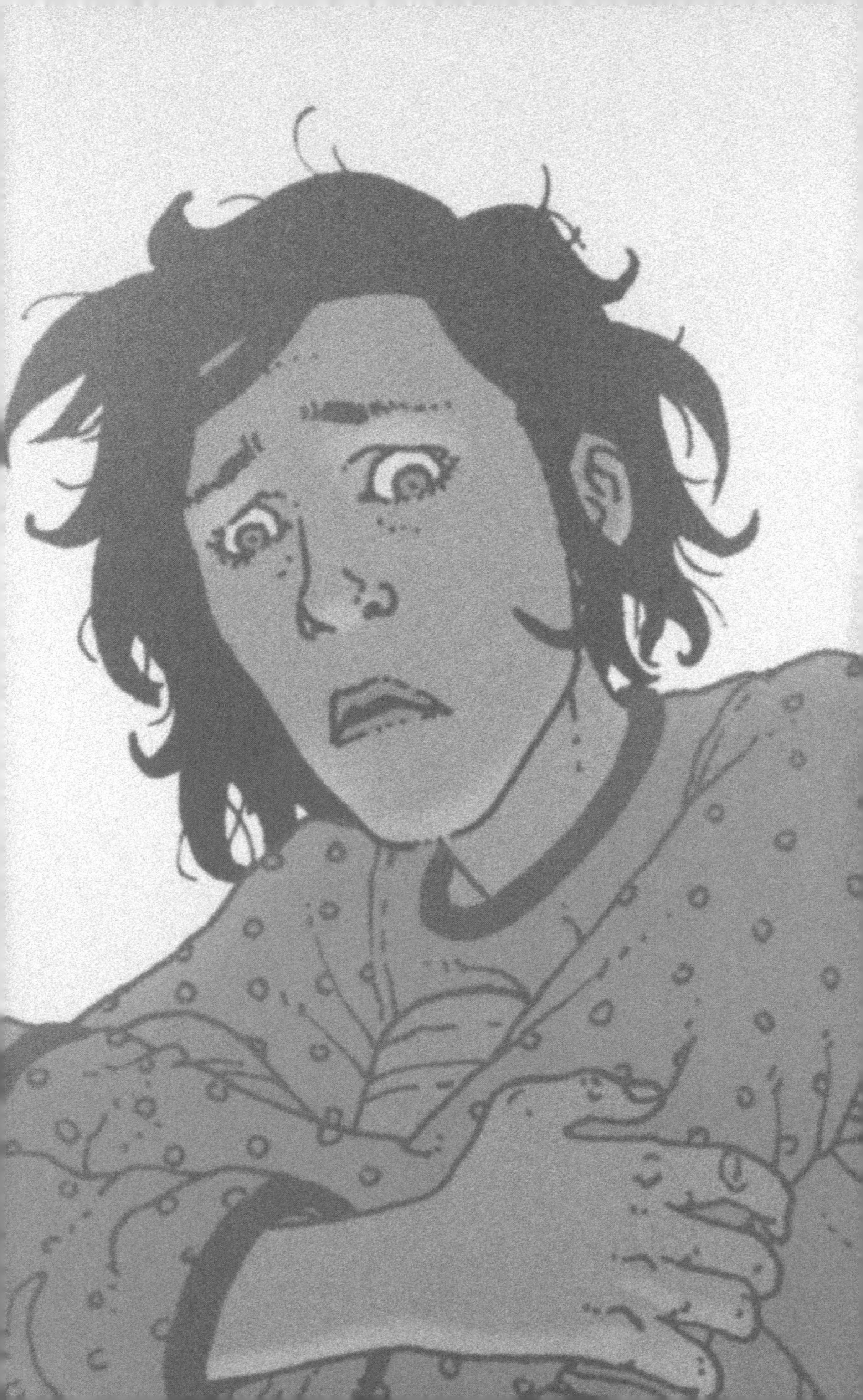

CHAPTER III
"Harold"

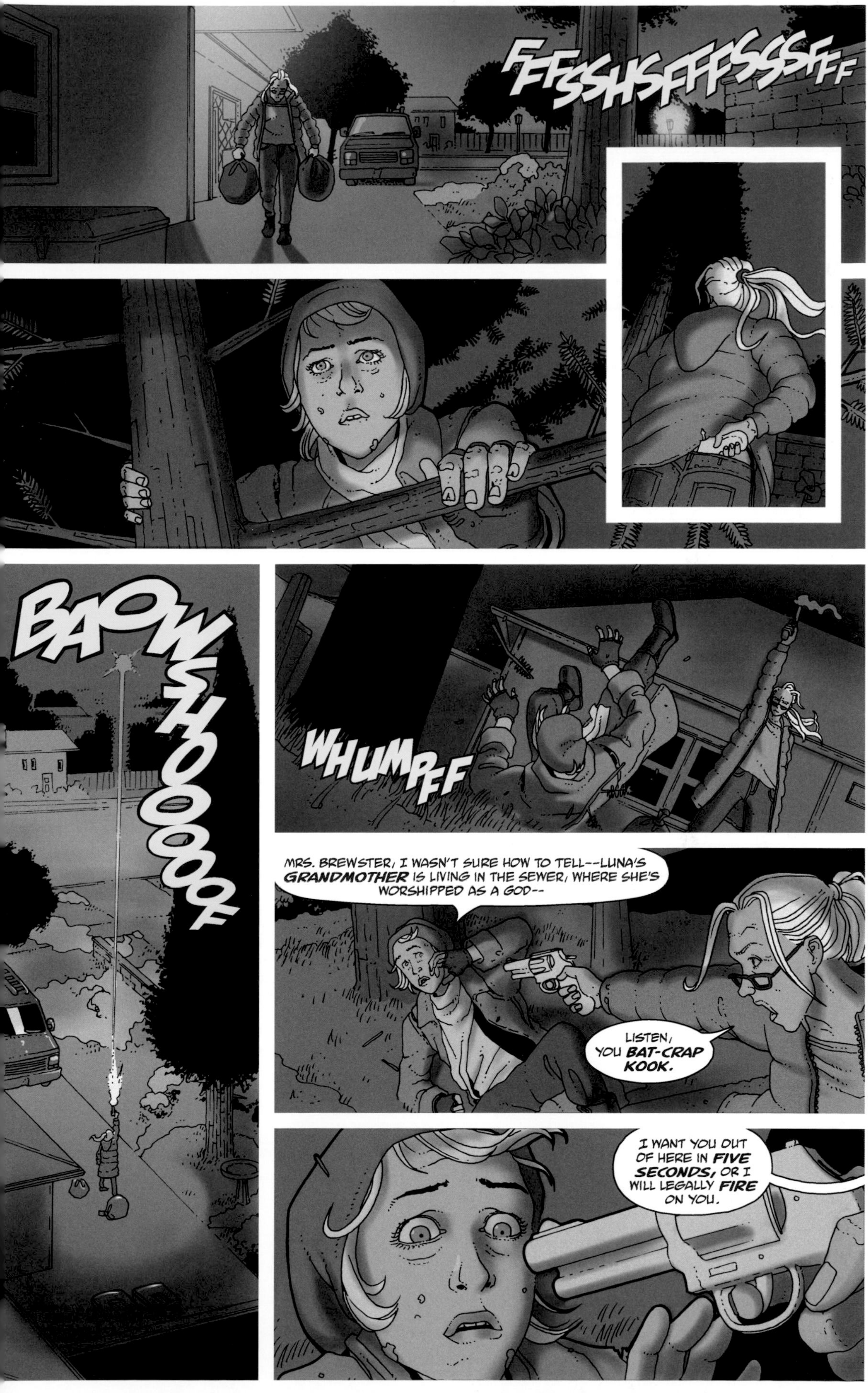
FFFSSHSFFFSSSFFF
BAOWSHOOOOOOF
WHUMPFF
MRS. BREWSTER, I WASN'T SURE HOW TO TELL--LUNA'S GRANDMOTHER IS LIVING IN THE SEWER, WHERE SHE'S WORSHIPPED AS A GOD--
LISTEN, YOU BAT-CRAP KOOK.
I WANT YOU OUT OF HERE IN FIVE SECONDS, OR I WILL LEGALLY FIRE ON YOU.

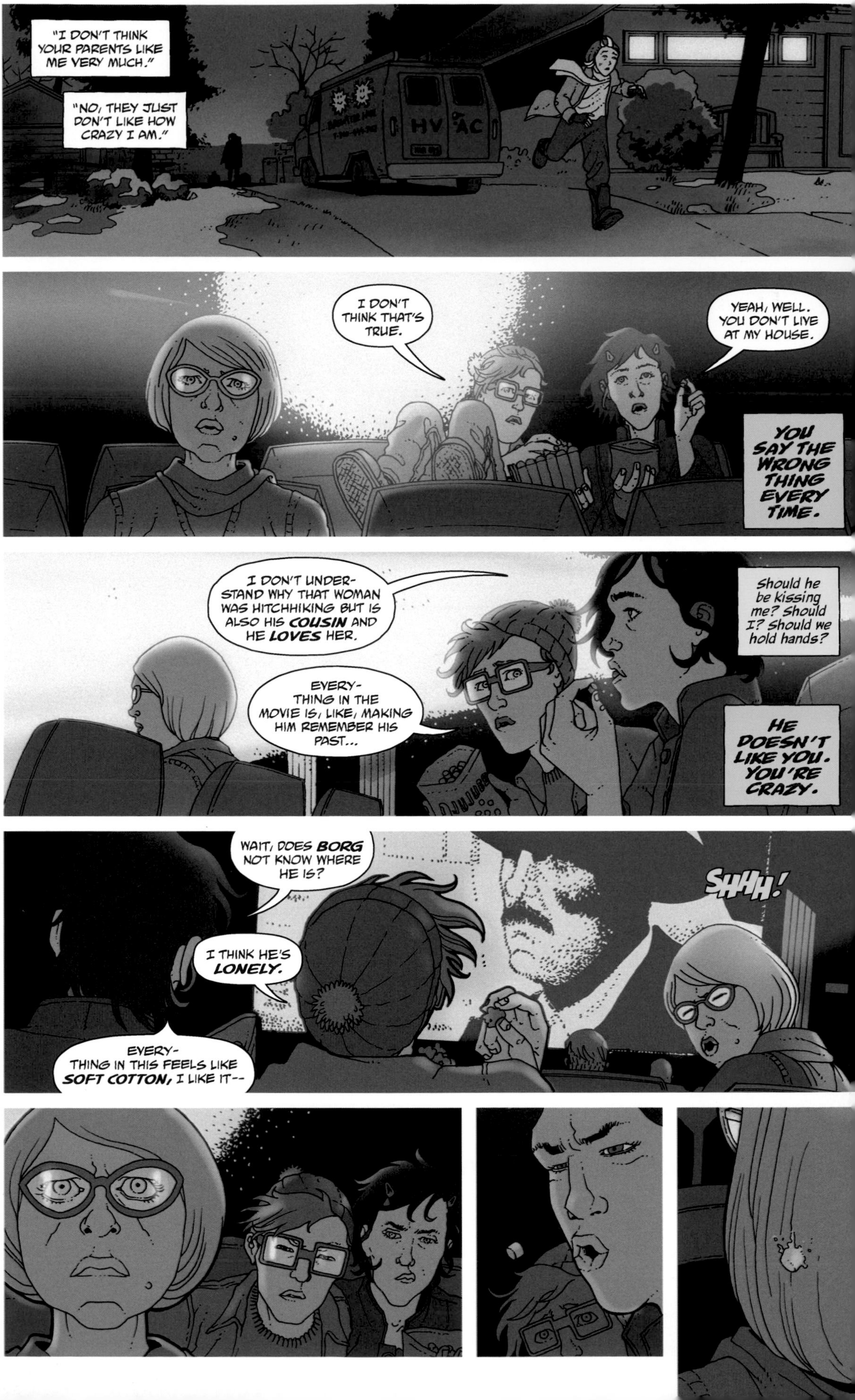
"I DON'T THINK YOUR PARENTS LIKE ME VERY MUCH."
"NO, THEY JUST DON'T LIKE HOW CRAZY I AM."
HV AC
I DON'T THINK THAT'S TRUE.
YEAH, WELL. YOU DON'T LIVE AT MY HOUSE.
YOU SAY THE WRONG THING EVERY TIME.
I DON'T UNDER-STAND WHY THAT WOMAN WAS HITCHHIKING BUT IS ALSO HIS COUSIN AND HE LOVES HER.
Should he be kissing me? Should I? Should we hold hands?
EVERY-THING IN THE MOVIE IS, LIKE, MAKING HIM REMEMBER HIS PAST...
HE DOESN'T LIKE YOU. YOU'RE CRAZY.
WAIT, DOES BORG NOT KNOW WHERE HE IS?
SHHH!
I THINK HE'S LONELY.
EVERY-THING IN THIS FEELS LIKE SOFT COTTON, I LIKE IT--

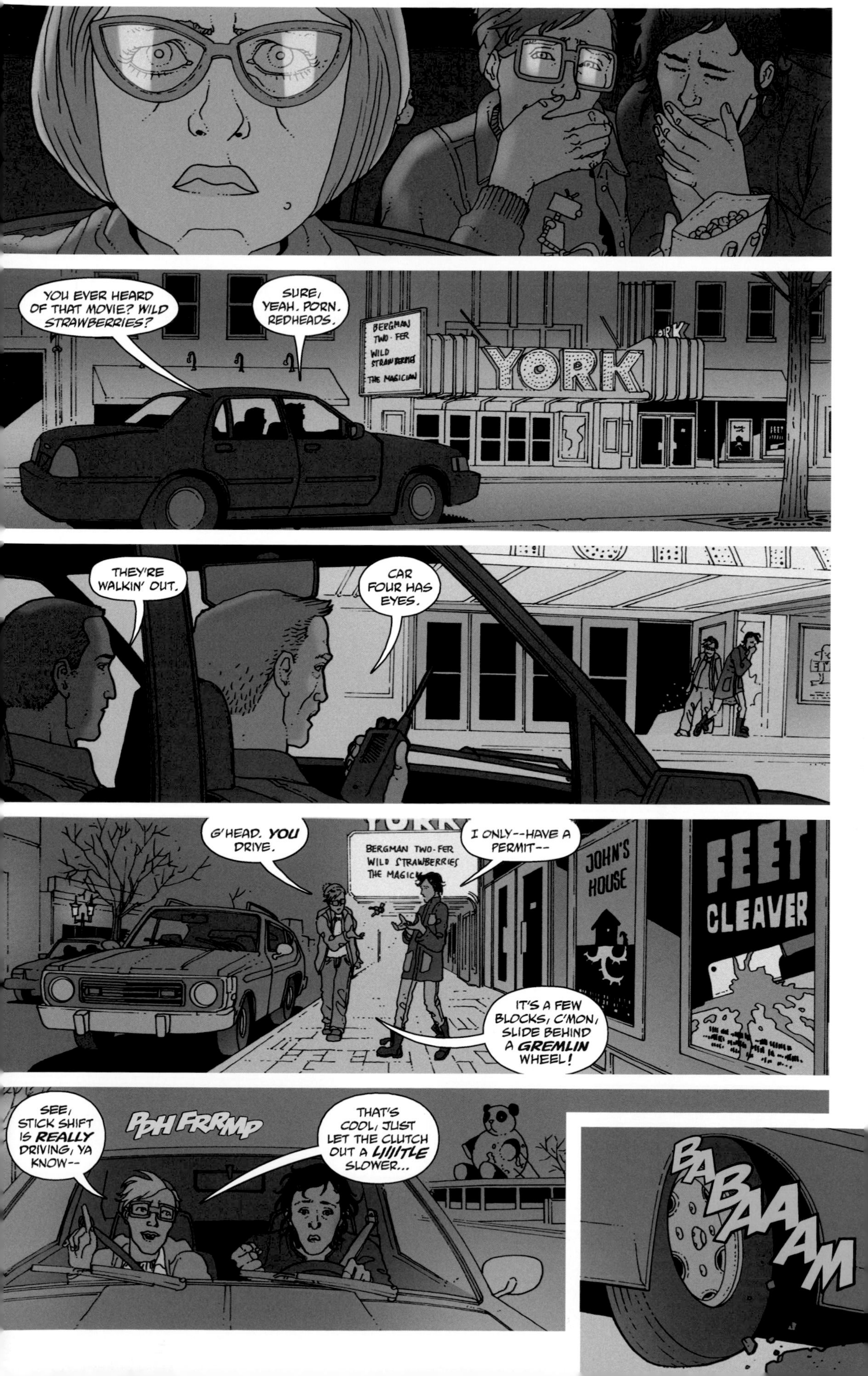
YOU EVER HEARD OF THAT MOVIE? WILD STRAWBERRIES?
SURE, YEAH. PORN. REDHEADS.
BERGMAN TWO-FER WILD STRAWBERRIES THE MAGICIAN
YORK
THEY'RE WALKIN' OUT.
CAR FOUR HAS EYES.
G'HEAD. YOU DRIVE.
BERGMAN TWO-FER WILD STRAWBERRIES THE MAGIC
I ONLY--HAVE A PERMIT--
JOHN'S HOUSE
FEET CLEAVER
IT'S A FEW BLOCKS, C'MON, SLIDE BEHIND A GREMLIN WHEEL!
SEE, STICK SHIFT IS REALLY DRIVING, YA KNOW--
PPH FRRMP
THAT'S COOL, JUST LET THE CLUTCH OUT A LIIIITLE SLOWER...
BABAAAM

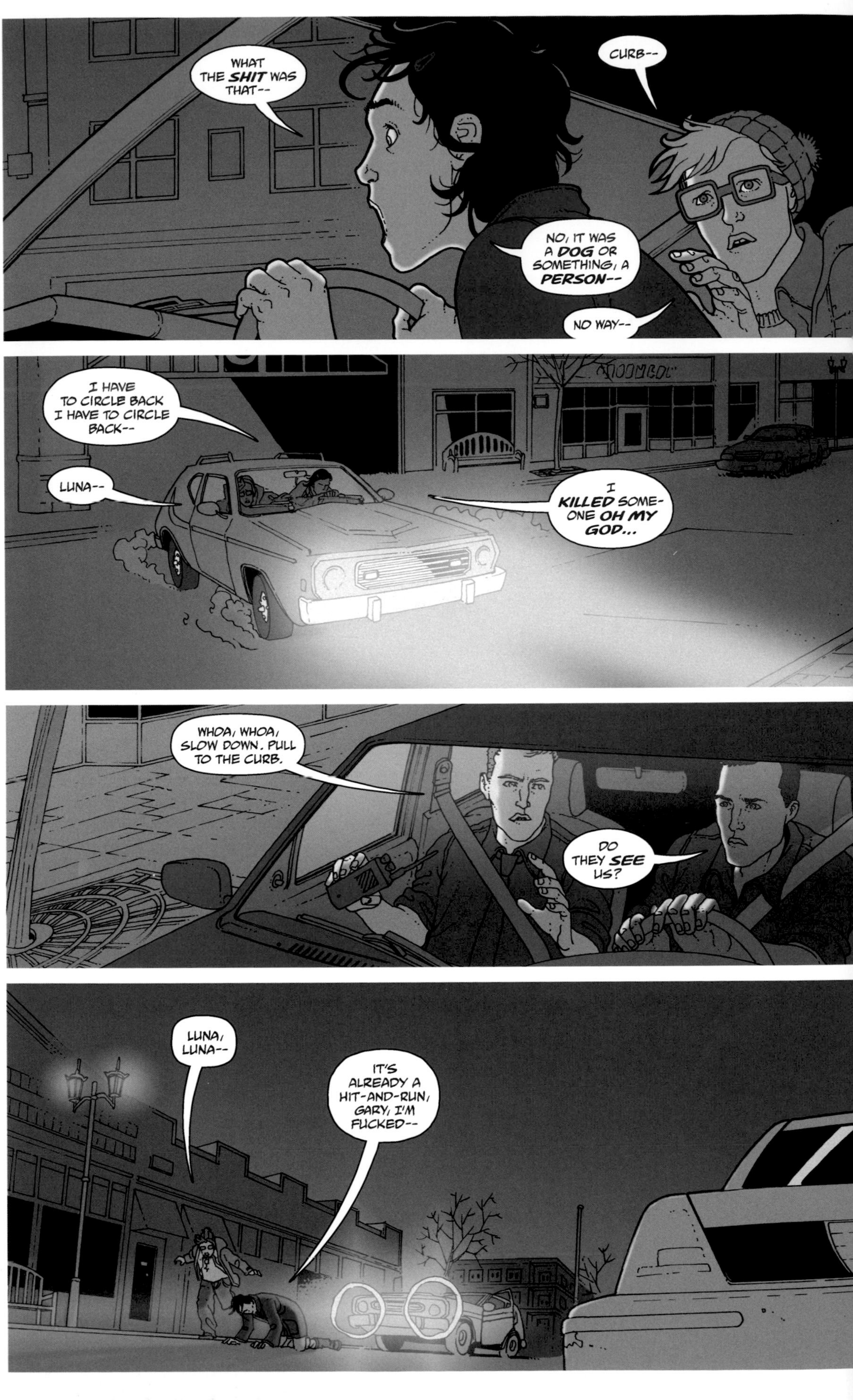
WHAT THE SHIT WAS THAT--
CURB--
NO, IT WAS A DOG OR SOMETHING, A PERSON--
NO WAY--
I HAVE TO CIRCLE BACK I HAVE TO CIRCLE BACK--
LUNA--
I KILLED SOME-ONE OH MY GOD...
WHOA, WHOA, SLOW DOWN. PULL TO THE CURB.
DO THEY SEE US?
LUNA, LUNA--
IT'S ALREADY A HIT-AND-RUN, GARY, I'M FUCKED--

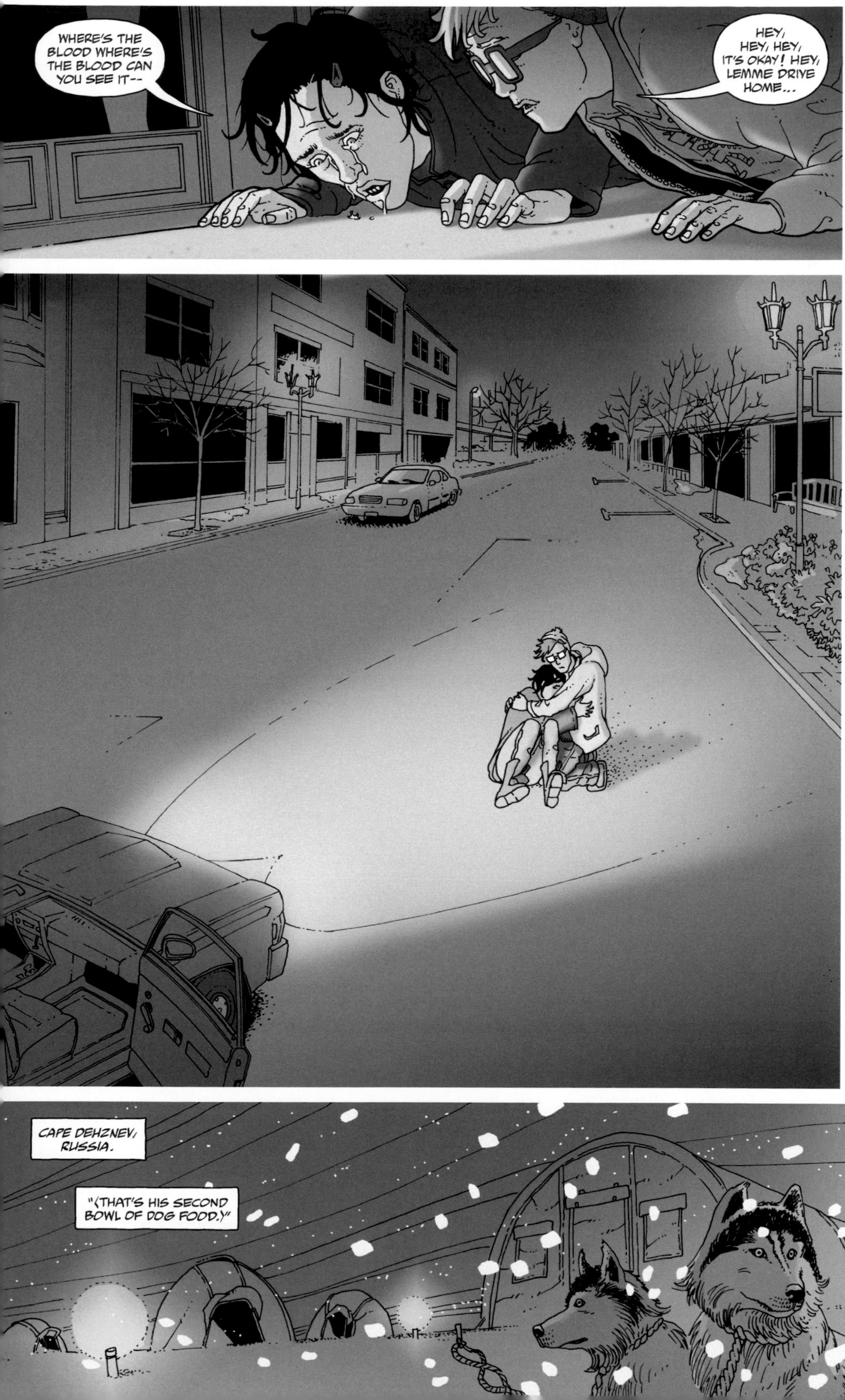
WHERE'S THE BLOOD WHERE'S THE BLOOD CAN YOU SEE IT--
HEY, HEY, HEY, IT'S OKAY! HEY, LEMME DRIVE HOME...
CAPE DEHZNEV, RUSSIA.
"(THAT'S HIS SECOND BOWL OF DOG FOOD.)"

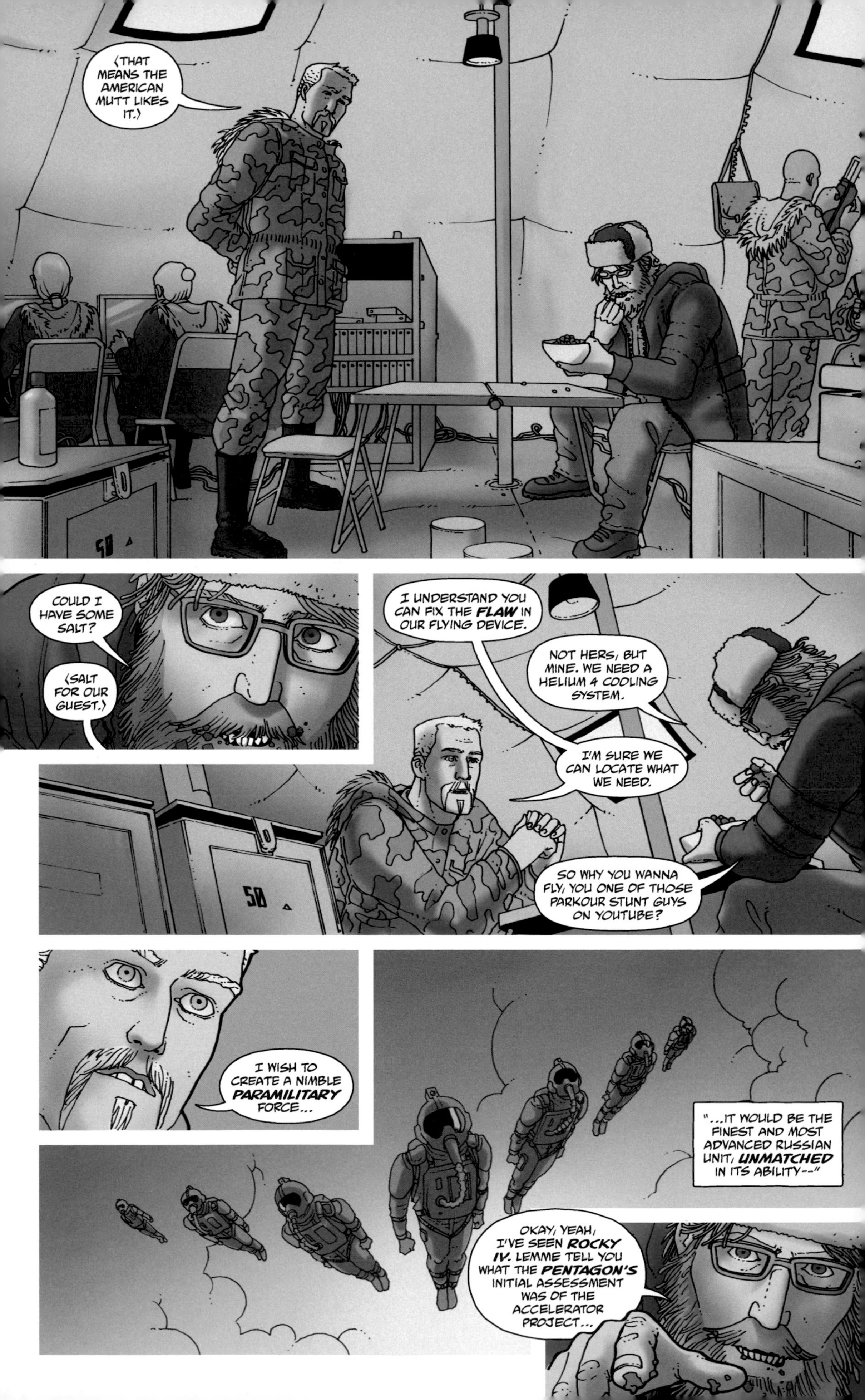

‹THAT MEANS THE AMERICAN MUTT LIKES IT.›
COULD I HAVE SOME SALT?
‹SALT FOR OUR GUEST.›
I UNDERSTAND YOU CAN FIX THE **FLAW** IN OUR FLYING DEVICE.
NOT HERS, BUT MINE. WE NEED A HELIUM 4 COOLING SYSTEM.
I'M SURE WE CAN LOCATE WHAT WE NEED.
SO WHY YOU WANNA FLY, YOU ONE OF THOSE PARKOUR STUNT GUYS ON YOUTUBE?
I WISH TO CREATE A NIMBLE **PARAMILITARY** FORCE...
"...IT WOULD BE THE FINEST AND MOST ADVANCED RUSSIAN UNIT, **UNMATCHED** IN ITS ABILITY--"
OKAY, YEAH, I'VE SEEN **ROCKY IV.** LEMME TELL YOU WHAT THE **PENTAGON'S** INITIAL ASSESSMENT WAS OF THE ACCELERATOR PROJECT...

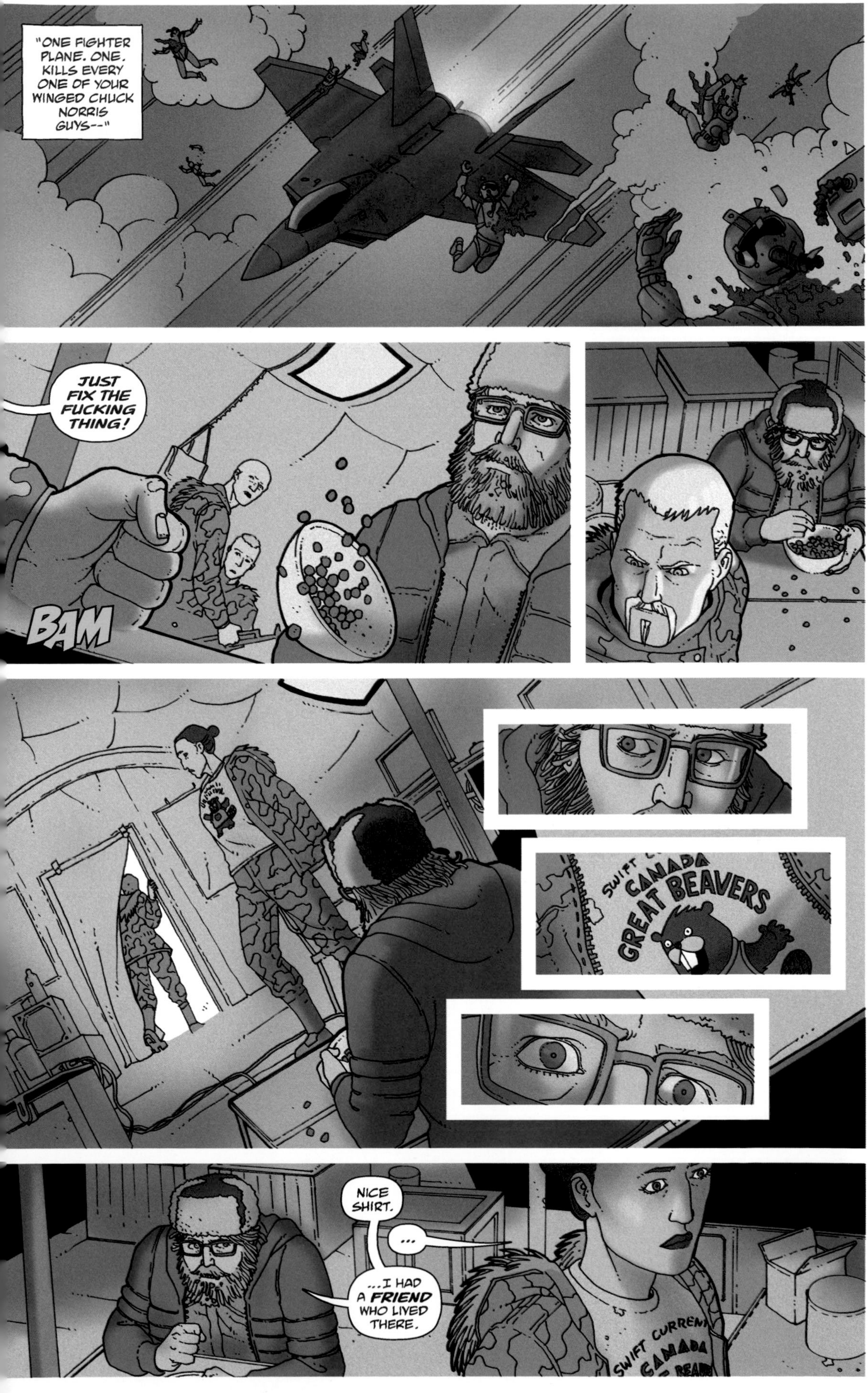
"ONE FIGHTER PLANE. ONE. KILLS EVERY ONE OF YOUR WINGED CHUCK NORRIS GUYS--"
JUST FIX THE FUCKING THING!
BAM
SWIFT CURRENT CANADA GREAT BEAVERS
NICE SHIRT.
...
...I HAD A FRIEND WHO LIVED THERE.

YOU HIT THE PERSON SO HARD THEIR BODY FLEW INTO A FRONT LAWN. OF COURSE IT WASN'T IN THE STREET.

THE POLICE WILL BE HERE ANY MINUTE.

RUBBERBALL RUBBERBALL RUBBERBALL

SUPERFLUIDS

ALIEN

ORDERS

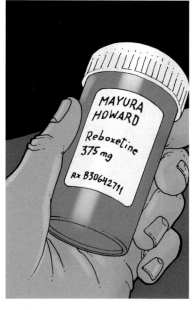

MAYURA HOWARD

Reboxetine
375 mg

Rx B30642711

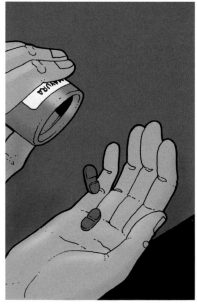

Here goes nothing--

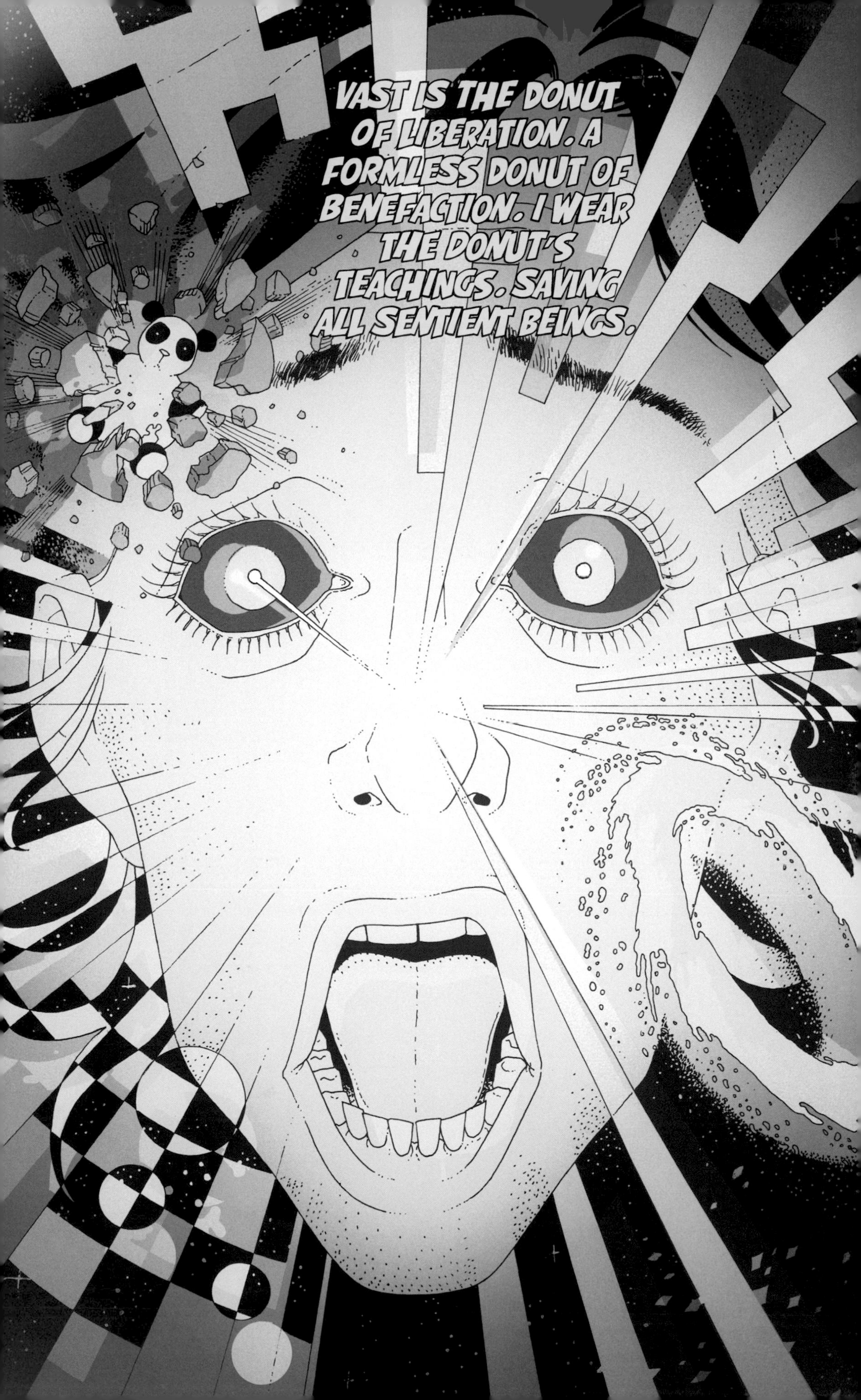
VAST IS THE DONUT OF LIBERATION. A FORMLESS DONUT OF BENEFACTION. I WEAR THE DONUT'S TEACHINGS. SAVING ALL SENTIENT BEINGS.

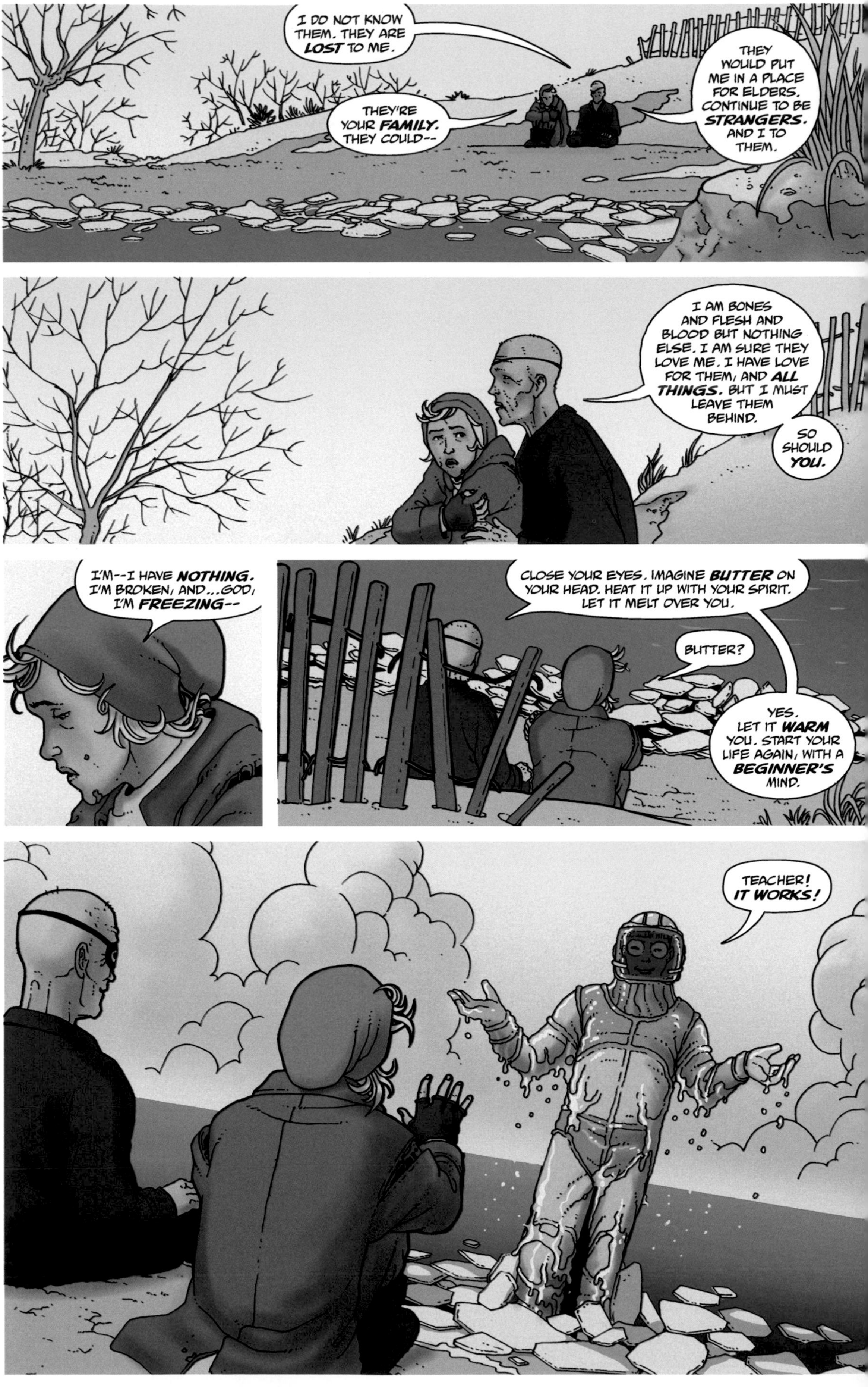
I DO NOT KNOW THEM. THEY ARE LOST TO ME.
THEY'RE YOUR FAMILY. THEY COULD--
THEY WOULD PUT ME IN A PLACE FOR ELDERS. CONTINUE TO BE STRANGERS. AND I TO THEM.
I AM BONES AND FLESH AND BLOOD BUT NOTHING ELSE. I AM SURE THEY LOVE ME. I HAVE LOVE FOR THEM, AND ALL THINGS. BUT I MUST LEAVE THEM BEHIND.
SO SHOULD YOU.
I'M--I HAVE NOTHING. I'M BROKEN, AND...GOD, I'M FREEZING--
CLOSE YOUR EYES. IMAGINE BUTTER ON YOUR HEAD. HEAT IT UP WITH YOUR SPIRIT. LET IT MELT OVER YOU.
BUTTER?
YES. LET IT WARM YOU. START YOUR LIFE AGAIN, WITH A BEGINNER'S MIND.
TEACHER! IT WORKS!

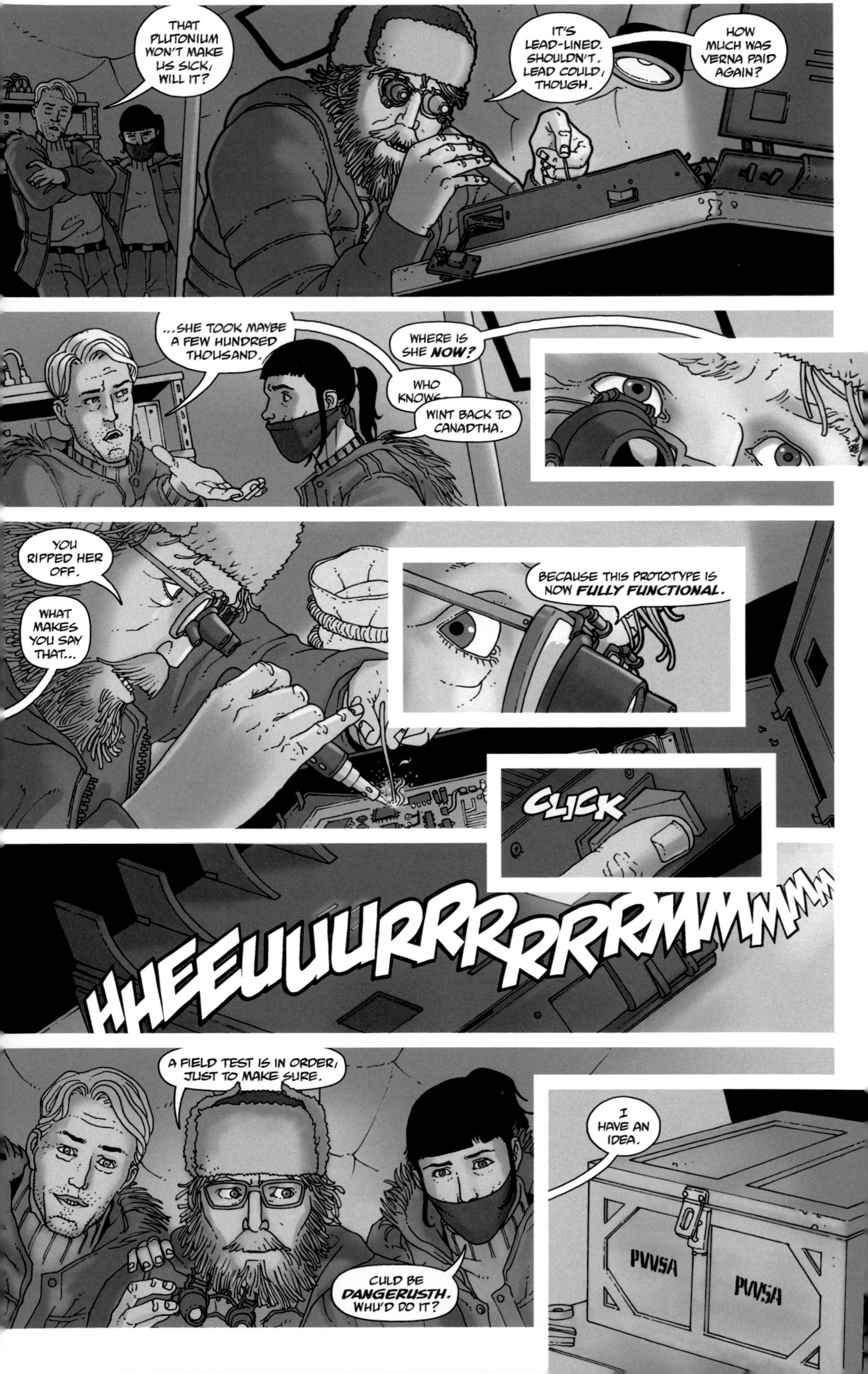
THAT PLUTONIUM WON'T MAKE US SICK, WILL IT?
IT'S LEAD-LINED. SHOULDN'T. LEAD COULD, THOUGH.
HOW MUCH WAS VERNA PAID AGAIN?
...SHE TOOK MAYBE A FEW HUNDRED THOUSAND.
WHERE IS SHE NOW?
WHO KNOWS--
WINT BACK TO CANADTHA.
YOU RIPPED HER OFF.
WHAT MAKES YOU SAY THAT...
BECAUSE THIS PROTOTYPE IS NOW FULLY FUNCTIONAL.
CLICK
HHEEUUURRRRRRMMMMMM
A FIELD TEST IS IN ORDER, JUST TO MAKE SURE.
CULD BE DANGERUSTH. WHU'D DO IT?
I HAVE AN IDEA.
PVVSA
PVVSA

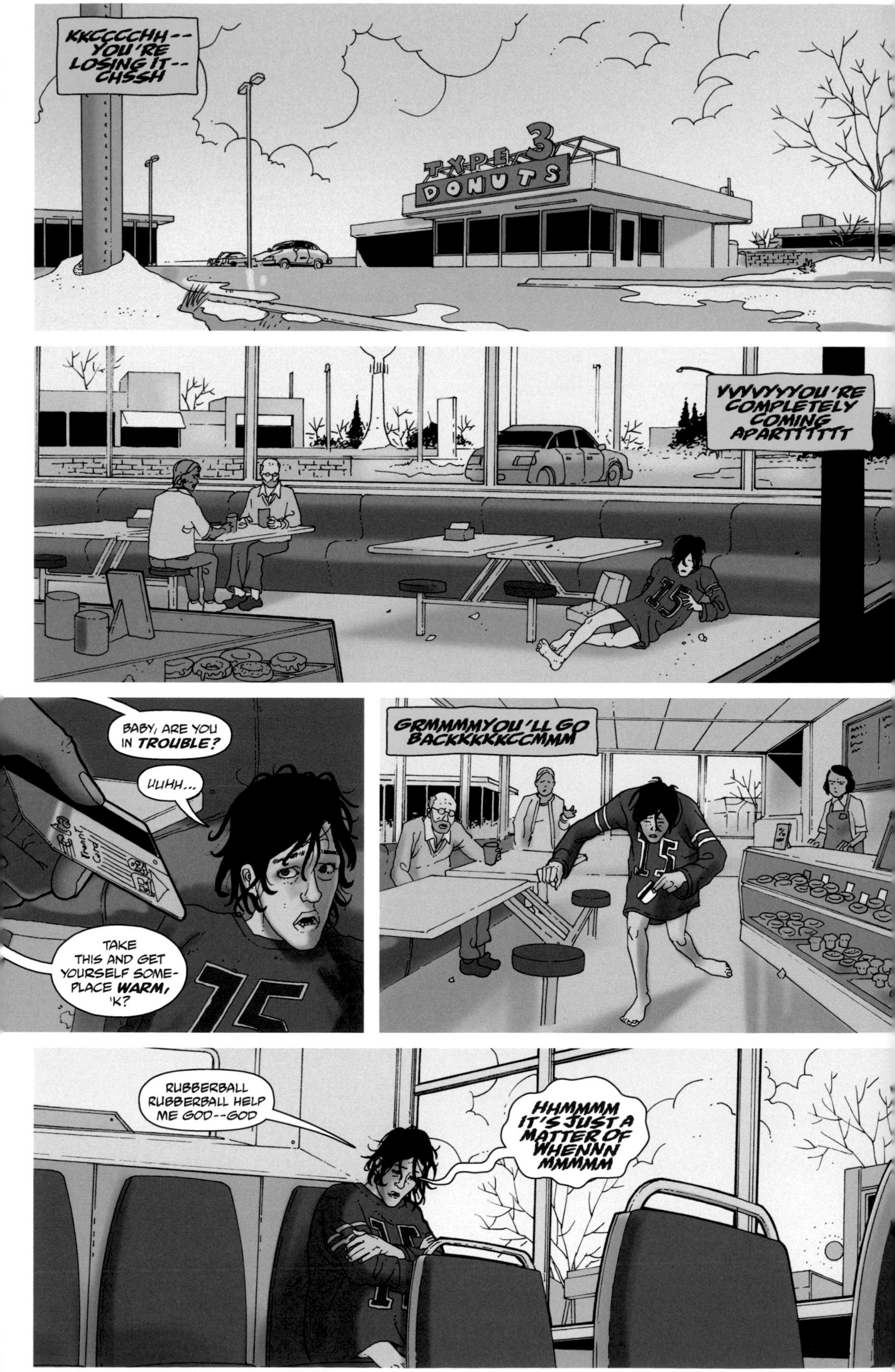
KKCCCCHH--
YOU'RE
LOSING IT--
CHSSH
TYPE 3
DONUTS
YYYYYYYOU'RE
COMPLETELY
COMING
APARTTTTTTT
BABY, ARE YOU IN TROUBLE?
UUHH...
TAKE THIS AND GET YOURSELF SOME-PLACE WARM, 'K?
GRMMMMYOU'LL GO BACKKKKKCCMMM
RUBBERBALL RUBBERBALL HELP ME GOD--GOD
HHMMMM IT'S JUST A MATTER OF WHENNN MMMMM

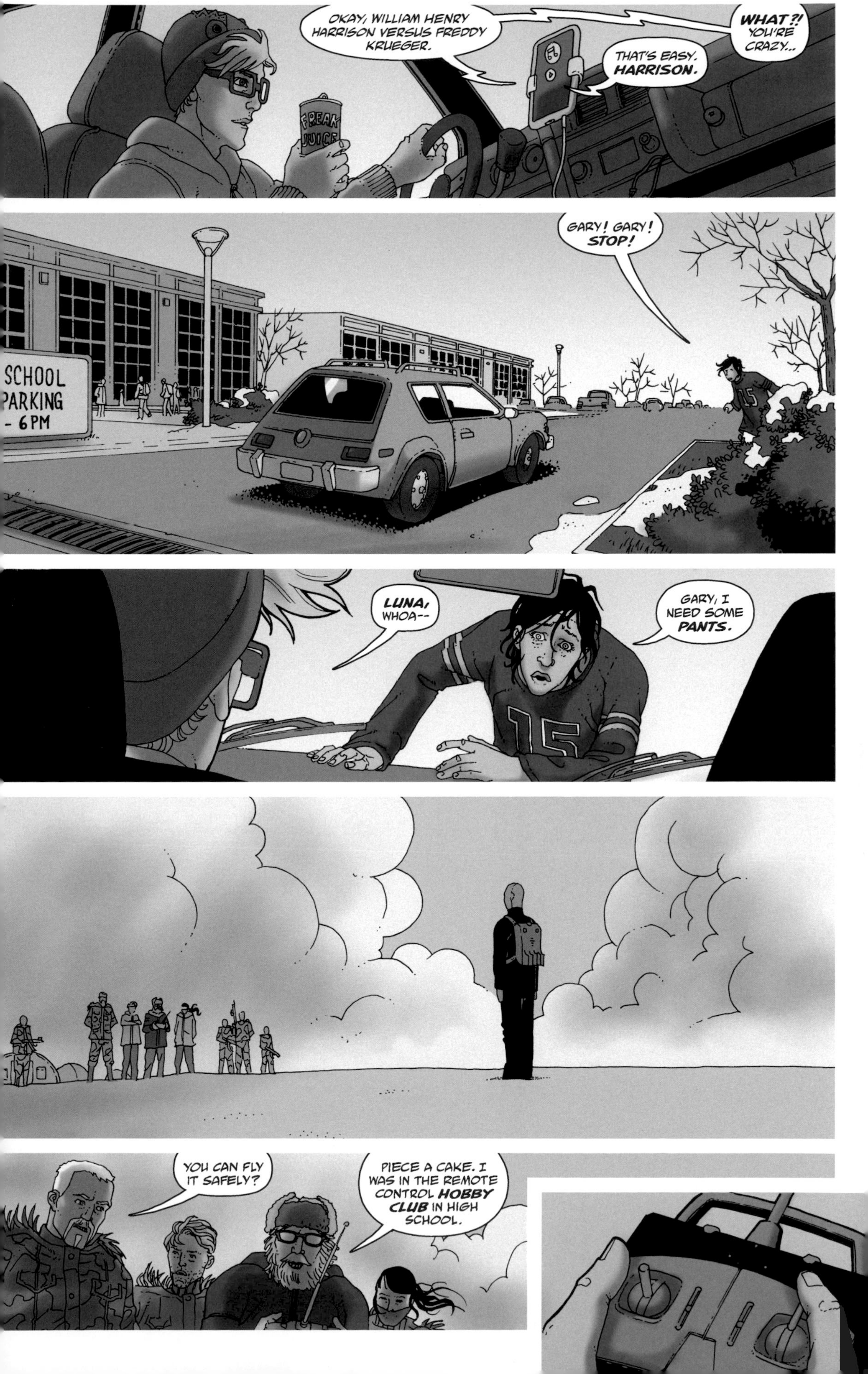
OKAY, WILLIAM HENRY HARRISON VERSUS FREDDY KRUEGER.
THAT'S EASY. HARRISON.
WHAT?! YOU'RE CRAZY...
FREAK JUICE
SCHOOL PARKING - 6PM
GARY! GARY! STOP!
LUNA, WHOA--
GARY, I NEED SOME PANTS.
YOU CAN FLY IT SAFELY?
PIECE A CAKE. I WAS IN THE REMOTE CONTROL HOBBY CLUB IN HIGH SCHOOL.

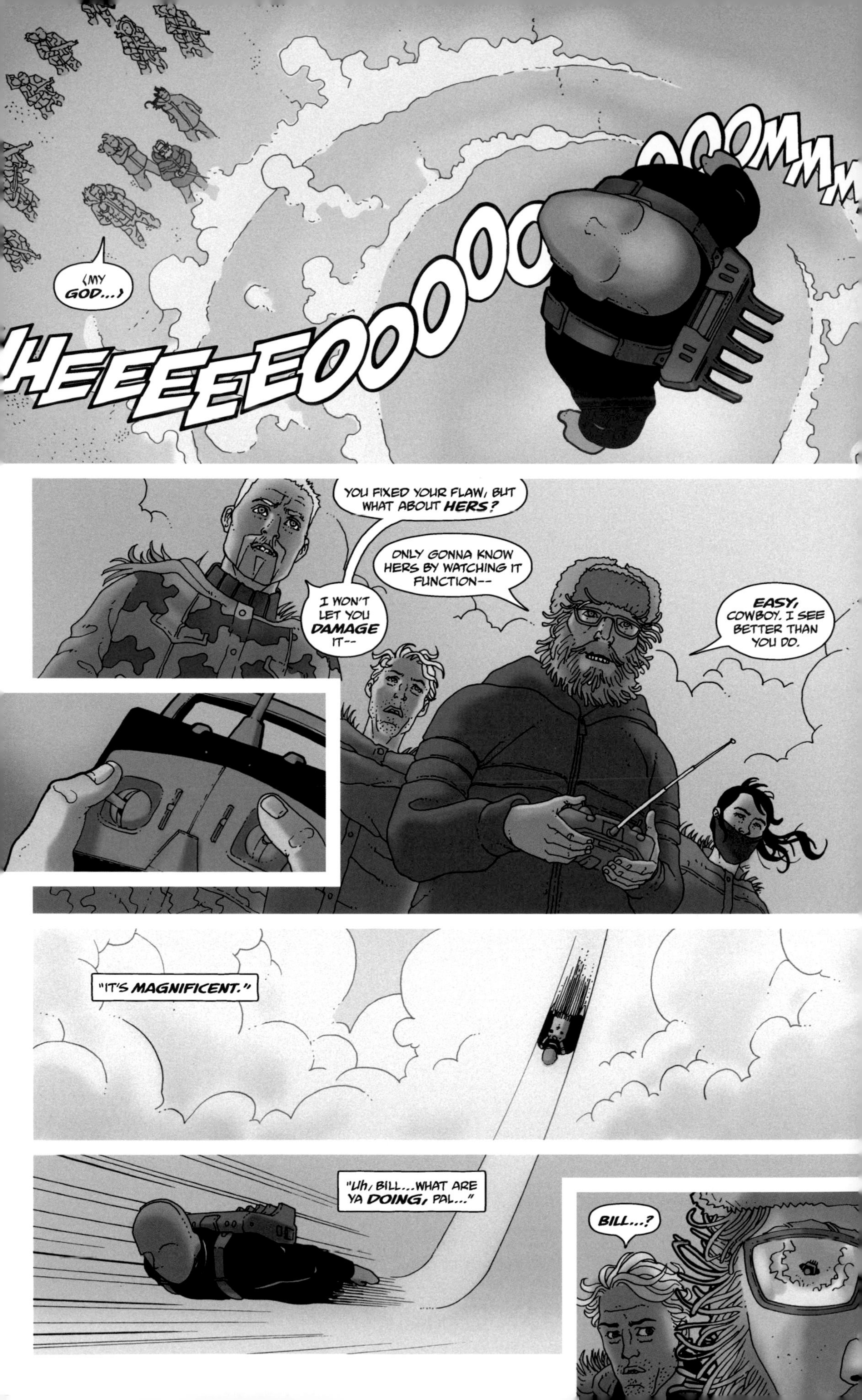
⟨MY GOD...⟩
HEEEEEOOOOOOOOOOOOMMMM
YOU FIXED YOUR FLAW, BUT WHAT ABOUT HERS?
I WON'T LET YOU DAMAGE IT--
ONLY GONNA KNOW HERS BY WATCHING IT FUNCTION--
EASY, COWBOY. I SEE BETTER THAN YOU DO.
"IT'S MAGNIFICENT."
"UH, BILL...WHAT ARE YA DOING, PAL..."
BILL...?

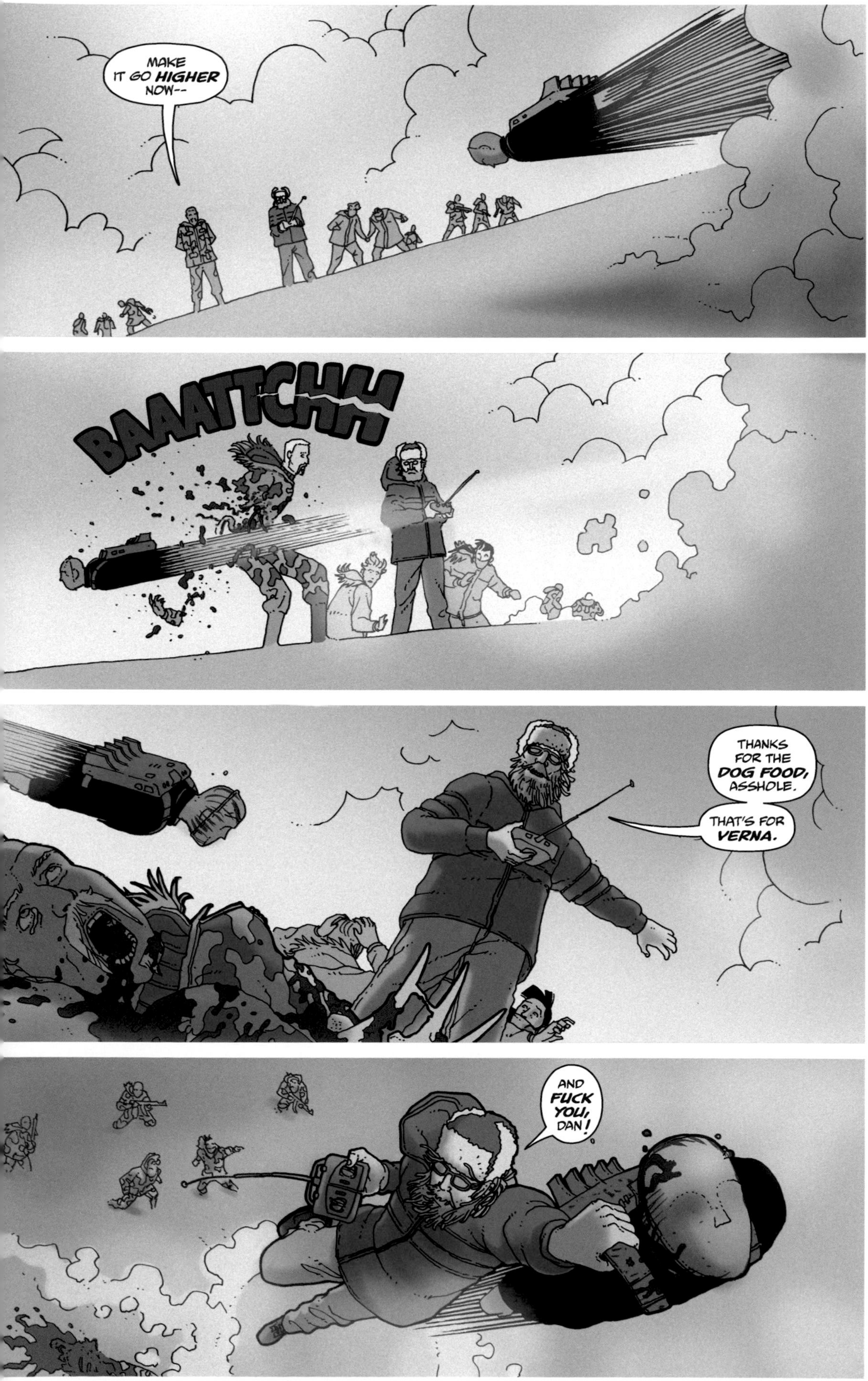
MAKE IT GO HIGHER NOW--
BAAATTCHH
THANKS FOR THE DOG FOOD, ASSHOLE.
THAT'S FOR VERNA.
AND FUCK YOU, DAN!

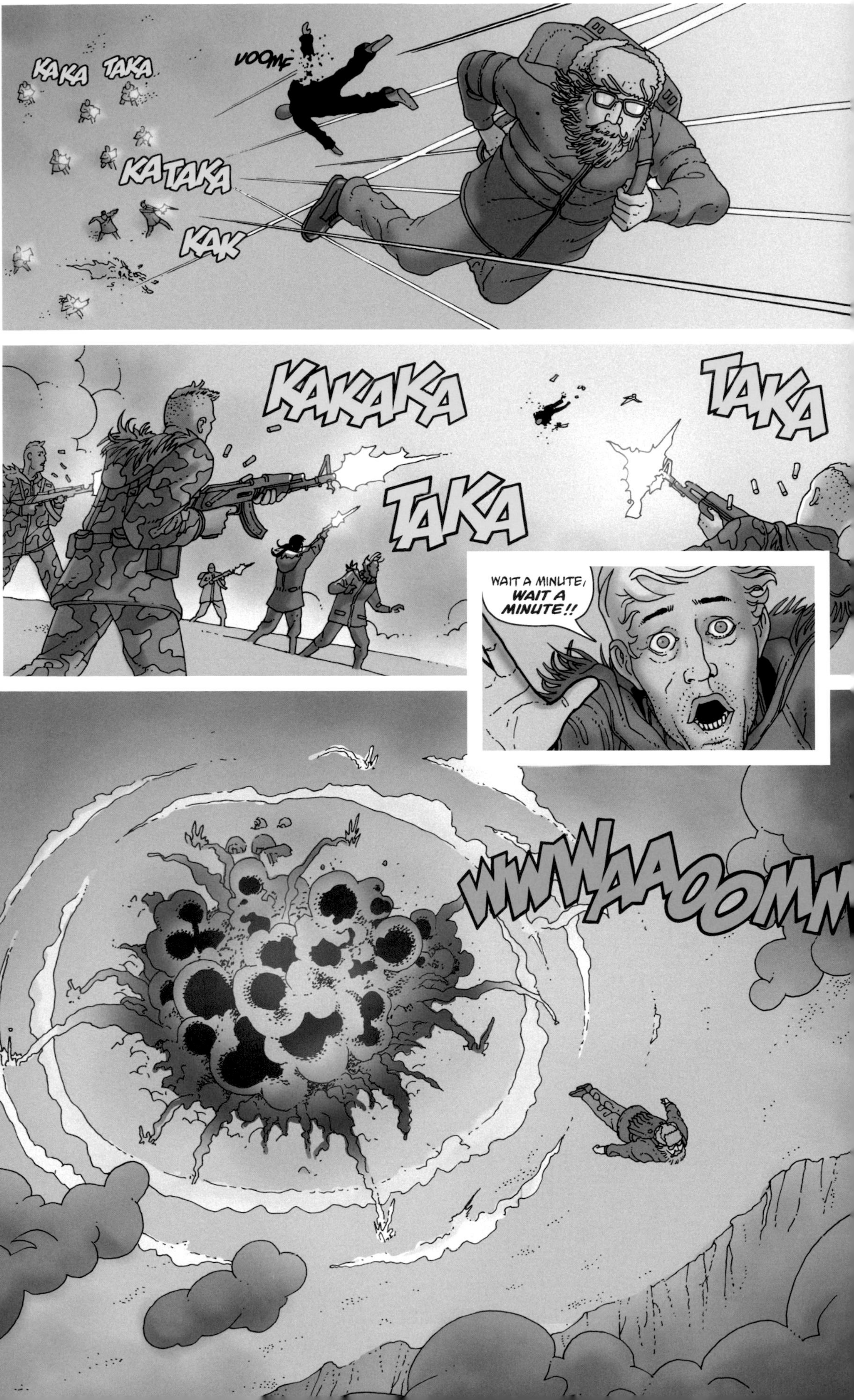
KAKA TAKA
VOOMF
KATAKA
KAK
KAKAKA
TAKA
TAKA
WAIT A MINUTE, WAIT A MINUTE!!
WWWAAOOMM

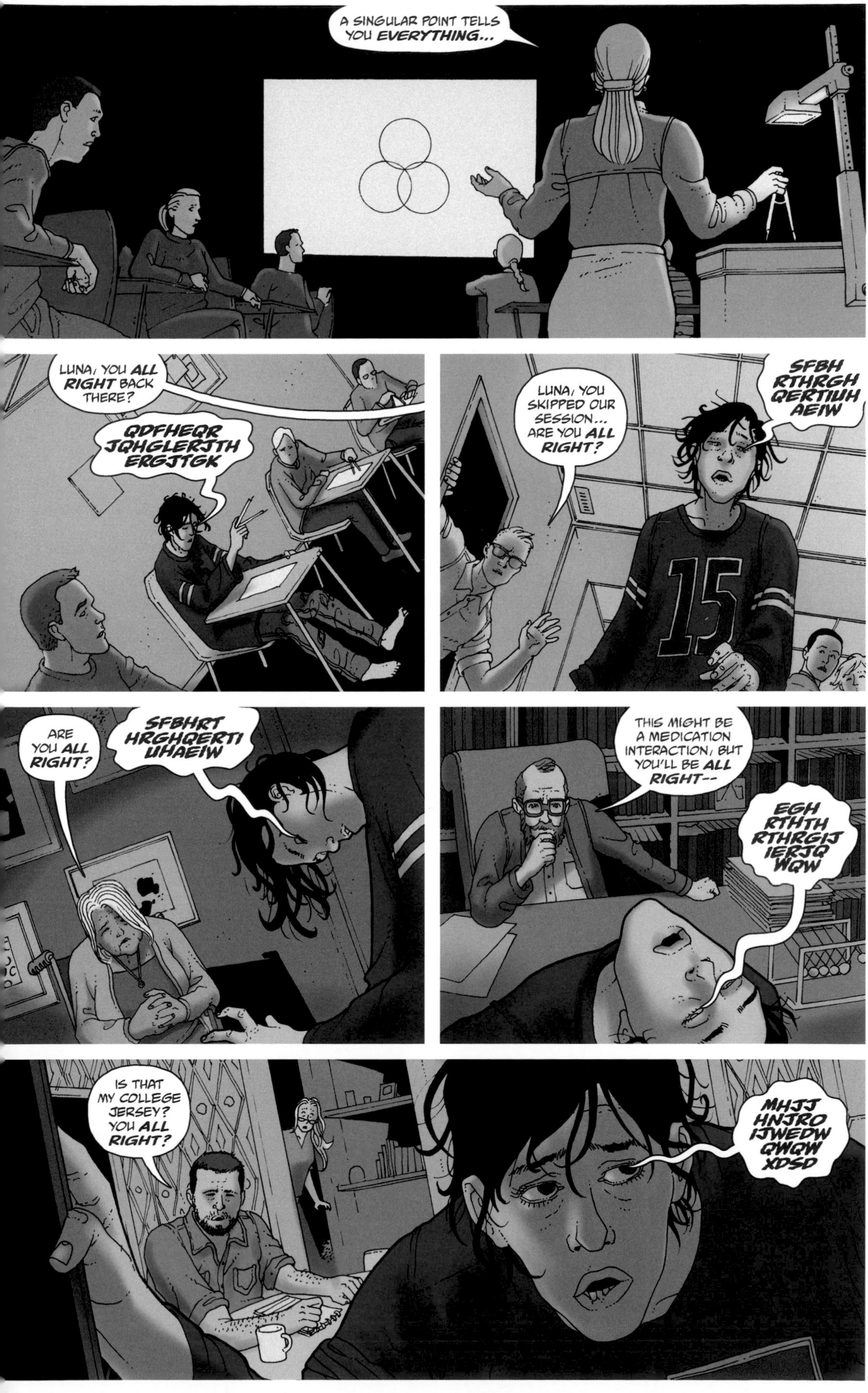
A SINGULAR POINT TELLS YOU EVERYTHING...
LUNA, YOU ALL RIGHT BACK THERE?
QDFHEQR JQHGLERJTH ERGJTGK
LUNA, YOU SKIPPED OUR SESSION... ARE YOU ALL RIGHT?
SFBH RTHRGH QERTIUH AEIW
15
ARE YOU ALL RIGHT?
SFBHRT HRGHQERTI UHAEIW
THIS MIGHT BE A MEDICATION INTERACTION, BUT YOU'LL BE ALL RIGHT--
EGH RTHTH RTHRGIJ IERJQ WQW
IS THAT MY COLLEGE JERSEY? YOU ALL RIGHT?
MHJJ HNJRO IJWEDW QWQW XDSD

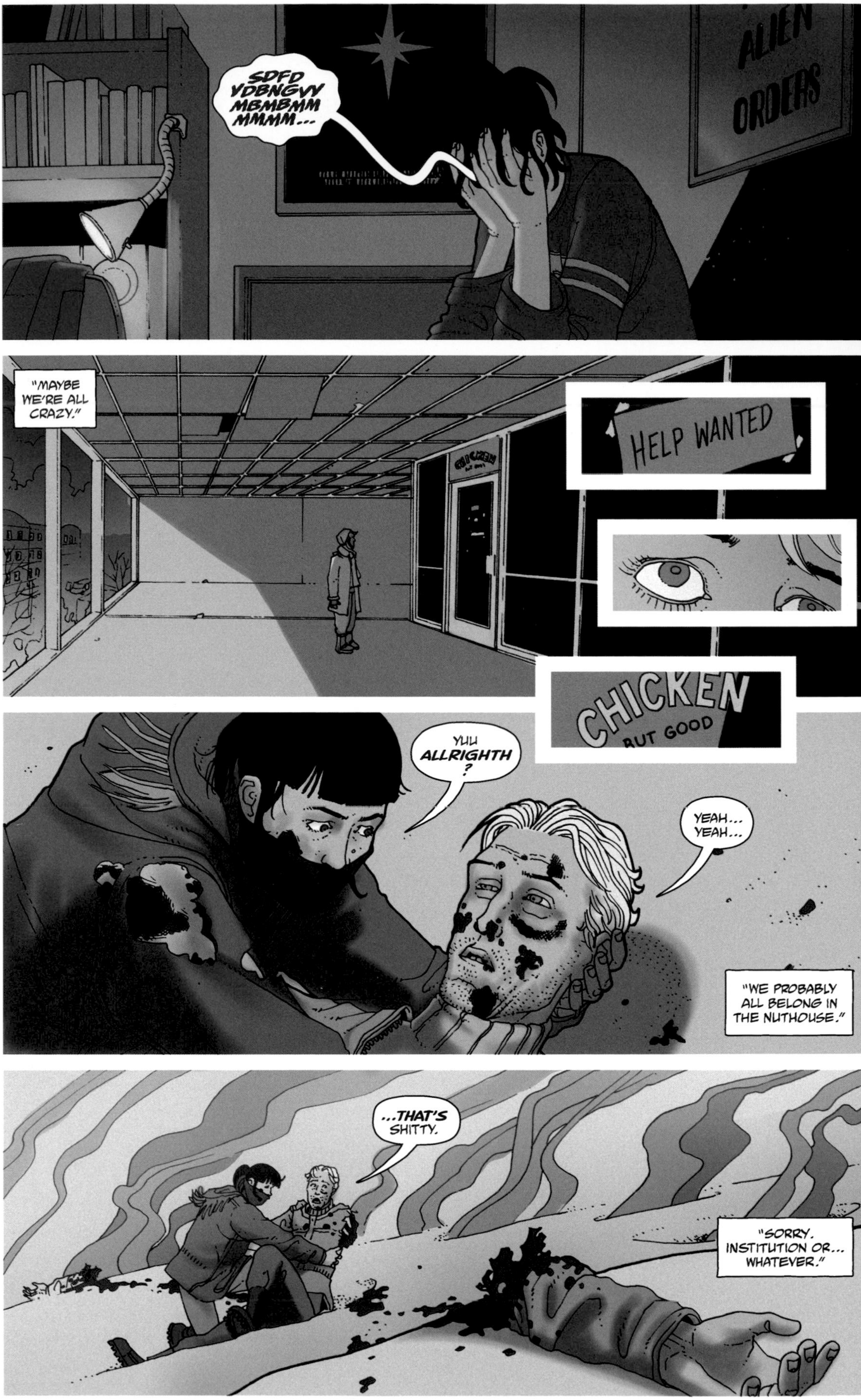
SDFD YDBNGVY MBMBMM MMMM...
ALIEN ORDERS
"MAYBE WE'RE ALL CRAZY."
HELP WANTED
CHICKEN BUT GOOD
YUU ALLRIGHTH ?
YEAH... YEAH...
"WE PROBABLY ALL BELONG IN THE NUTHOUSE."
...THAT'S SHITTY.
"SORRY. INSTITUTION OR... WHATEVER."

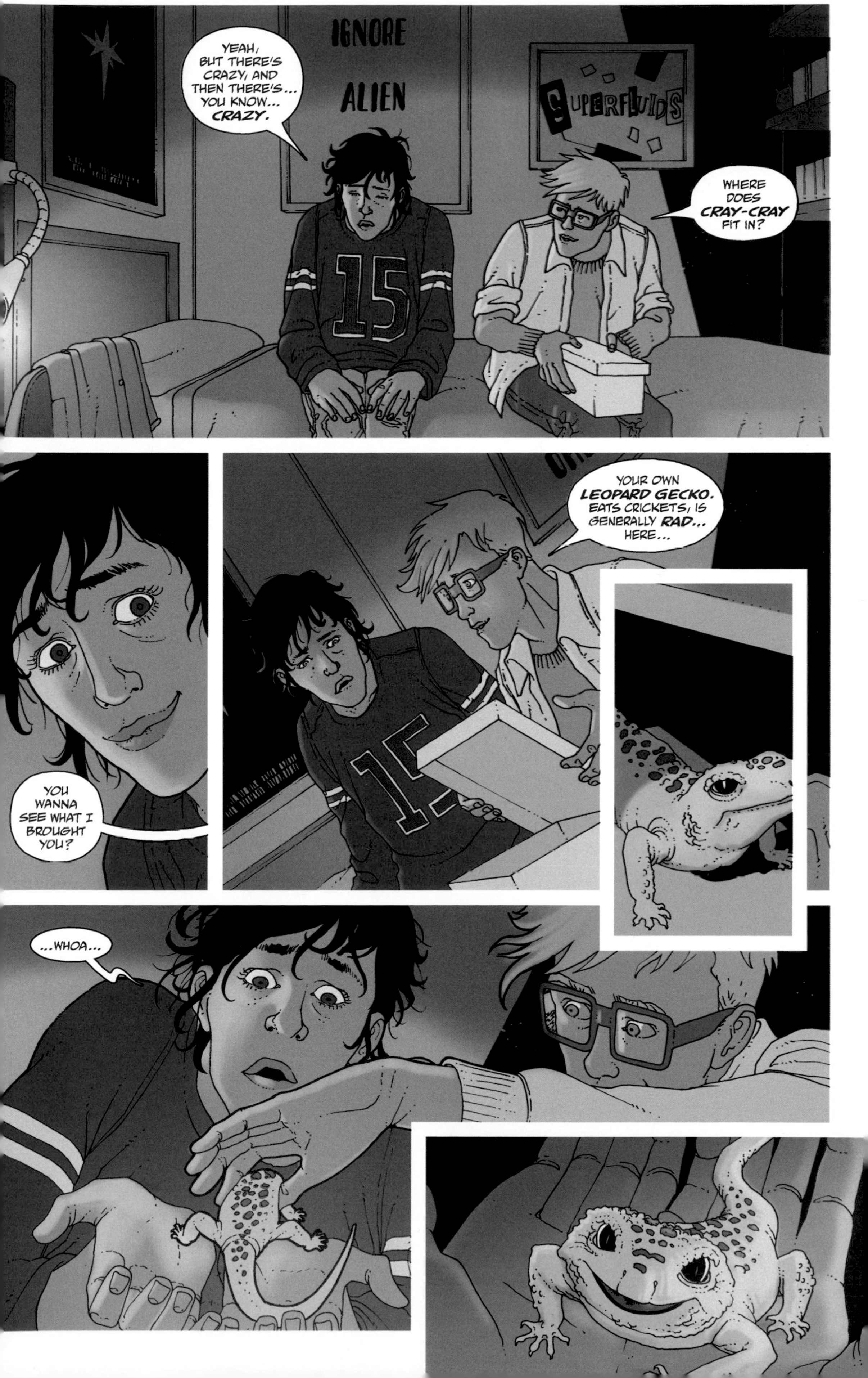
IGNORE
ALIEN
SUPERFLUIDS
YEAH, BUT THERE'S CRAZY, AND THEN THERE'S... YOU KNOW... CRAZY.
WHERE DOES CRAY-CRAY FIT IN?
YOU WANNA SEE WHAT I BROUGHT YOU?
YOUR OWN LEOPARD GECKO. EATS CRICKETS, IS GENERALLY RAD... HERE...
...WHOA...

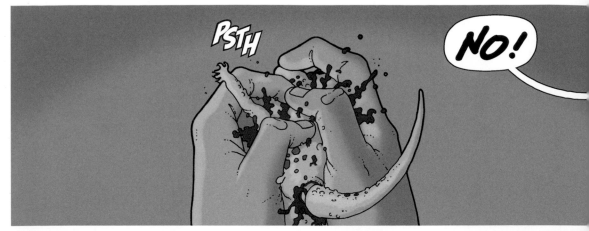

PSTH

NO!

GARY I CAN'T I CAN'T I CAN'T I CAN'T--

...OKAY... I THOUGHT YOU'D LIKE HIM--

I DO, I'M JUST...NOT READY--

IGNORE ALIEN ORDERS

SUPERFLUIDS

SORRY, I THINK MY MEDS... I'M JUST HAVING A *BAD* DAY...

YOU KNOW...WE DON'T *HAVE TO* DRIVE DOWN TO GRASSHOPPER, TO SEE...WHO-EVER'S DOWN THERE...

WHAT DO YOU MEAN?

WE COULD GO *SOMEWHERE ELSE*. JUST HANG OUT. LIKE--GO CAMPING OR SOME-THING. JUST US.

THAT SOUNDS... THAT ACTUALLY SOUNDS... *AWESOME.*

YEAH?

YEAH, DUDE.

I STILL WANT YOU TO TELL ME ABOUT THE *FLYING WOMAN* SOMEDAY, THOUGH.

...SOMEDAY. HEY. LET'S NAME OUR GECKO *BORG.*

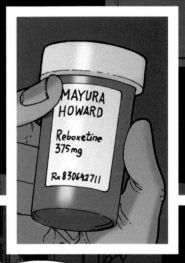

MAYURA
HOWARD

Reboxetine
375mg

Rx 830642711

...EY.

I'M GLAD. THAT...BOY... MAKES YOU... *HAPPY.*

BUT, IF YOU EVER FEEL...LIKE THAT WOMAN DID. *MAYURA.* PROMISE ME YOU'LL TELL ME.

...OKAY.

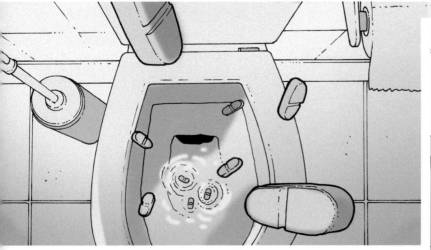

I NEED TO BE FREE OF YOU.

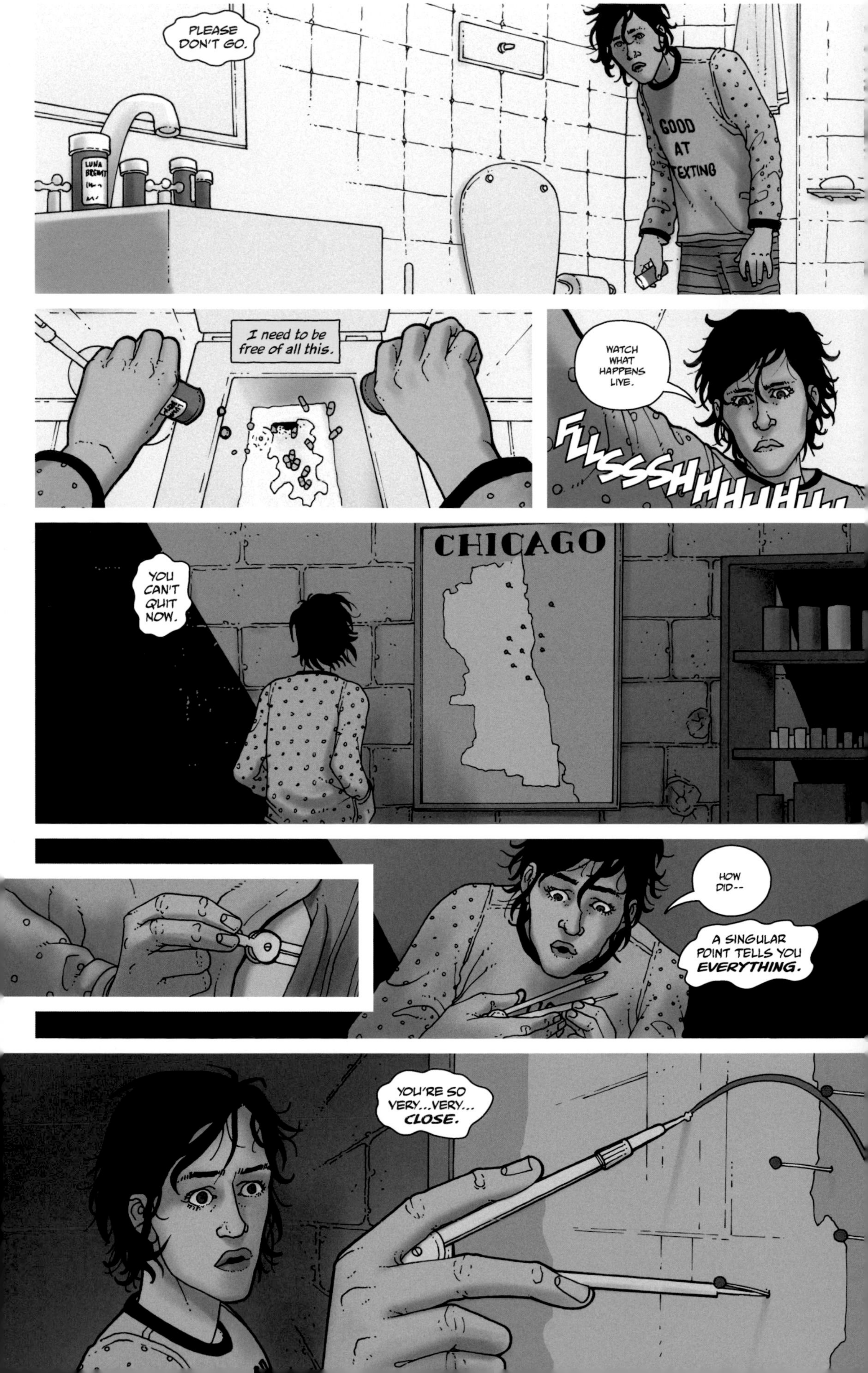
PLEASE DON'T GO.
GOOD AT TEXTING
LUNA BREMT
I need to be free of all this.
WATCH WHAT HAPPENS LIVE.
FLUSSSSHHHHHH
CHICAGO
YOU CAN'T QUIT NOW.
HOW DID--
A SINGULAR POINT TELLS YOU EVERYTHING.
YOU'RE SO VERY...VERY... CLOSE.

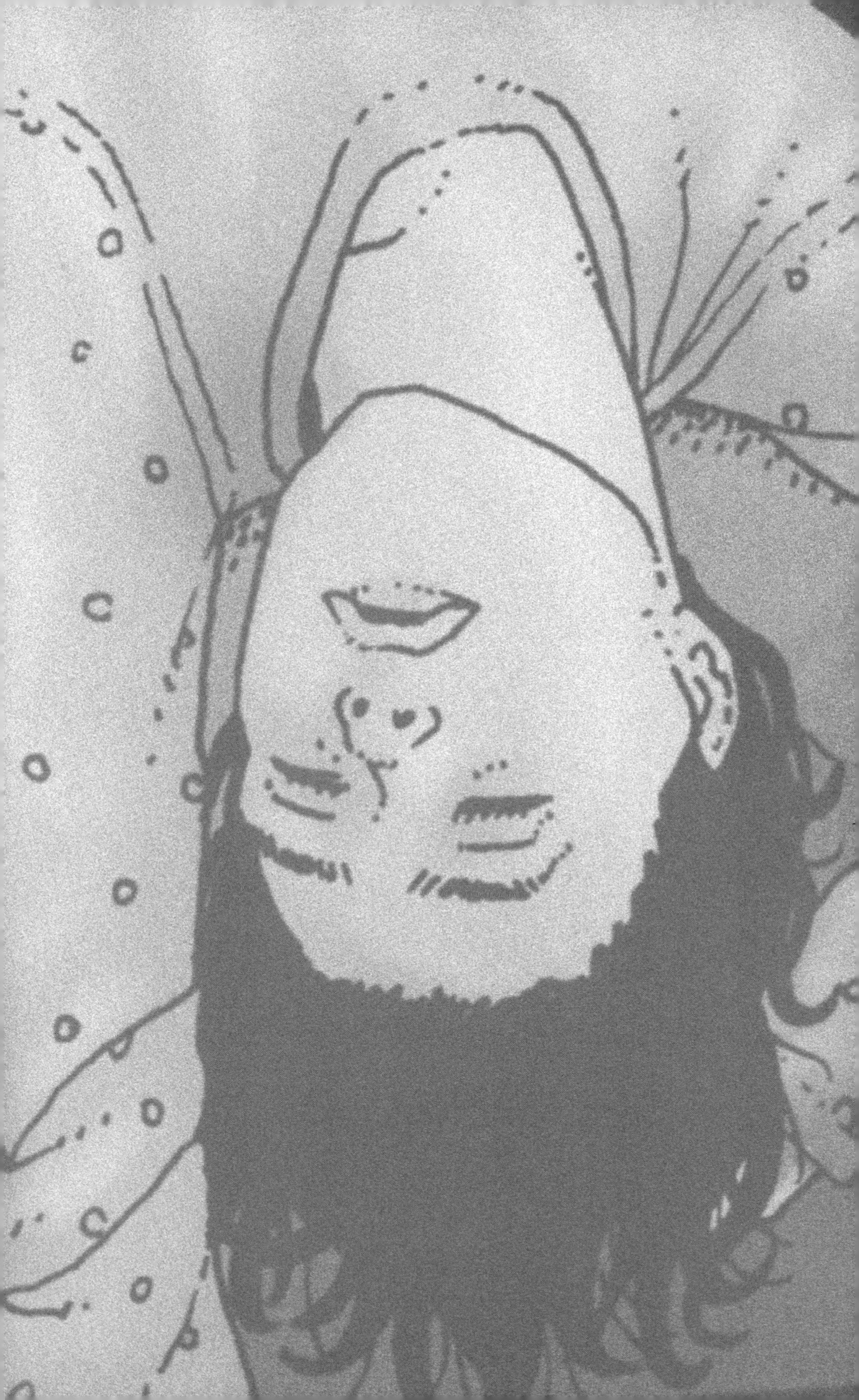

CHAPTER IV
"Dipshit"

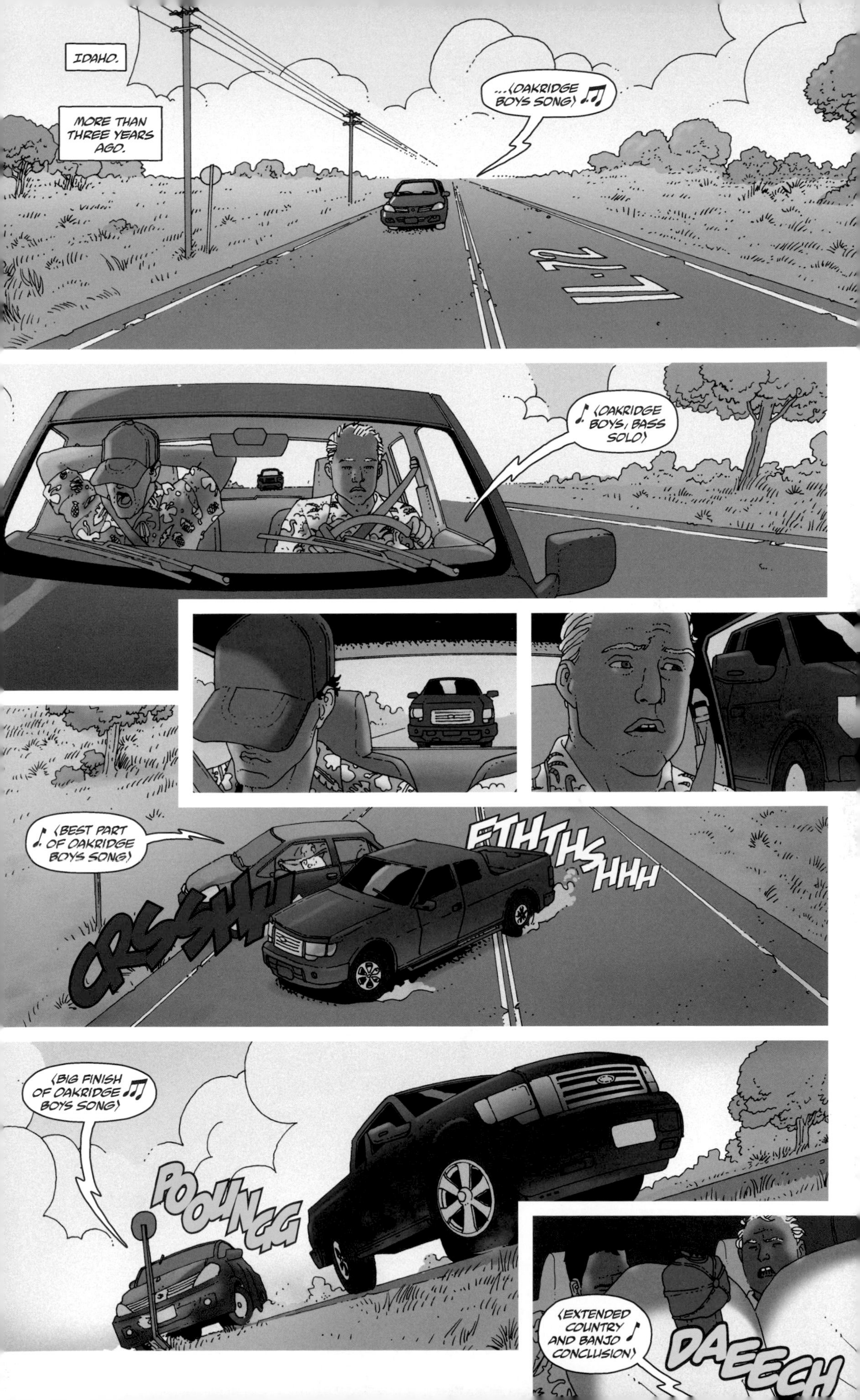
IDAHO.
MORE THAN THREE YEARS AGO.
...(OAKRIDGE BOYS SONG) ♫
♪ (OAKRIDGE BOYS, BASS SOLO)
♪ (BEST PART OF OAKRIDGE BOYS SONG)
FTHTHSHHH
CRSSHH
(BIG FINISH OF OAKRIDGE BOYS SONG) ♫
POOUNGG
(EXTENDED COUNTRY AND BANJO CONCLUSION) ♪
DAEECH

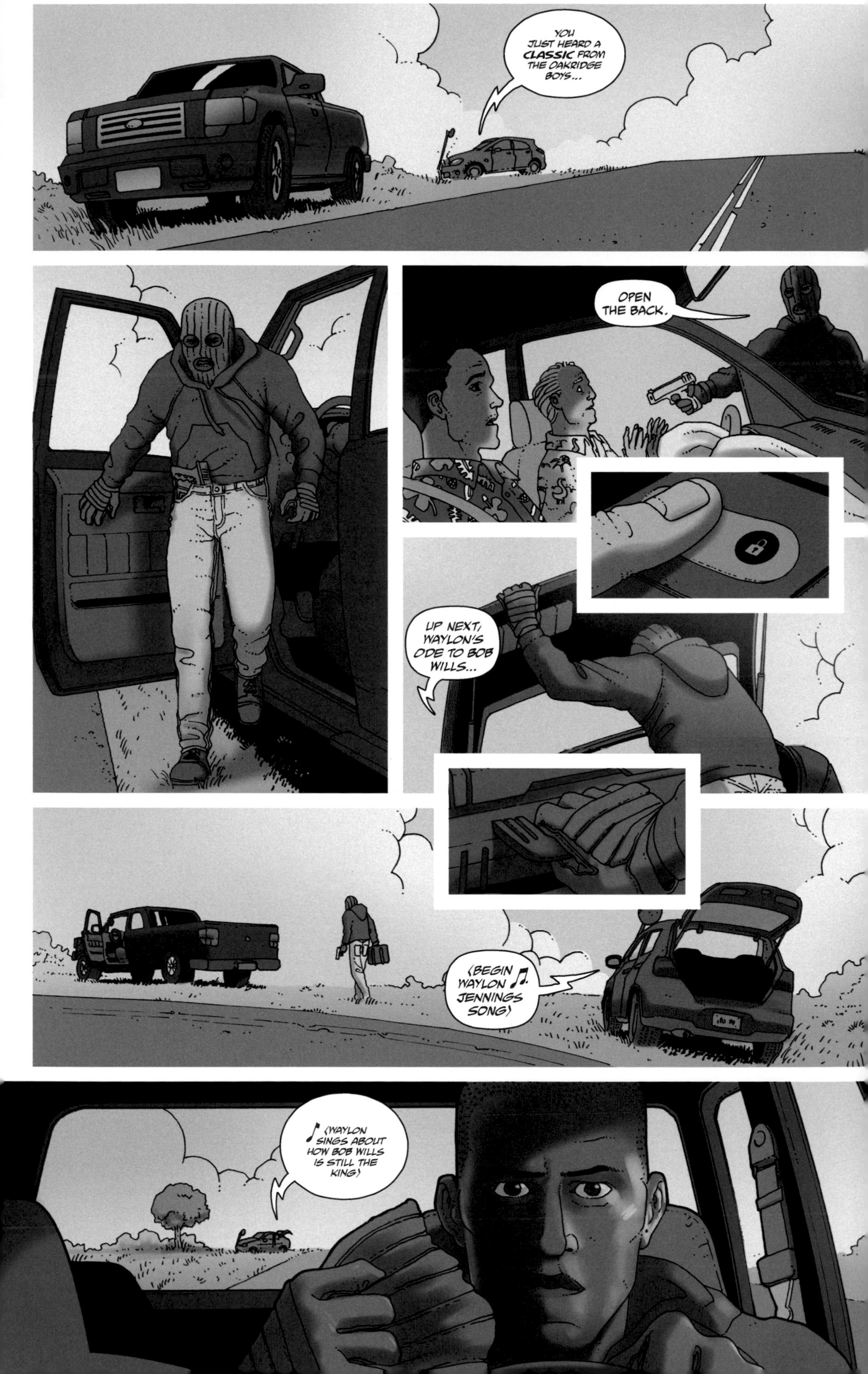
YOU JUST HEARD A CLASSIC FROM THE OAKRIDGE BOYS...
OPEN THE BACK.
UP NEXT, WAYLON'S ODE TO BOB WILLS...
⟨BEGIN WAYLON JENNINGS SONG⟩
⟨WAYLON SINGS ABOUT HOW BOB WILLS IS STILL THE KING⟩

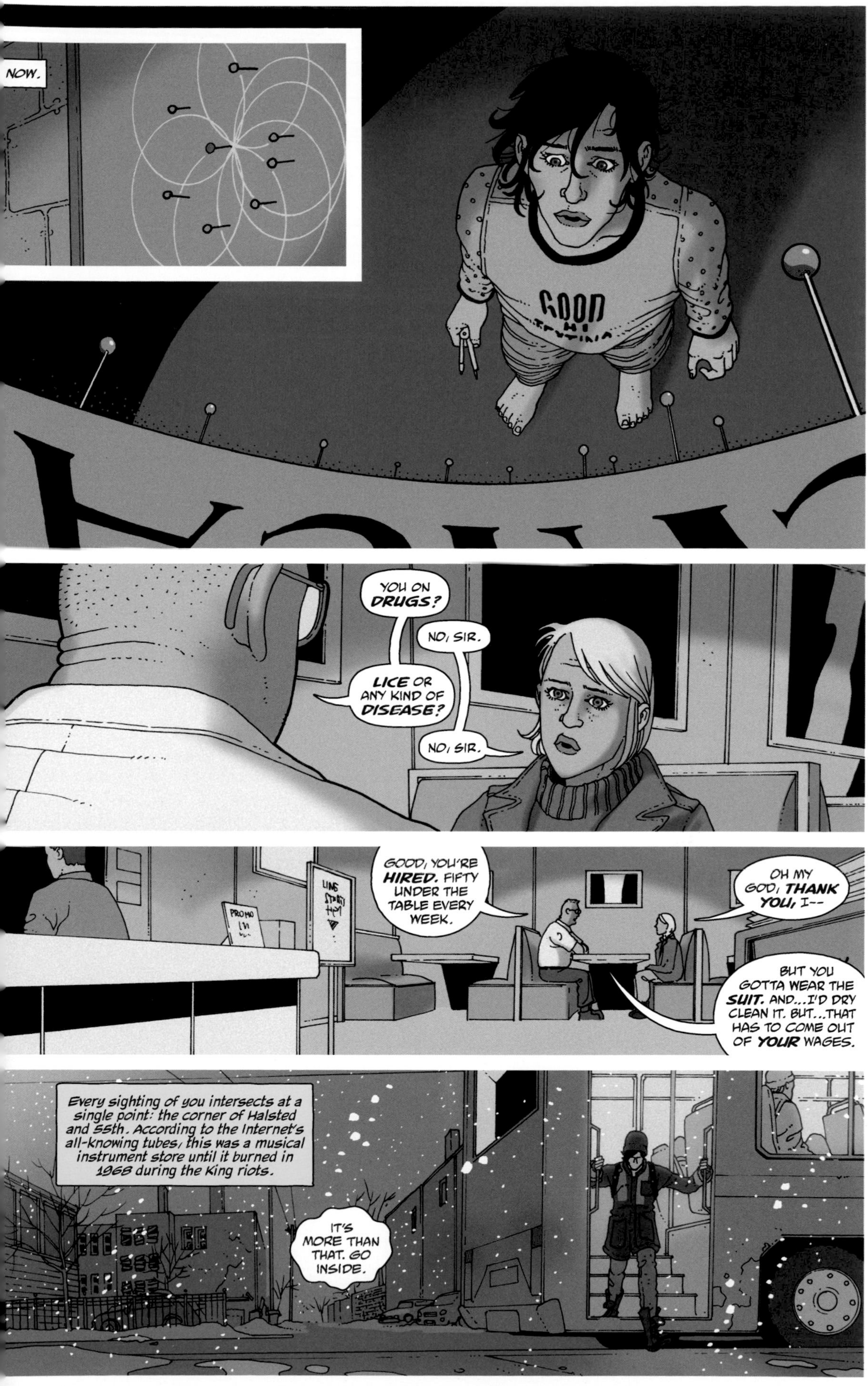
NOW.
YOU ON DRUGS?
NO, SIR.
LICE OR ANY KIND OF DISEASE?
NO, SIR.
GOOD, YOU'RE HIRED. FIFTY UNDER THE TABLE EVERY WEEK.
OH MY GOD, THANK YOU, I--
BUT YOU GOTTA WEAR THE SUIT. AND...I'D DRY CLEAN IT. BUT...THAT HAS TO COME OUT OF YOUR WAGES.
Every sighting of you intersects at a single point: the corner of Halsted and 55th. According to the Internet's all-knowing tubes, this was a musical instrument store until it burned in 1968 during the King riots.
IT'S MORE THAN THAT. GO INSIDE.

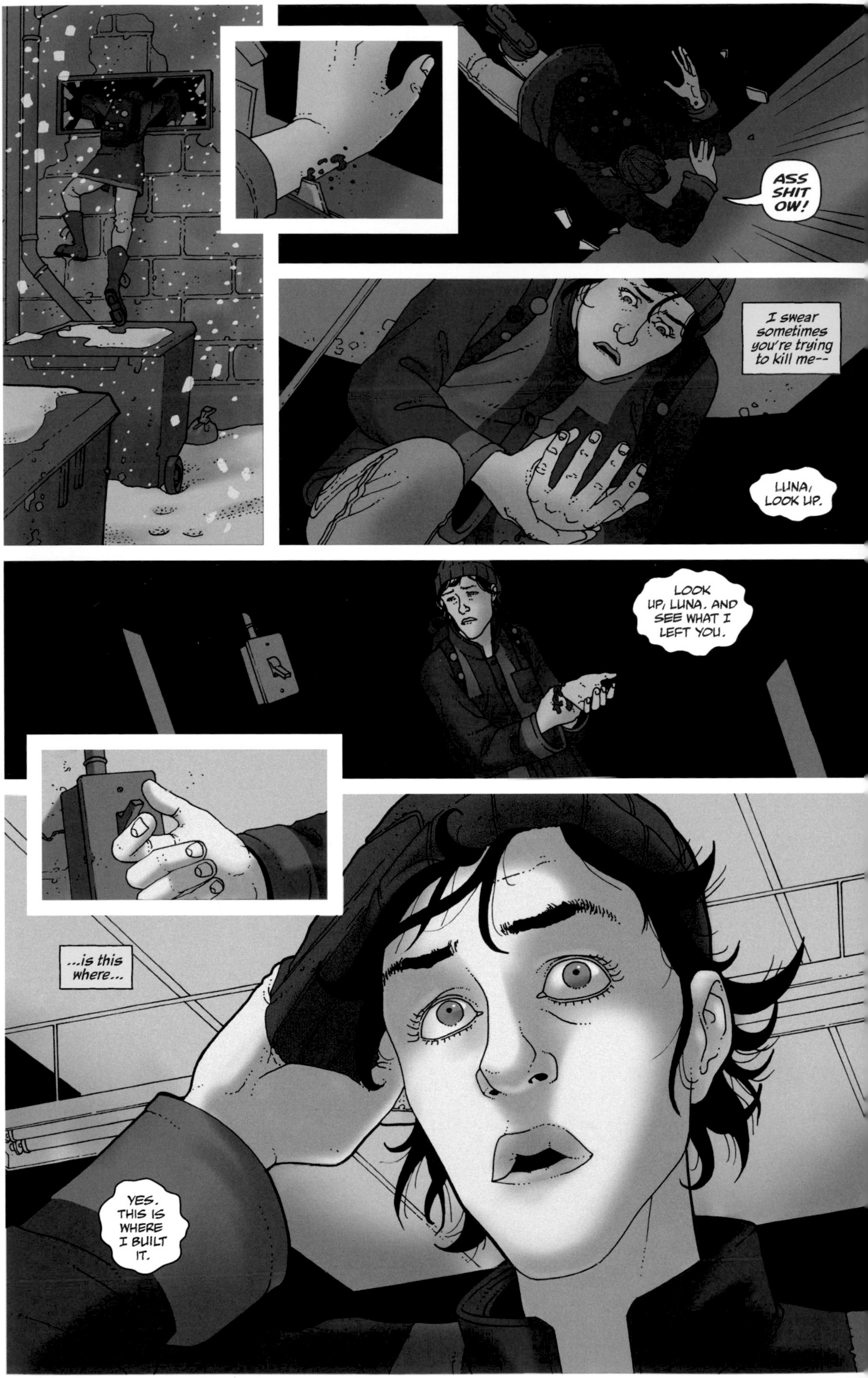
ASS SHIT OW!
I swear sometimes you're trying to kill me--
LUNA, LOOK UP.
LOOK UP, LUNA. AND SEE WHAT I LEFT YOU.
...is this where...
YES. THIS IS WHERE I BUILT IT.

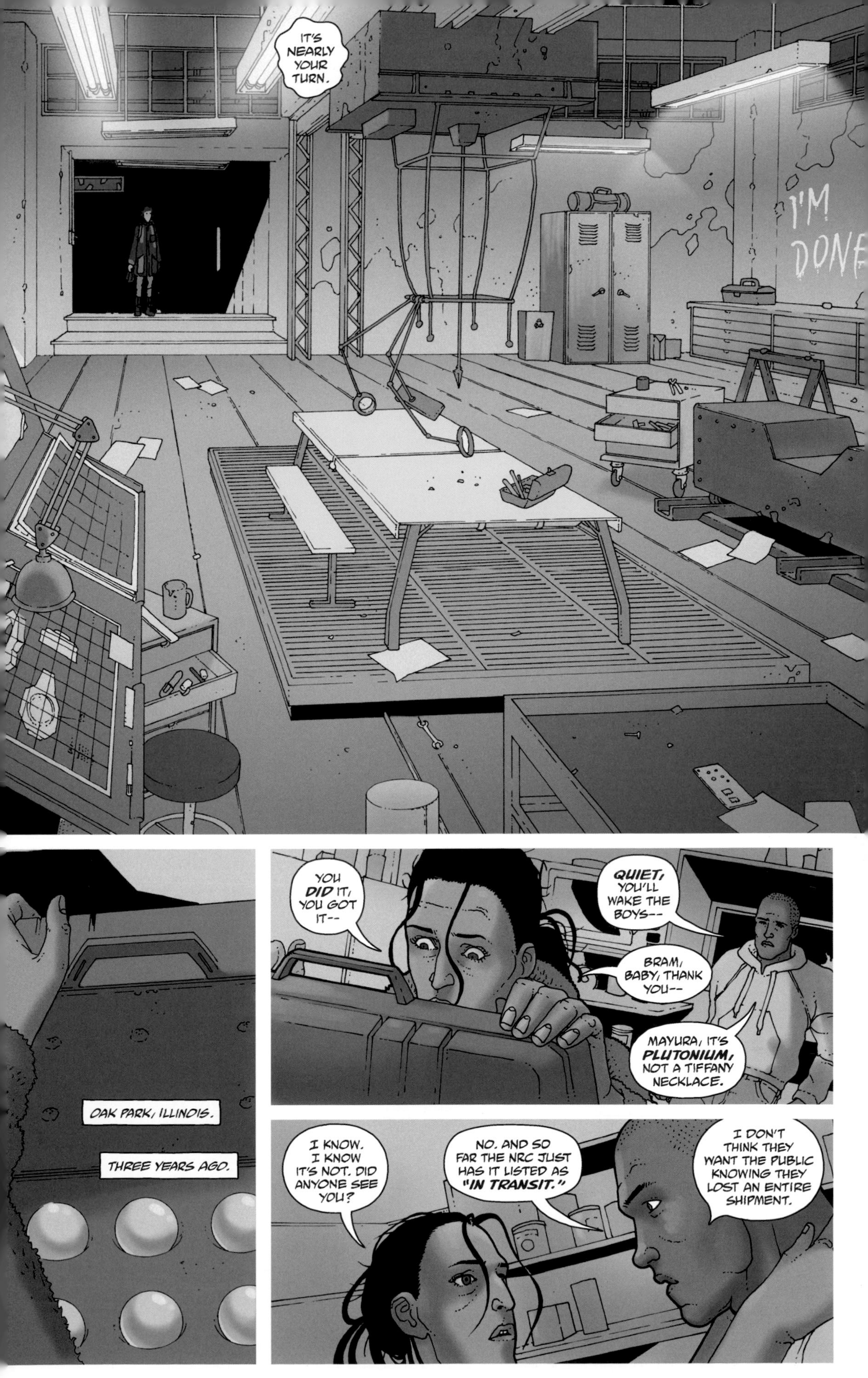
IT'S NEARLY YOUR TURN.
I'M DONE
OAK PARK, ILLINOIS.
THREE YEARS AGO.
YOU DID IT, YOU GOT IT--
QUIET, YOU'LL WAKE THE BOYS--
BRAM, BABY, THANK YOU--
MAYURA, IT'S PLUTONIUM, NOT A TIFFANY NECKLACE.
I KNOW. I KNOW IT'S NOT. DID ANYONE SEE YOU?
NO. AND SO FAR THE NRC JUST HAS IT LISTED AS "IN TRANSIT."
I DON'T THINK THEY WANT THE PUBLIC KNOWING THEY LOST AN ENTIRE SHIPMENT.

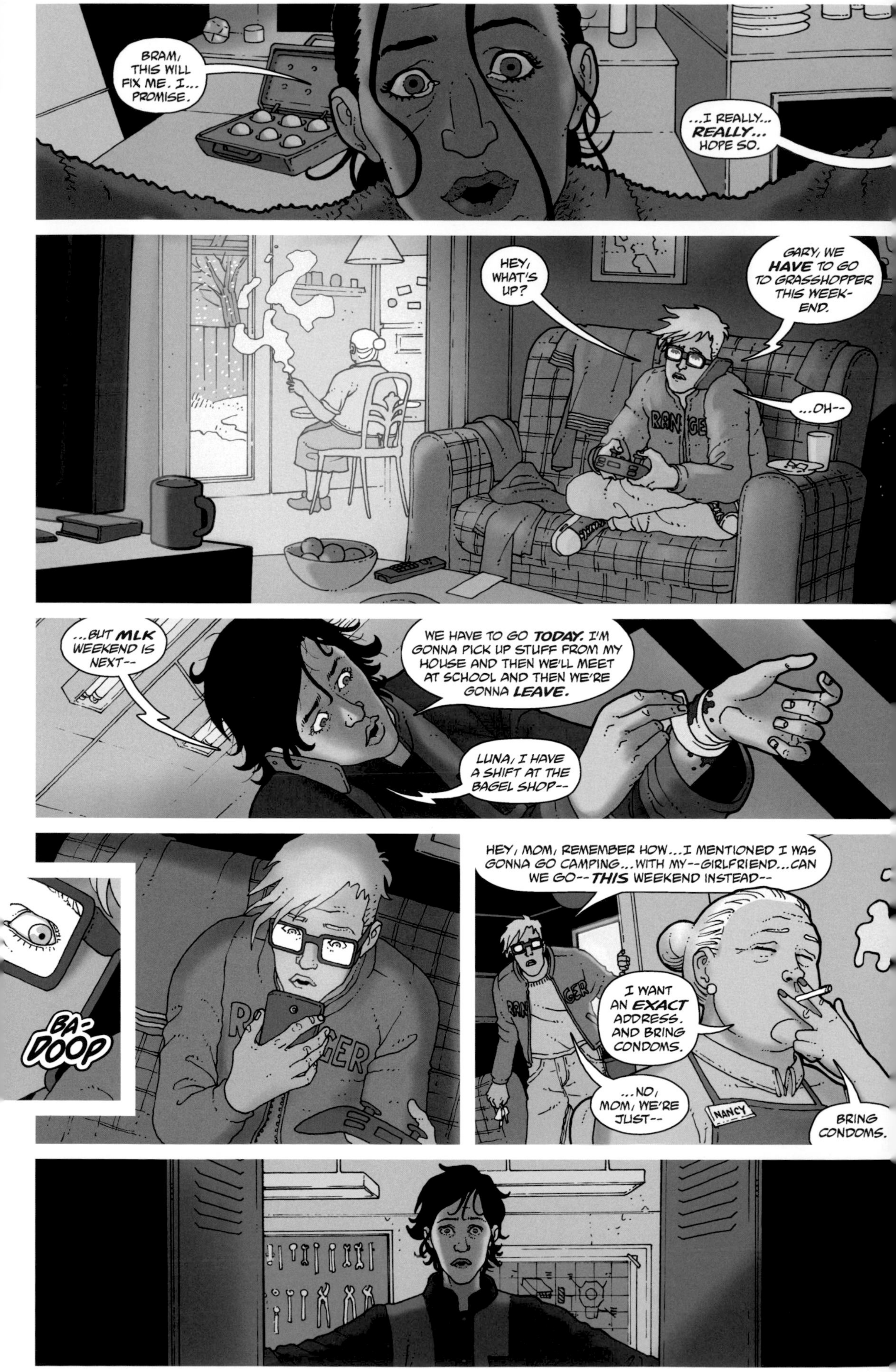
BRAM, THIS WILL FIX ME. I... PROMISE.
...I REALLY... REALLY... HOPE SO.
HEY, WHAT'S UP?
GARY, WE HAVE TO GO TO GRASSHOPPER THIS WEEK-END.
...OH--
...BUT MLK WEEKEND IS NEXT--
WE HAVE TO GO TODAY. I'M GONNA PICK UP STUFF FROM MY HOUSE AND THEN WE'LL MEET AT SCHOOL AND THEN WE'RE GONNA LEAVE.
LUNA, I HAVE A SHIFT AT THE BAGEL SHOP--
BA-DOOP
HEY, MOM, REMEMBER HOW...I MENTIONED I WAS GONNA GO CAMPING...WITH MY--GIRLFRIEND...CAN WE GO--THIS WEEKEND INSTEAD--
I WANT AN EXACT ADDRESS. AND BRING CONDOMS.
...NO, MOM, WE'RE JUST--
NANCY
BRING CONDOMS.

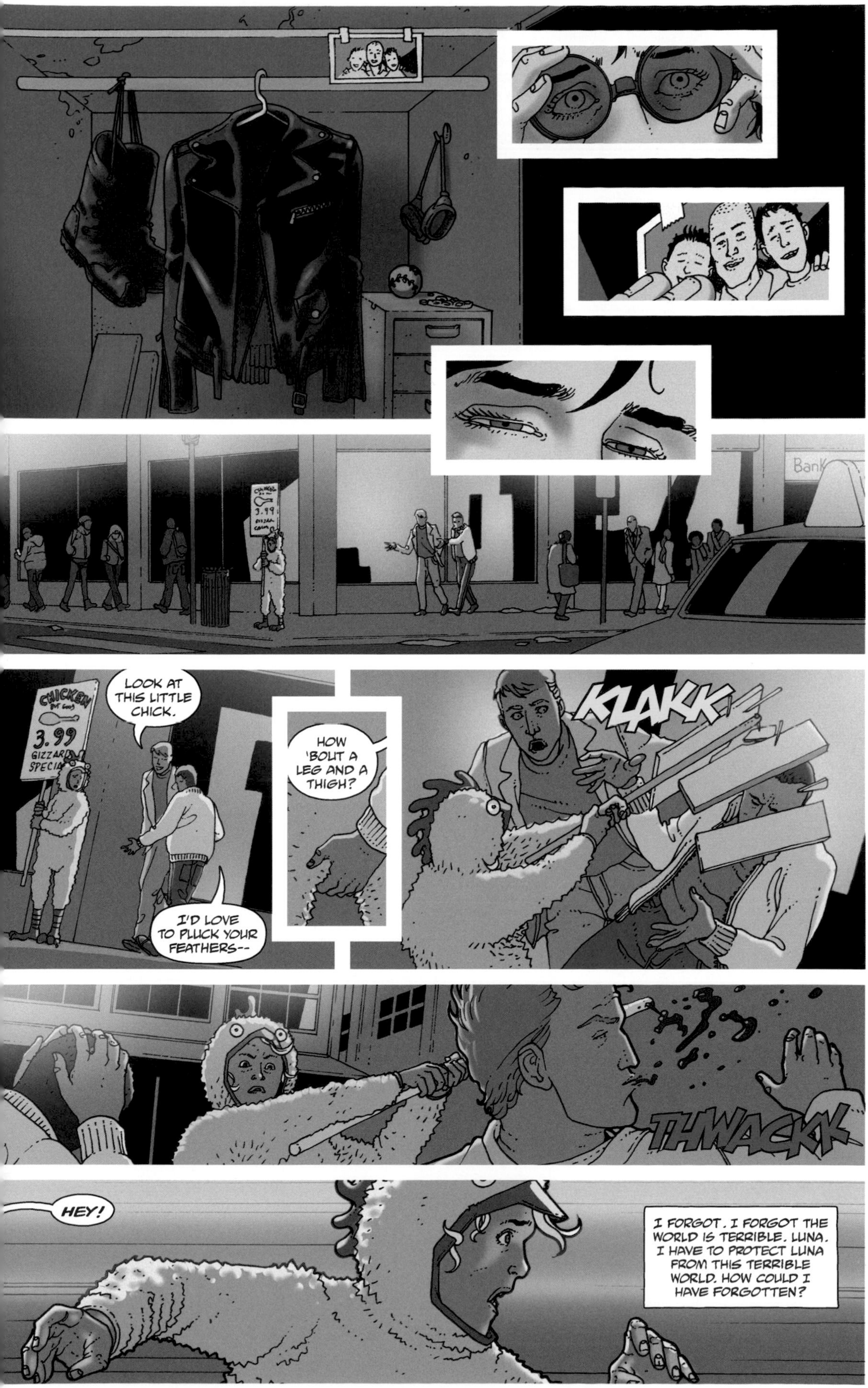
Bank
CHICKEN
3.99
GIZZARD SPECIAL
LOOK AT THIS LITTLE CHICK.
HOW 'BOUT A LEG AND A THIGH?
I'D LOVE TO PLUCK YOUR FEATHERS--
KLAKK
THWACKK
HEY!
I FORGOT. I FORGOT THE WORLD IS TERRIBLE. LUNA. I HAVE TO PROTECT LUNA FROM THIS TERRIBLE WORLD. HOW COULD I HAVE FORGOTTEN?

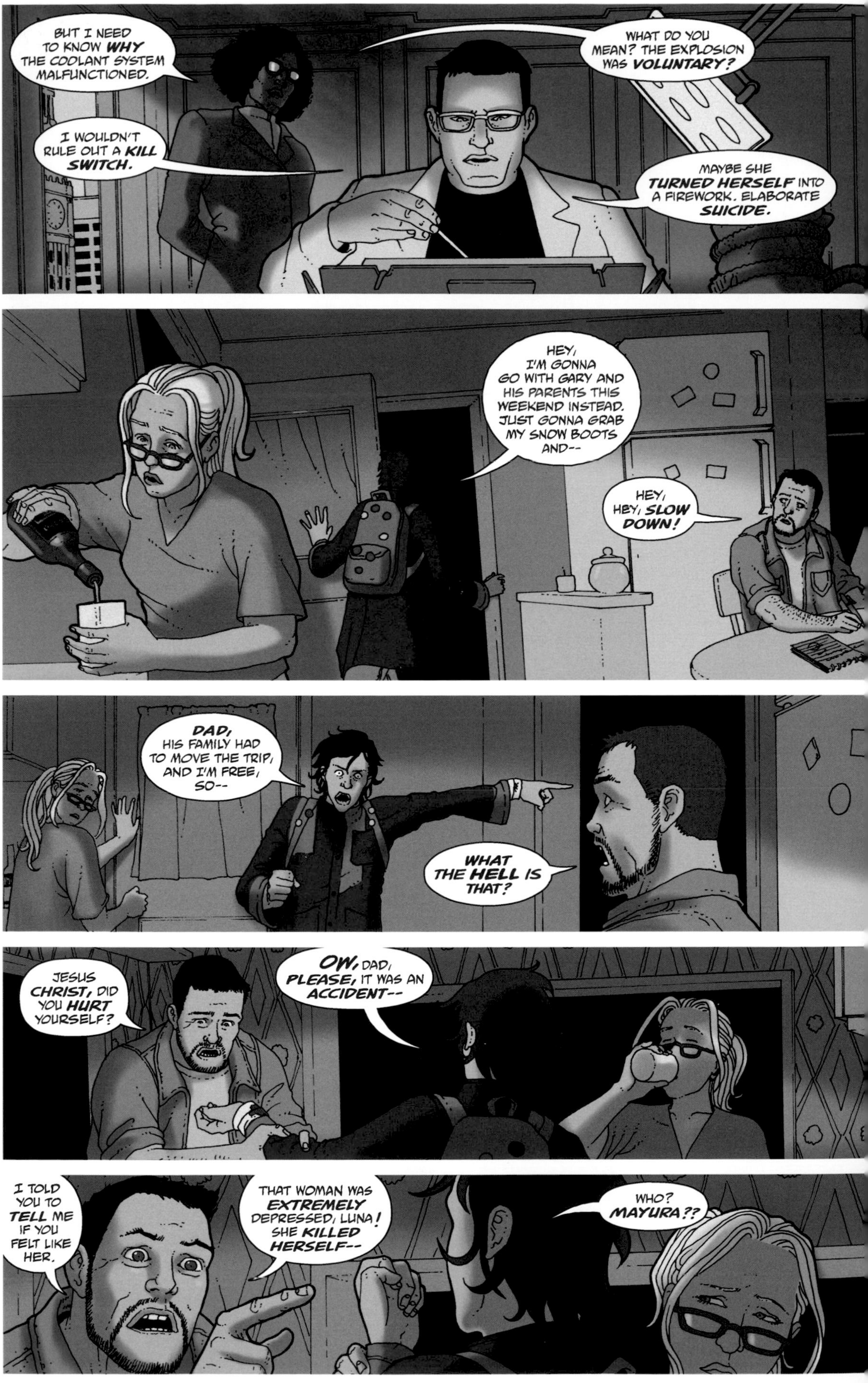
BUT I NEED TO KNOW WHY THE COOLANT SYSTEM MALFUNCTIONED.
WHAT DO YOU MEAN? THE EXPLOSION WAS VOLUNTARY?
I WOULDN'T RULE OUT A KILL SWITCH.
MAYBE SHE TURNED HERSELF INTO A FIREWORK. ELABORATE SUICIDE.
HEY, I'M GONNA GO WITH GARY AND HIS PARENTS THIS WEEKEND INSTEAD. JUST GONNA GRAB MY SNOW BOOTS AND--
HEY, HEY, SLOW DOWN!
DAD, HIS FAMILY HAD TO MOVE THE TRIP, AND I'M FREE, SO--
WHAT THE HELL IS THAT?
JESUS CHRIST, DID YOU HURT YOURSELF?
OW, DAD, PLEASE, IT WAS AN ACCIDENT--
I TOLD YOU TO TELL ME IF YOU FELT LIKE HER.
THAT WOMAN WAS EXTREMELY DEPRESSED, LUNA! SHE KILLED HERSELF--
WHO? MAYURA??

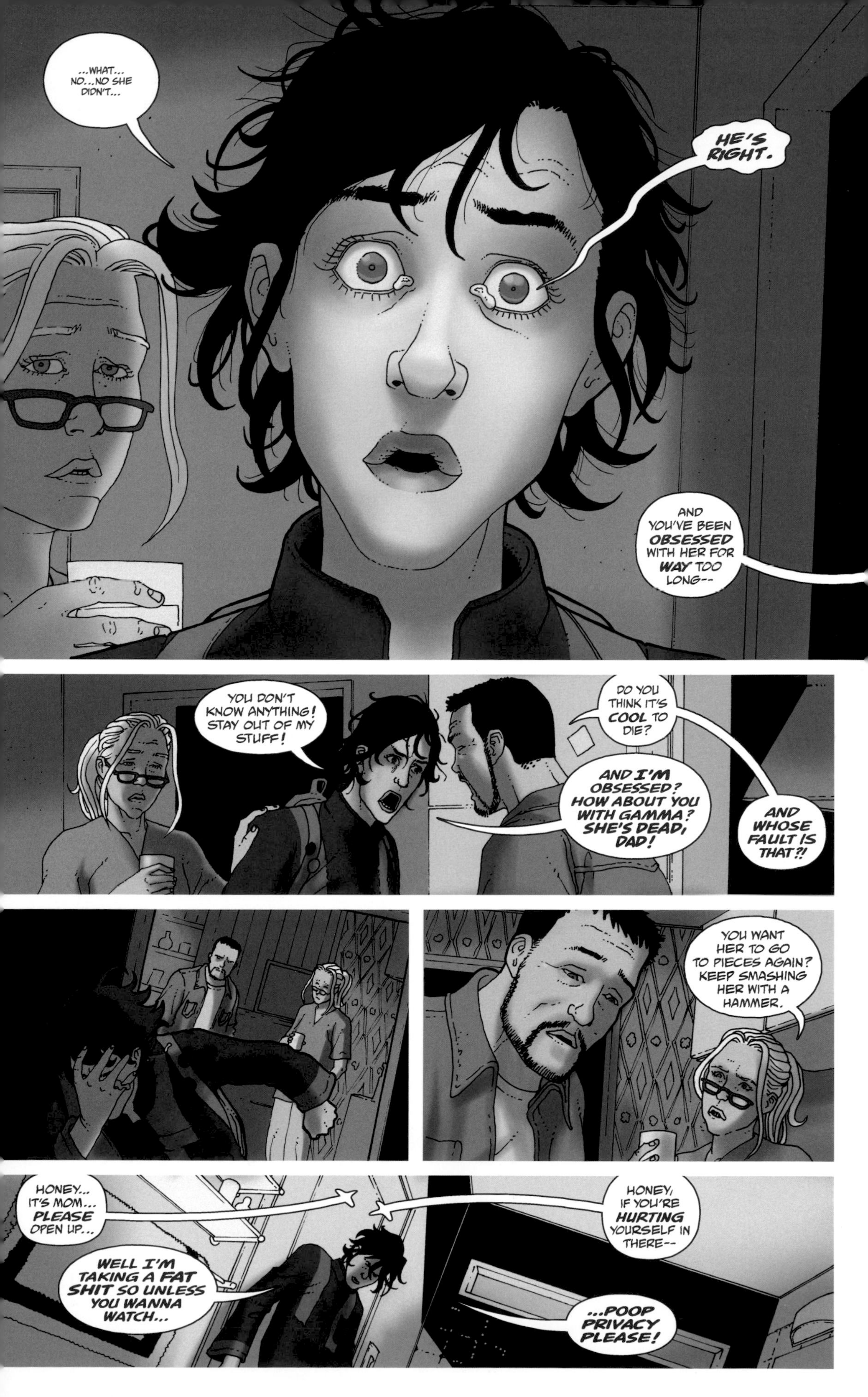
...WHAT...
NO...NO SHE DIDN'T...
HE'S RIGHT.
AND YOU'VE BEEN OBSESSED WITH HER FOR WAY TOO LONG--
YOU DON'T KNOW ANYTHING! STAY OUT OF MY STUFF!
DO YOU THINK IT'S COOL TO DIE?
AND I'M OBSESSED? HOW ABOUT YOU WITH GAMMA? SHE'S DEAD, DAD!
AND WHOSE FAULT IS THAT?!
YOU WANT HER TO GO TO PIECES AGAIN? KEEP SMASHING HER WITH A HAMMER.
HONEY... IT'S MOM... PLEASE OPEN UP...
HONEY, IF YOU'RE HURTING YOURSELF IN THERE--
WELL I'M TAKING A FAT SHIT SO UNLESS YOU WANNA WATCH...
...POOP PRIVACY PLEASE!

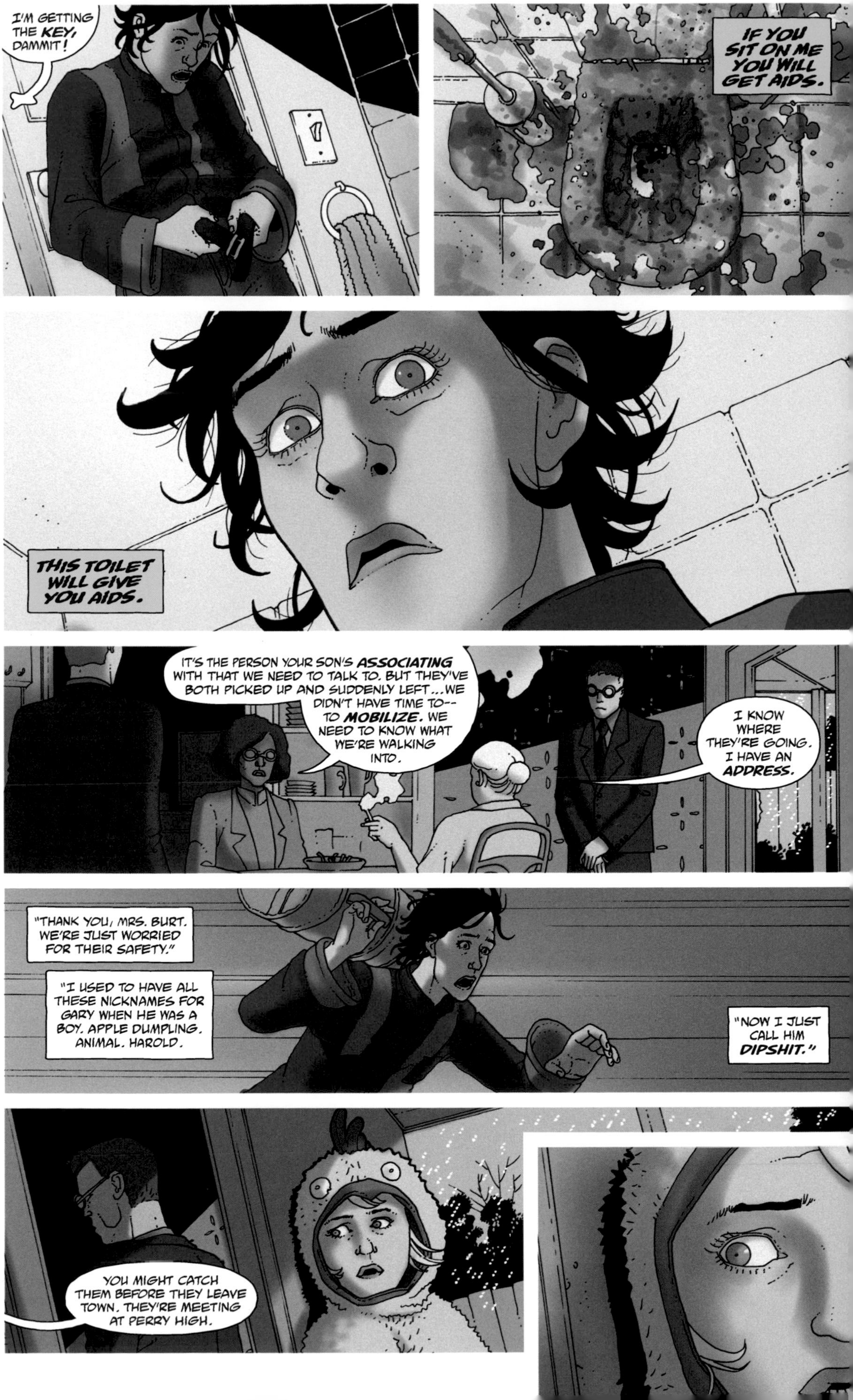
I'M GETTING THE KEY, DAMMIT!
IF YOU SIT ON ME YOU WILL GET AIDS.
THIS TOILET WILL GIVE YOU AIDS.
IT'S THE PERSON YOUR SON'S ASSOCIATING WITH THAT WE NEED TO TALK TO. BUT THEY'VE BOTH PICKED UP AND SUDDENLY LEFT... WE DIDN'T HAVE TIME TO-- TO MOBILIZE. WE NEED TO KNOW WHAT WE'RE WALKING INTO.
I KNOW WHERE THEY'RE GOING. I HAVE AN ADDRESS.
"THANK YOU, MRS. BURT. WE'RE JUST WORRIED FOR THEIR SAFETY."
"I USED TO HAVE ALL THESE NICKNAMES FOR GARY WHEN HE WAS A BOY. APPLE DUMPLING. ANIMAL. HAROLD.
"NOW I JUST CALL HIM DIPSHIT."
YOU MIGHT CATCH THEM BEFORE THEY LEAVE TOWN. THEY'RE MEETING AT PERRY HIGH.

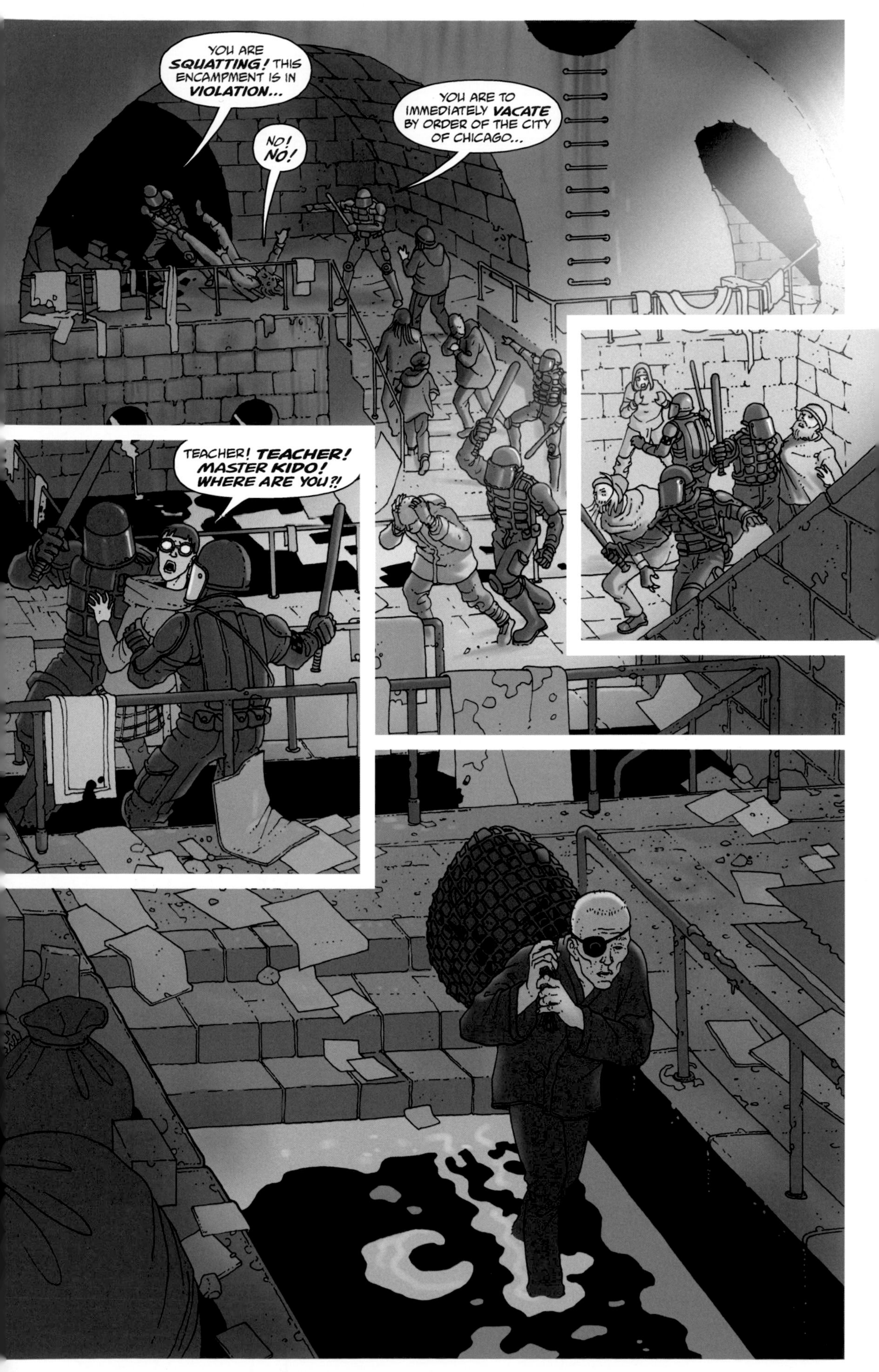
YOU ARE SQUATTING! THIS ENCAMPMENT IS IN VIOLATION...
NO! NO!
YOU ARE TO IMMEDIATELY VACATE BY ORDER OF THE CITY OF CHICAGO...
TEACHER! TEACHER! MASTER KIDO! WHERE ARE YOU?!

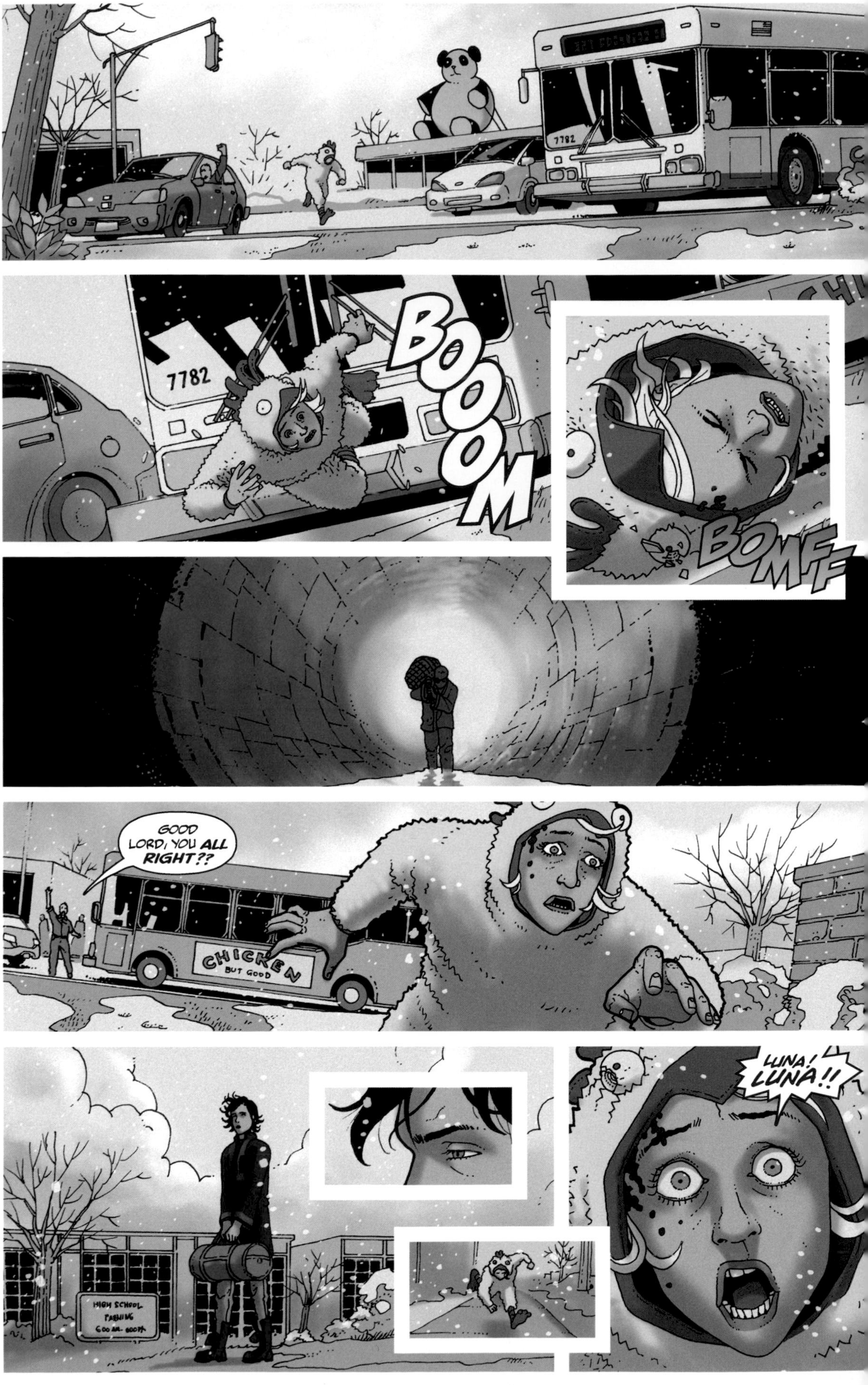
7782
BOOOM
BOMFF
GOOD LORD, YOU ALL RIGHT??
CHICKEN BUT GOOD
HIGH SCHOOL PARKING
LUNA! LUNA!!

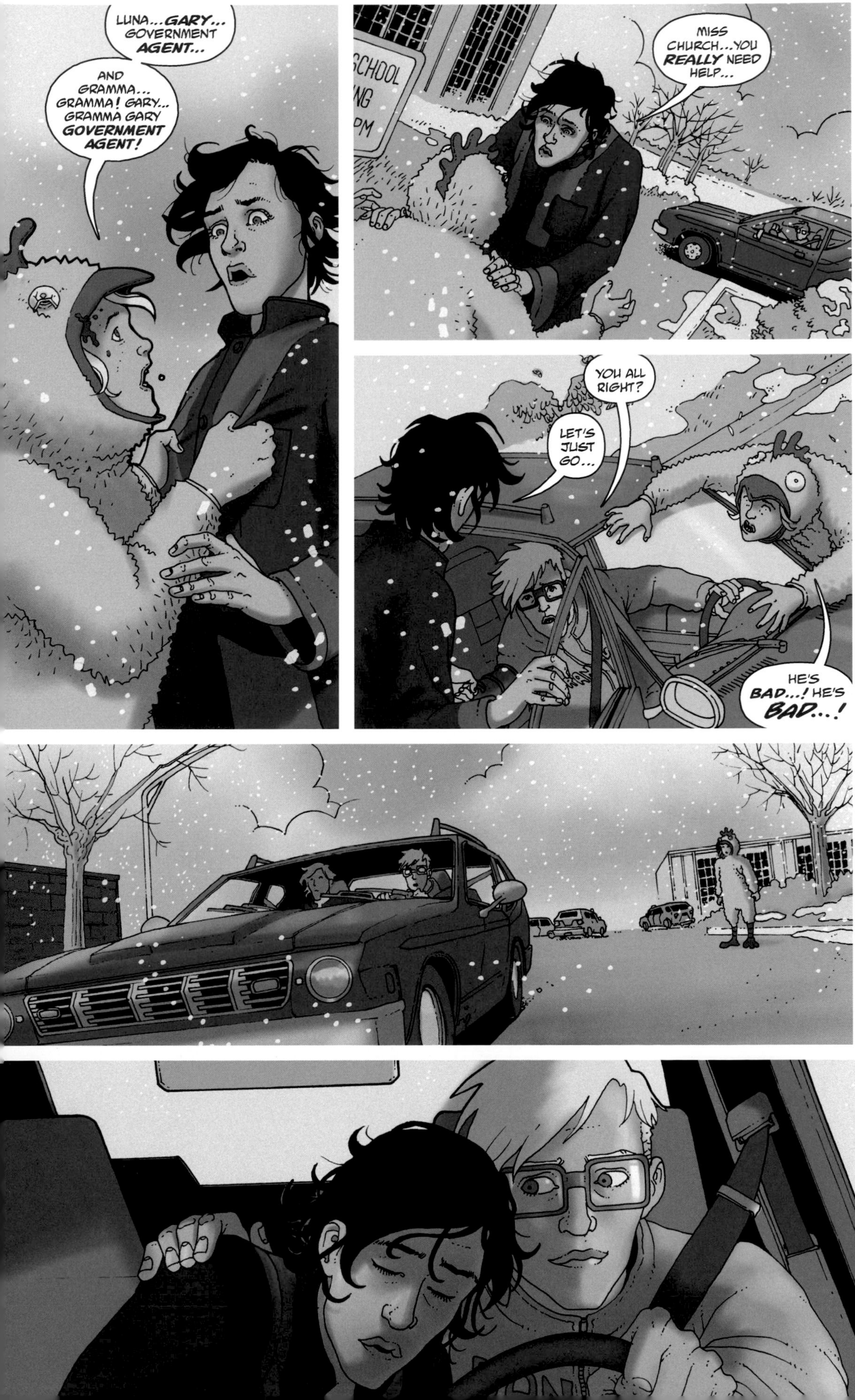
LUNA... GARY... GOVERNMENT AGENT...
AND GRAMMA... GRAMMA! GARY... GRAMMA GARY GOVERNMENT AGENT!
SCHOOL
NG
PM
MISS CHURCH... YOU REALLY NEED HELP...
YOU ALL RIGHT?
LET'S JUST GO...
HE'S BAD...! HE'S BAD...!

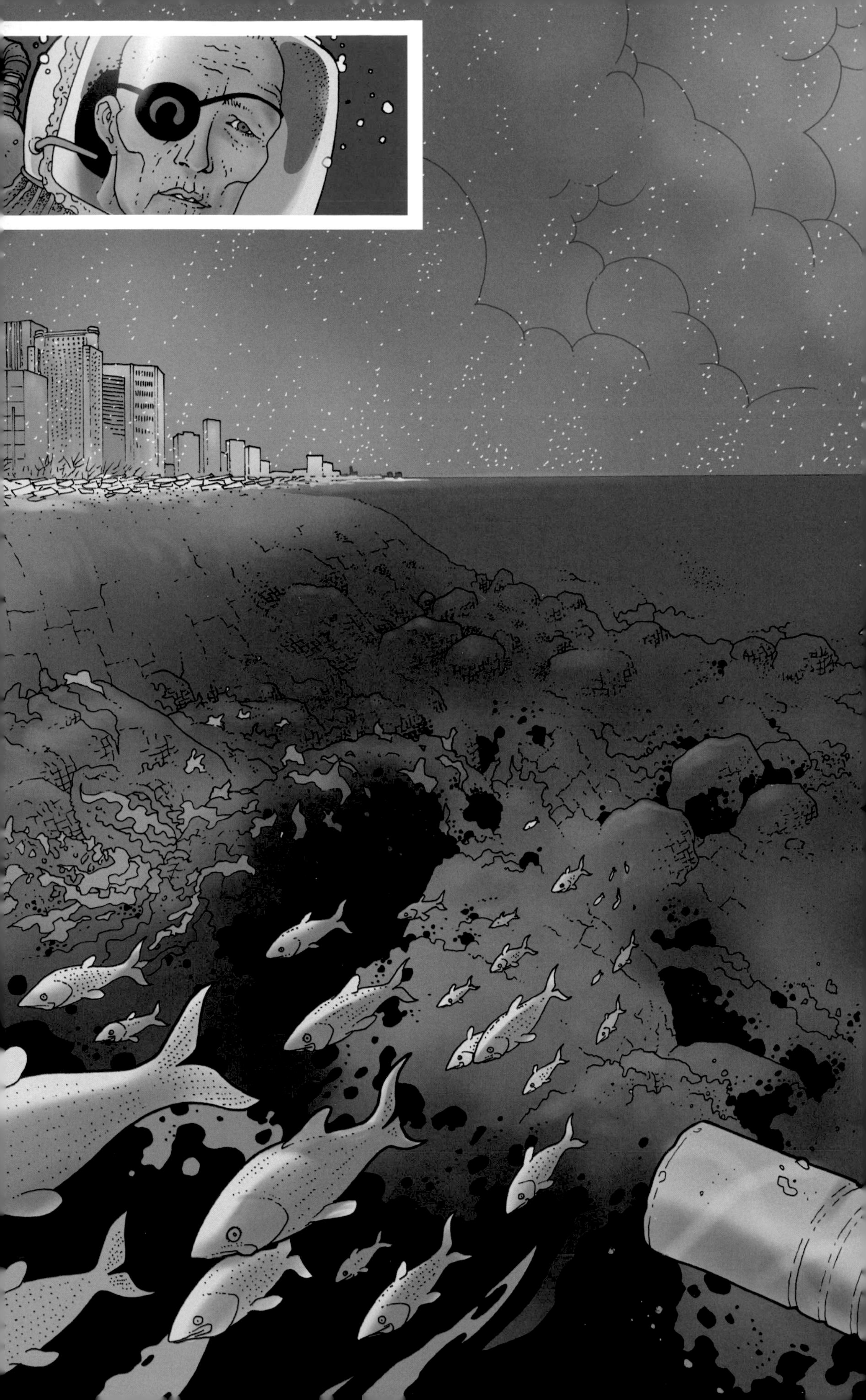

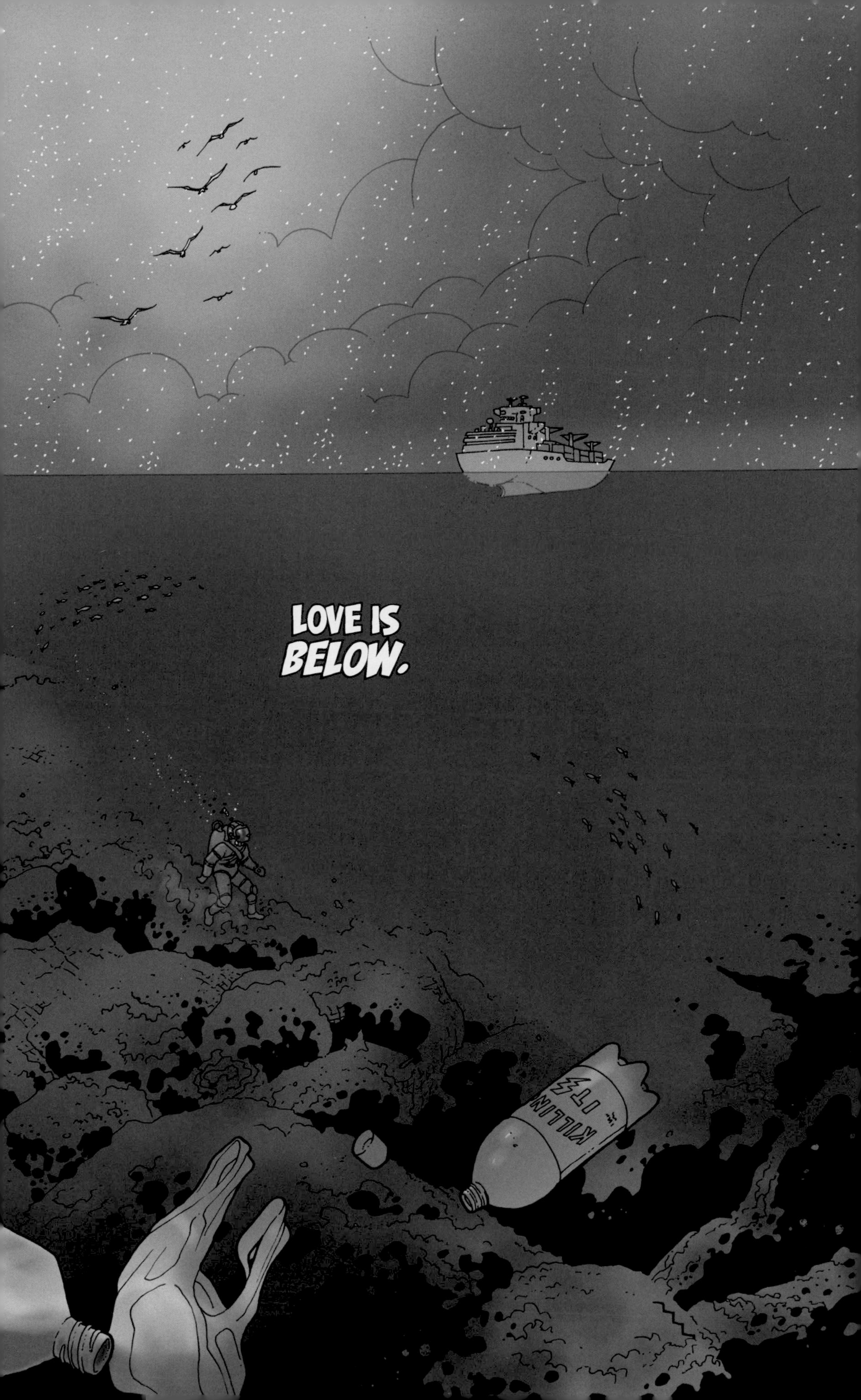
LOVE IS BELOW.

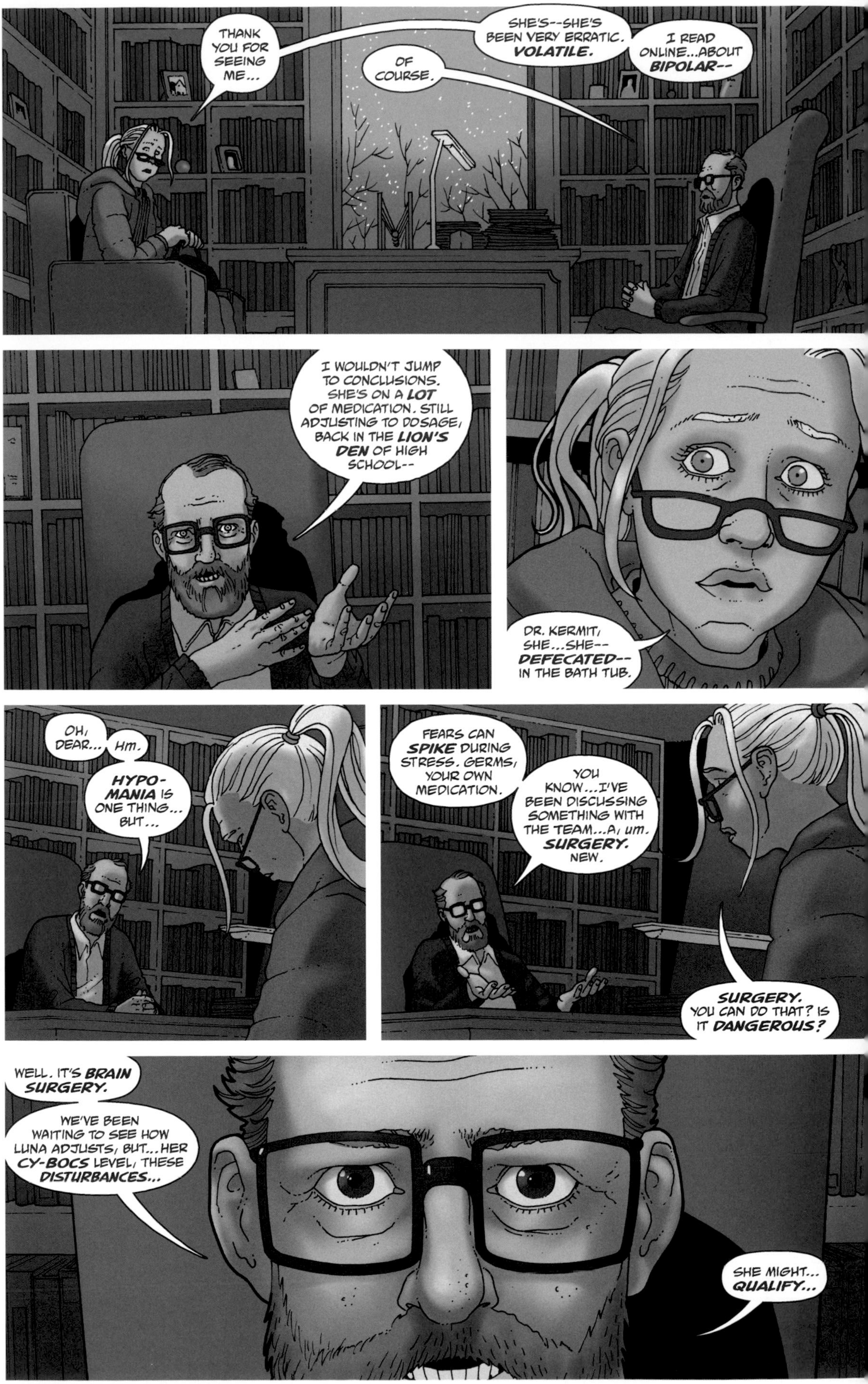
THANK YOU FOR SEEING ME...
OF COURSE.
SHE'S--SHE'S BEEN VERY ERRATIC. VOLATILE.
I READ ONLINE...ABOUT BIPOLAR--
I WOULDN'T JUMP TO CONCLUSIONS. SHE'S ON A LOT OF MEDICATION. STILL ADJUSTING TO DOSAGE, BACK IN THE LION'S DEN OF HIGH SCHOOL--
DR. KERMIT, SHE...SHE-- DEFECATED-- IN THE BATH TUB.
OH, DEAR...
Hm.
HYPO-MANIA IS ONE THING... BUT...
FEARS CAN SPIKE DURING STRESS. GERMS, YOUR OWN MEDICATION.
YOU KNOW...I'VE BEEN DISCUSSING SOMETHING WITH THE TEAM...A, um. SURGERY. NEW.
SURGERY. YOU CAN DO THAT? IS IT DANGEROUS?
WELL. IT'S BRAIN SURGERY.
WE'VE BEEN WAITING TO SEE HOW LUNA ADJUSTS, BUT...HER CY-BOCS LEVEL, THESE DISTURBANCES...
SHE MIGHT... QUALIFY...

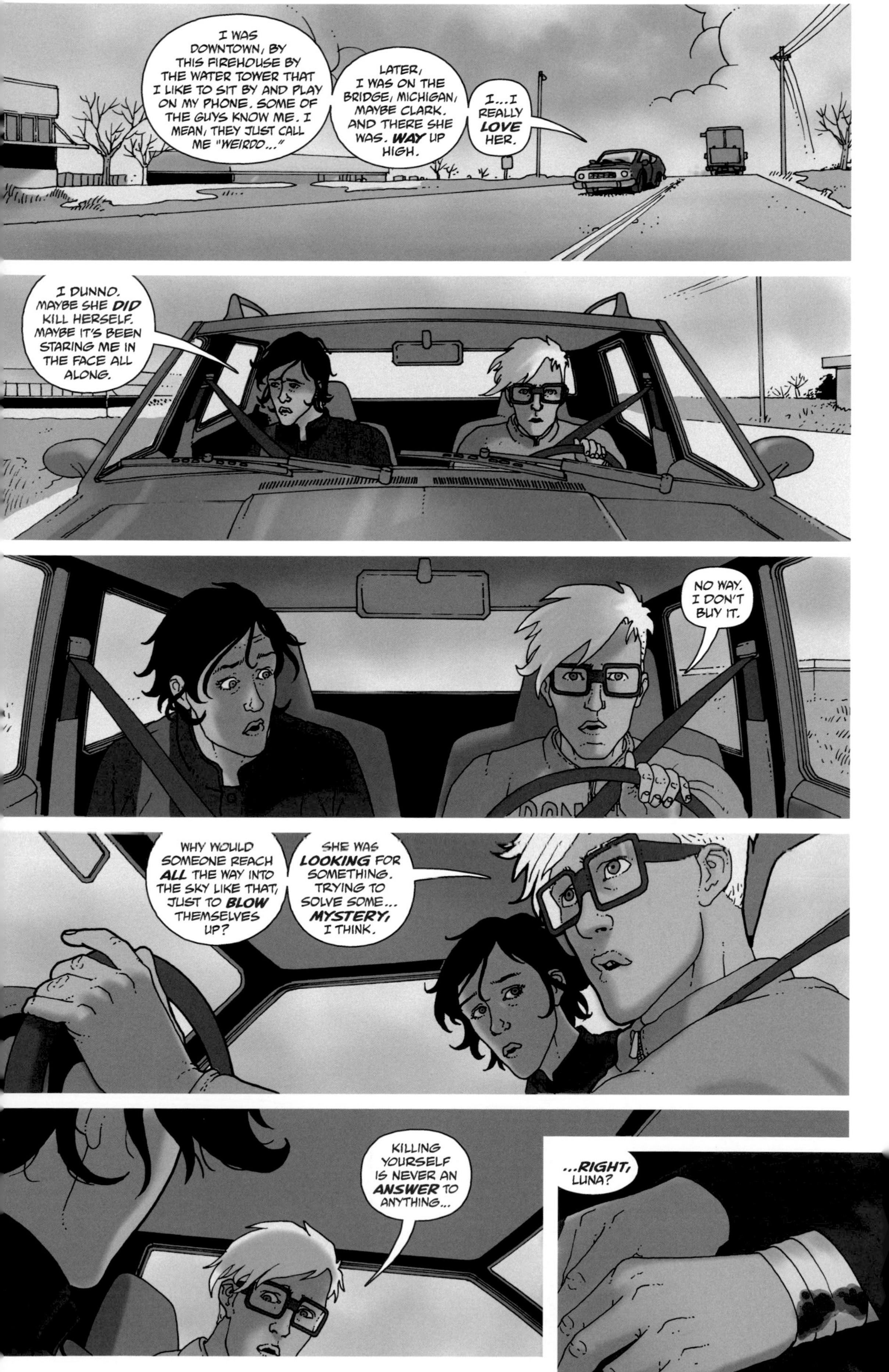
I WAS DOWNTOWN, BY THIS FIREHOUSE BY THE WATER TOWER THAT I LIKE TO SIT BY AND PLAY ON MY PHONE. SOME OF THE GUYS KNOW ME. I MEAN, THEY JUST CALL ME "WEIRDO..."
LATER, I WAS ON THE BRIDGE, MICHIGAN, MAYBE CLARK. AND THERE SHE WAS. WAY UP HIGH.
I...I REALLY LOVE HER.
I DUNNO. MAYBE SHE DID KILL HERSELF. MAYBE IT'S BEEN STARING ME IN THE FACE ALL ALONG.
NO WAY. I DON'T BUY IT.
WHY WOULD SOMEONE REACH ALL THE WAY INTO THE SKY LIKE THAT, JUST TO BLOW THEMSELVES UP?
SHE WAS LOOKING FOR SOMETHING. TRYING TO SOLVE SOME... MYSTERY, I THINK.
KILLING YOURSELF IS NEVER AN ANSWER TO ANYTHING...
...RIGHT, LUNA?

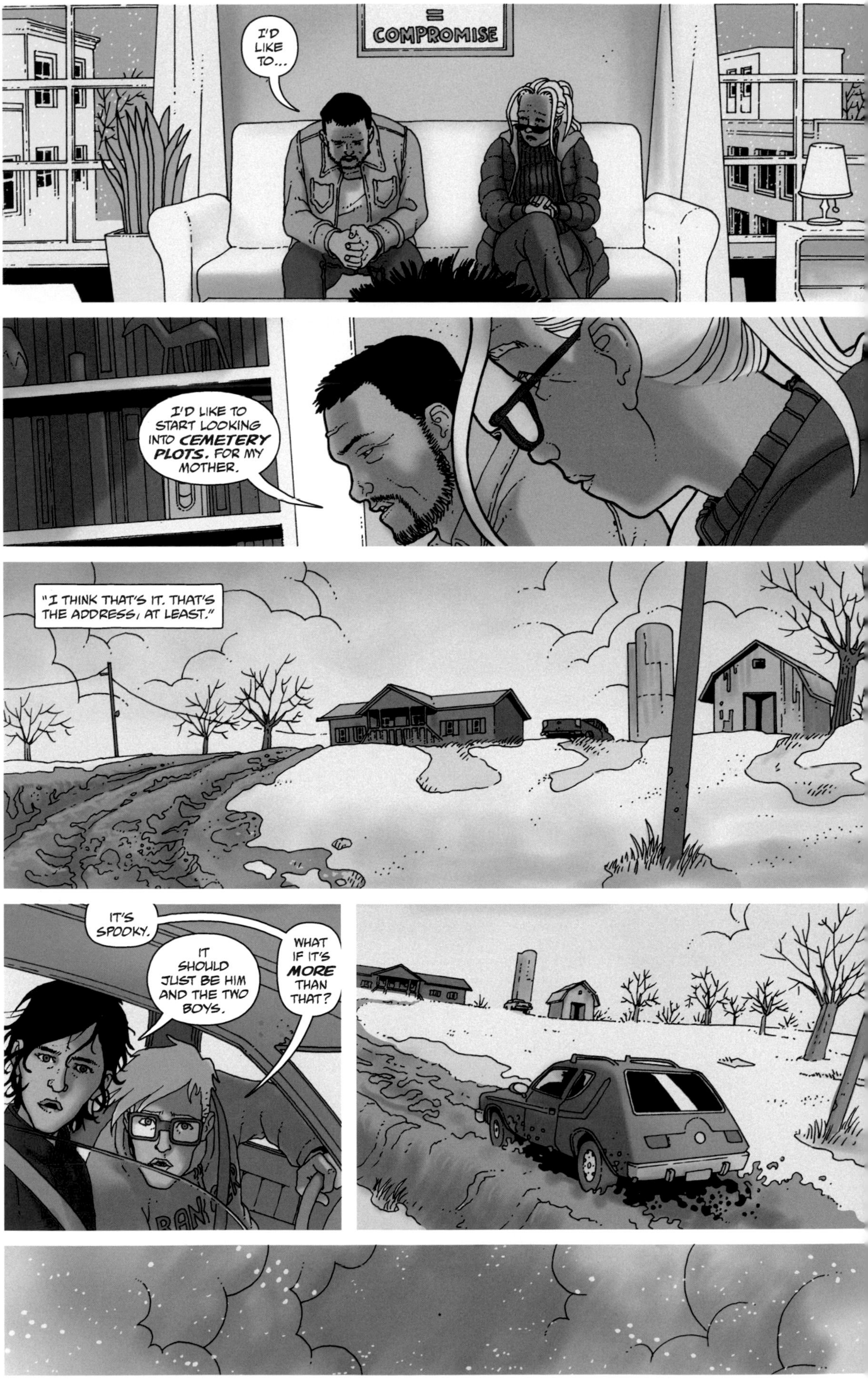
COMPROMISE
I'D LIKE TO...
I'D LIKE TO START LOOKING INTO CEMETERY PLOTS. FOR MY MOTHER.
"I THINK THAT'S IT. THAT'S THE ADDRESS, AT LEAST."
IT'S SPOOKY.
IT SHOULD JUST BE HIM AND THE TWO BOYS.
WHAT IF IT'S MORE THAN THAT?

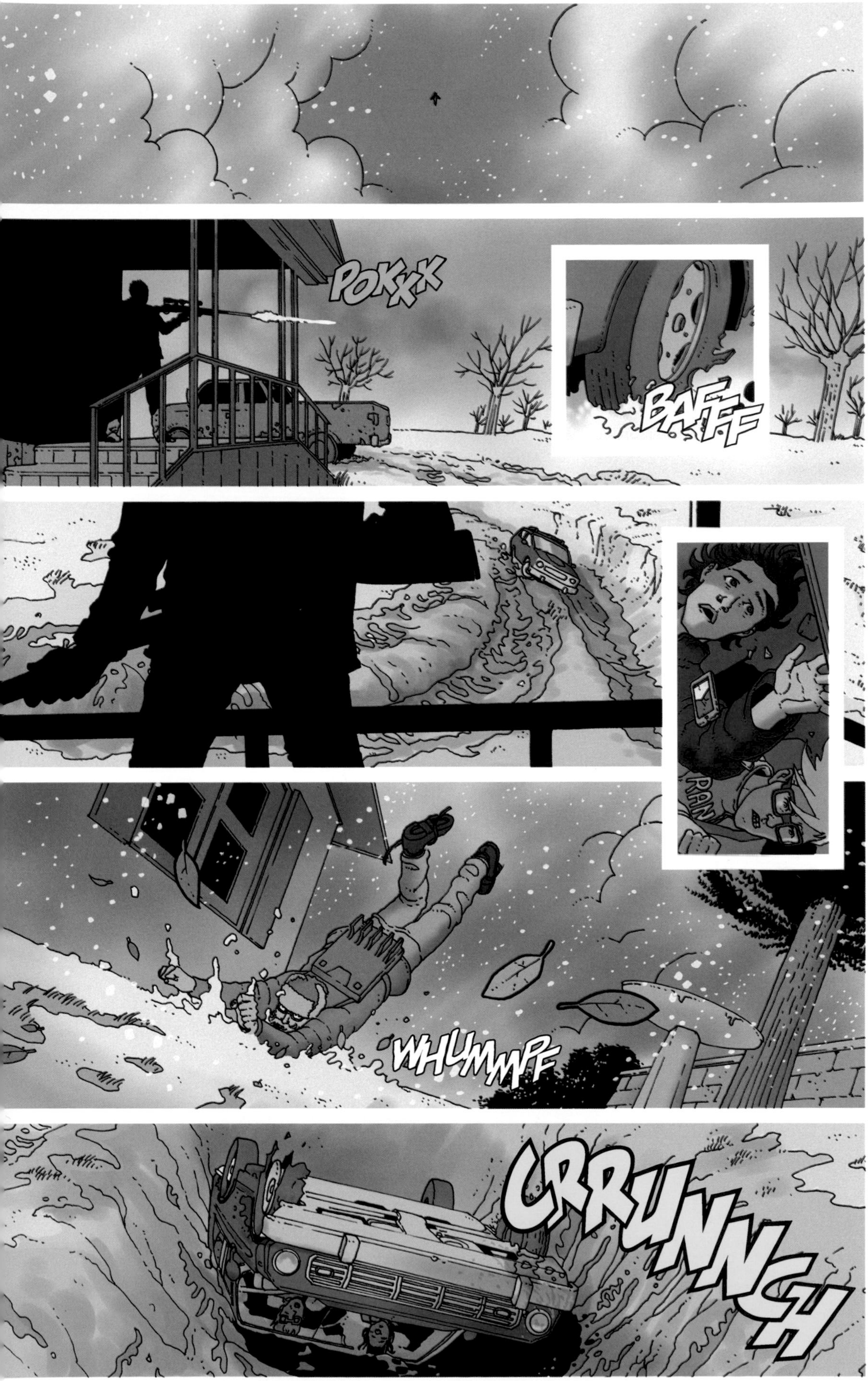

POKKK
BAFFF
RAN
WHUMMPF
CRRUNNCH

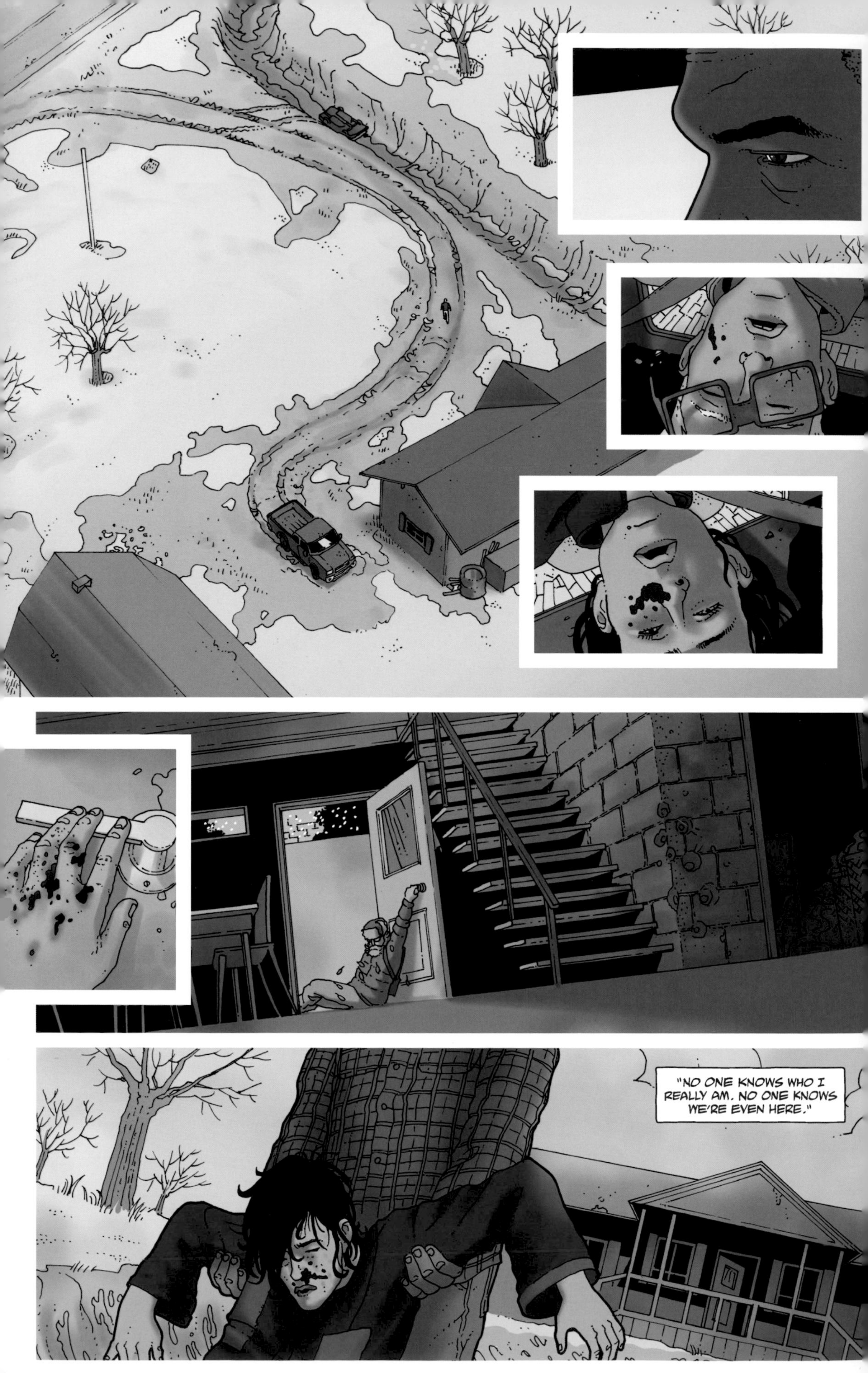
"NO ONE KNOWS WHO I REALLY AM. NO ONE KNOWS WE'RE EVEN HERE."

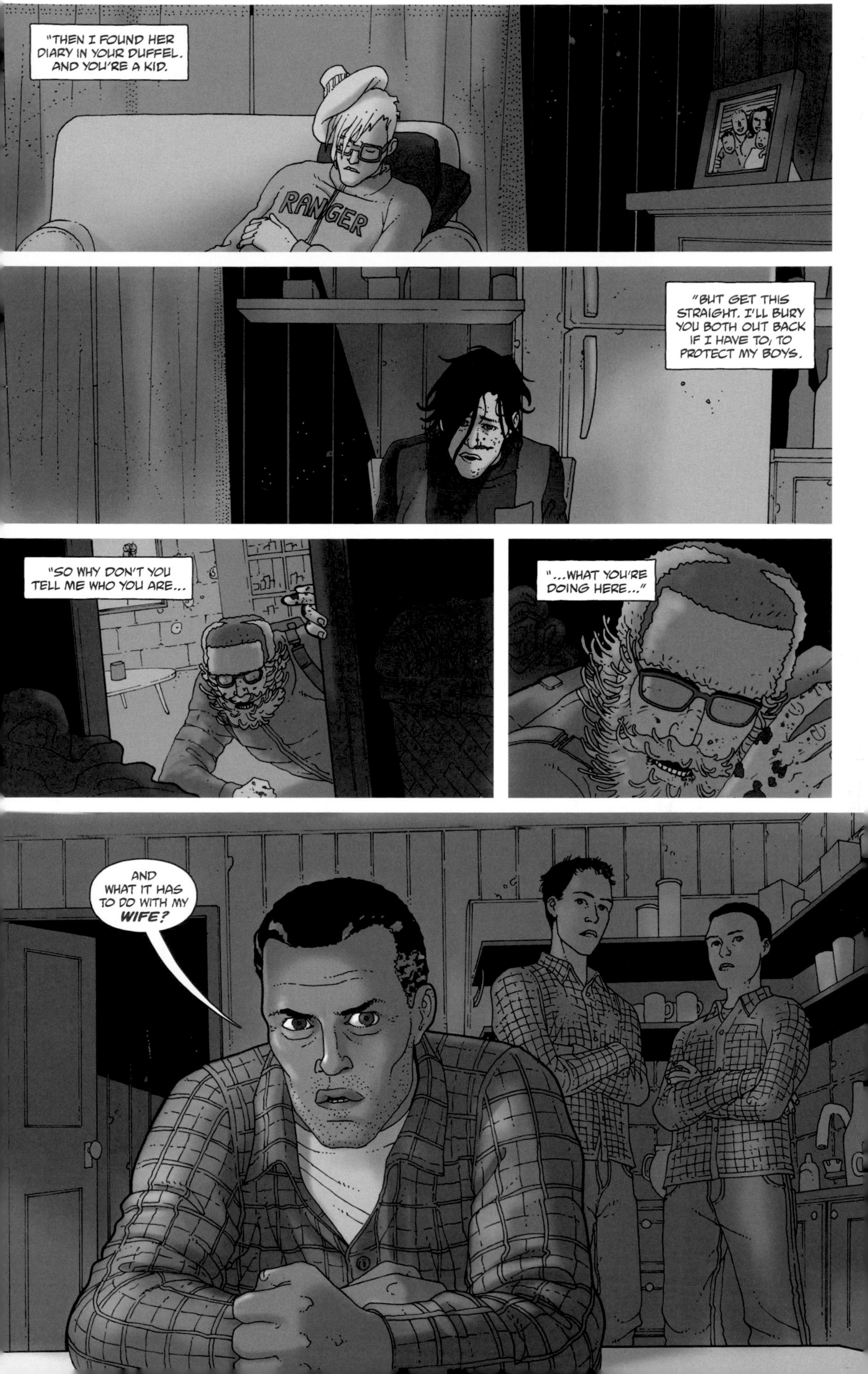
"THEN I FOUND HER DIARY IN YOUR DUFFEL. AND YOU'RE A KID.
"BUT GET THIS STRAIGHT. I'LL BURY YOU BOTH OUT BACK IF I HAVE TO, TO PROTECT MY BOYS.
RANGER
"SO WHY DON'T YOU TELL ME WHO YOU ARE...
"...WHAT YOU'RE DOING HERE..."
AND WHAT IT HAS TO DO WITH MY WIFE?

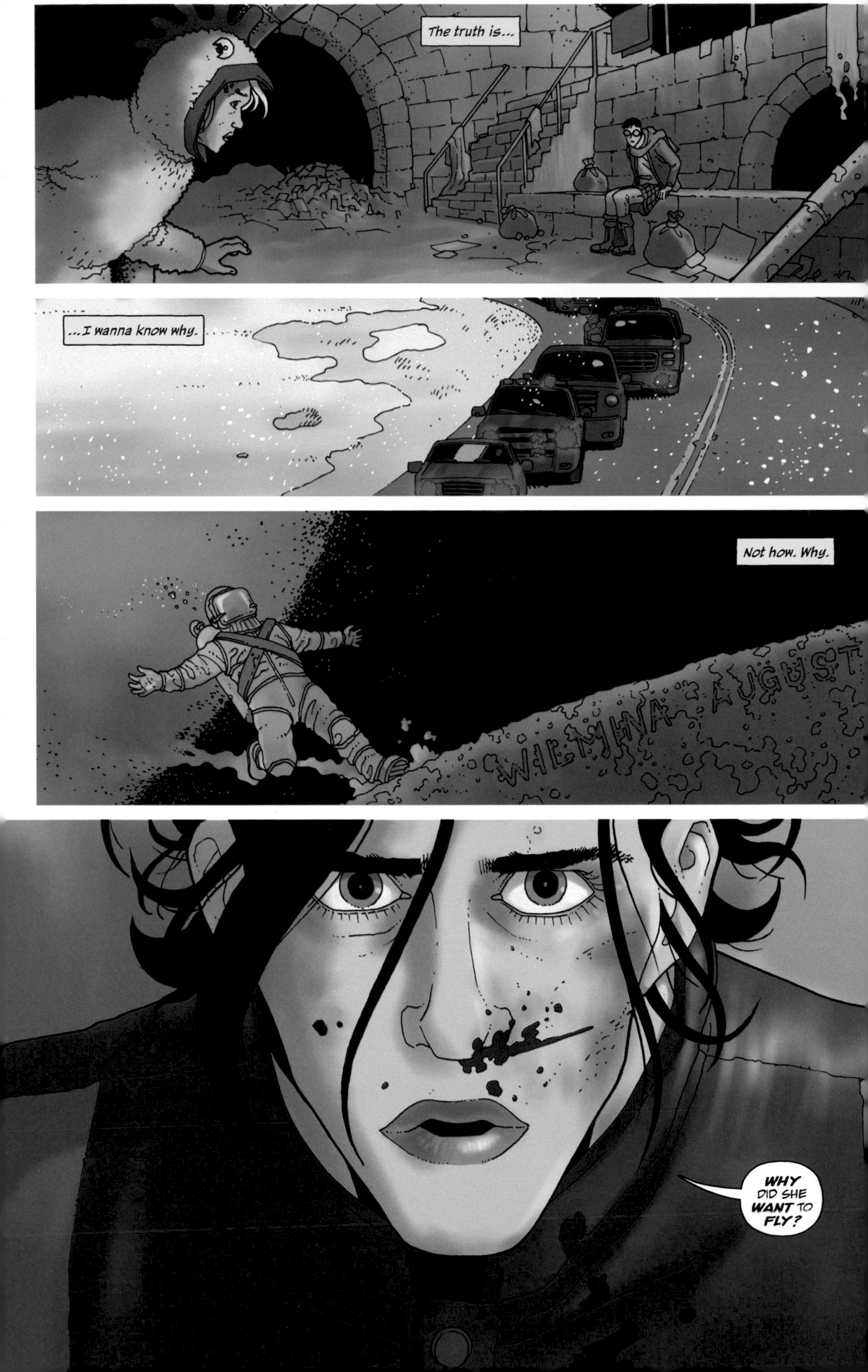
The truth is...
...I wanna know why.
Not how. Why.
WILMINA AUGUST
WHY DID SHE WANT TO FLY?

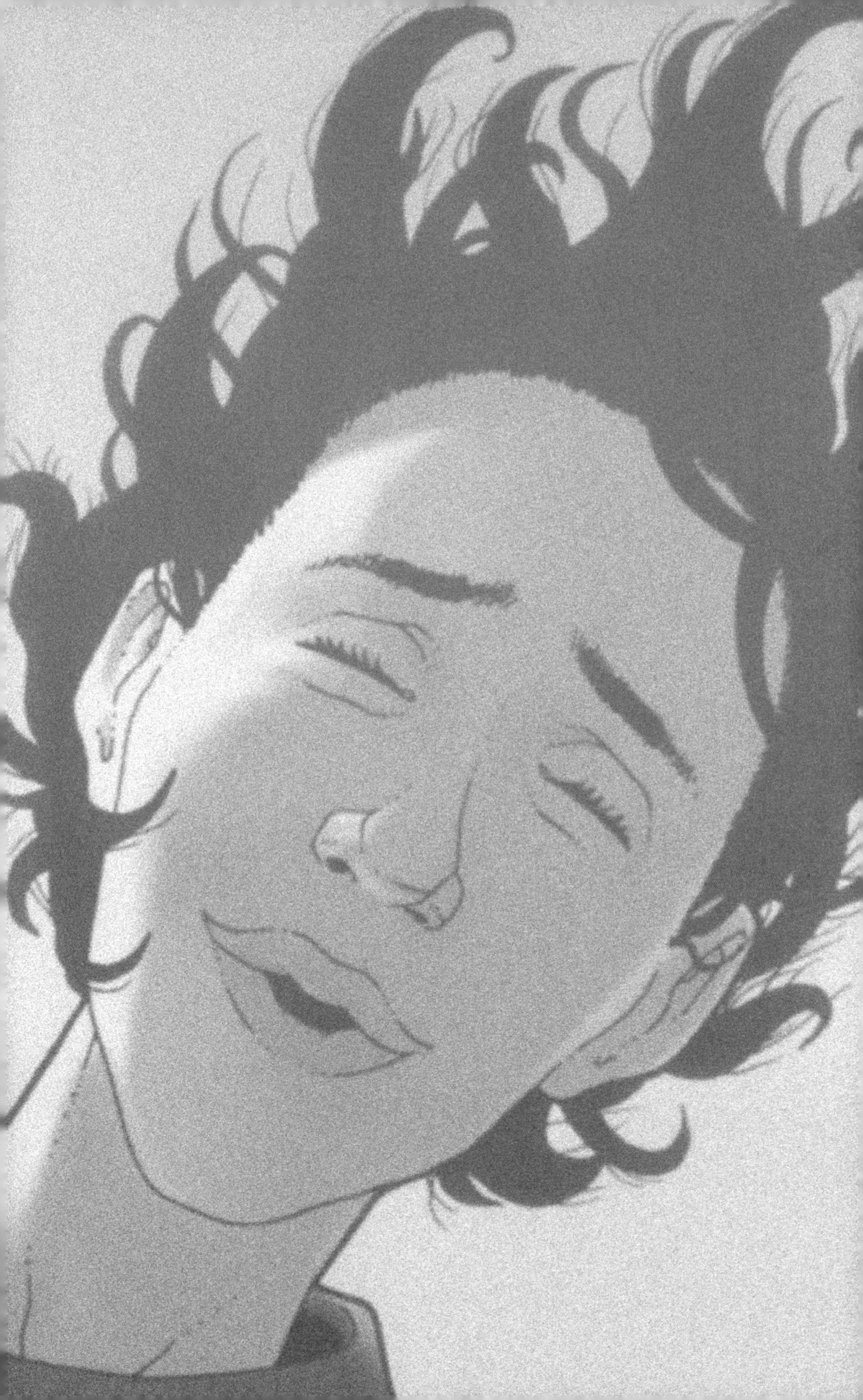

CHAPTER V
"Grounded"

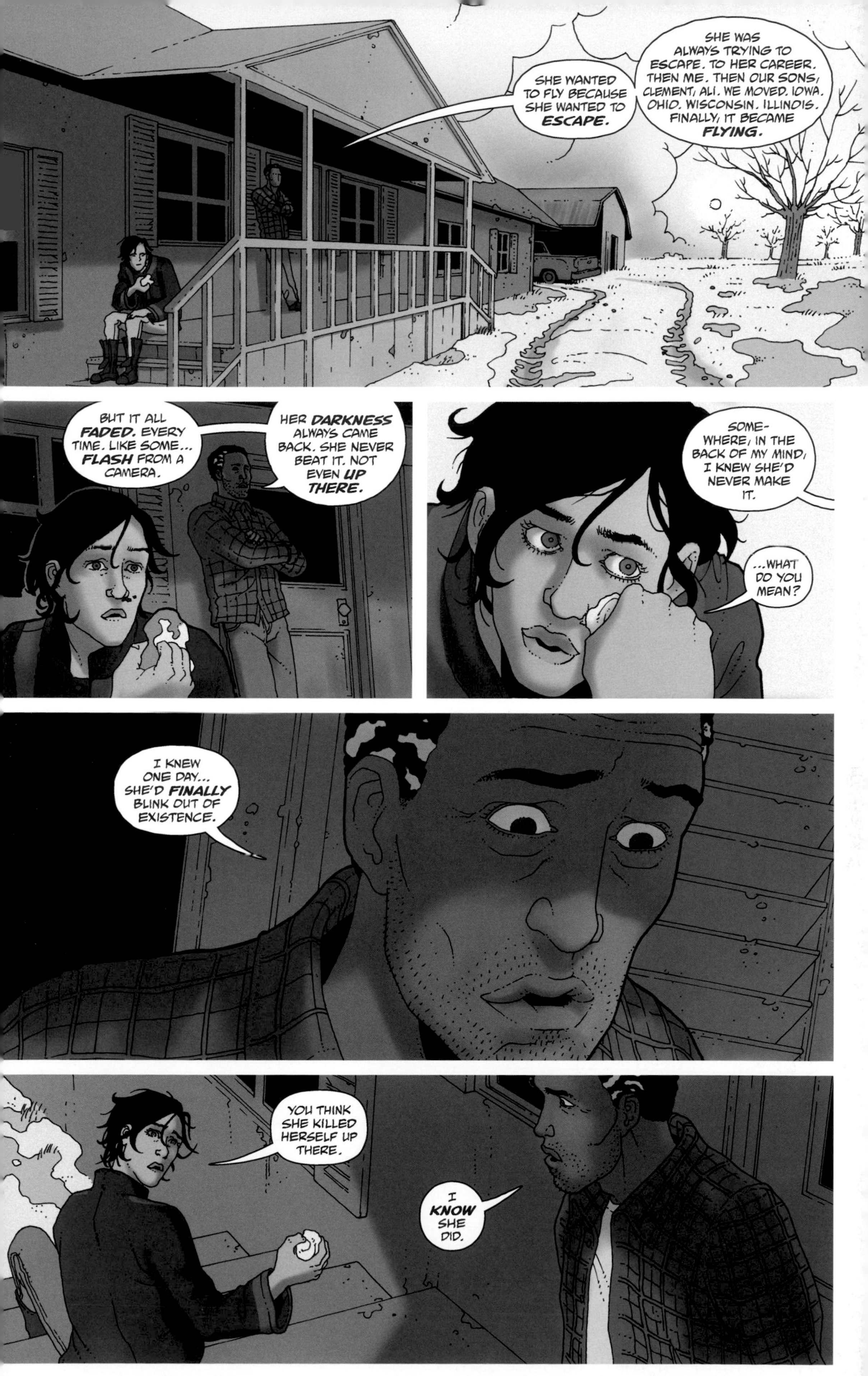
SHE WANTED TO FLY BECAUSE SHE WANTED TO ESCAPE.
SHE WAS ALWAYS TRYING TO ESCAPE. TO HER CAREER. THEN ME. THEN OUR SONS, CLEMENT, ALI. WE MOVED. IOWA. OHIO. WISCONSIN. ILLINOIS. FINALLY, IT BECAME FLYING.
BUT IT ALL FADED. EVERY TIME. LIKE SOME... FLASH FROM A CAMERA.
HER DARKNESS ALWAYS CAME BACK. SHE NEVER BEAT IT. NOT EVEN UP THERE.
SOME-WHERE, IN THE BACK OF MY MIND, I KNEW SHE'D NEVER MAKE IT.
...WHAT DO YOU MEAN?
I KNEW ONE DAY... SHE'D FINALLY BLINK OUT OF EXISTENCE.
YOU THINK SHE KILLED HERSELF UP THERE.
I KNOW SHE DID.

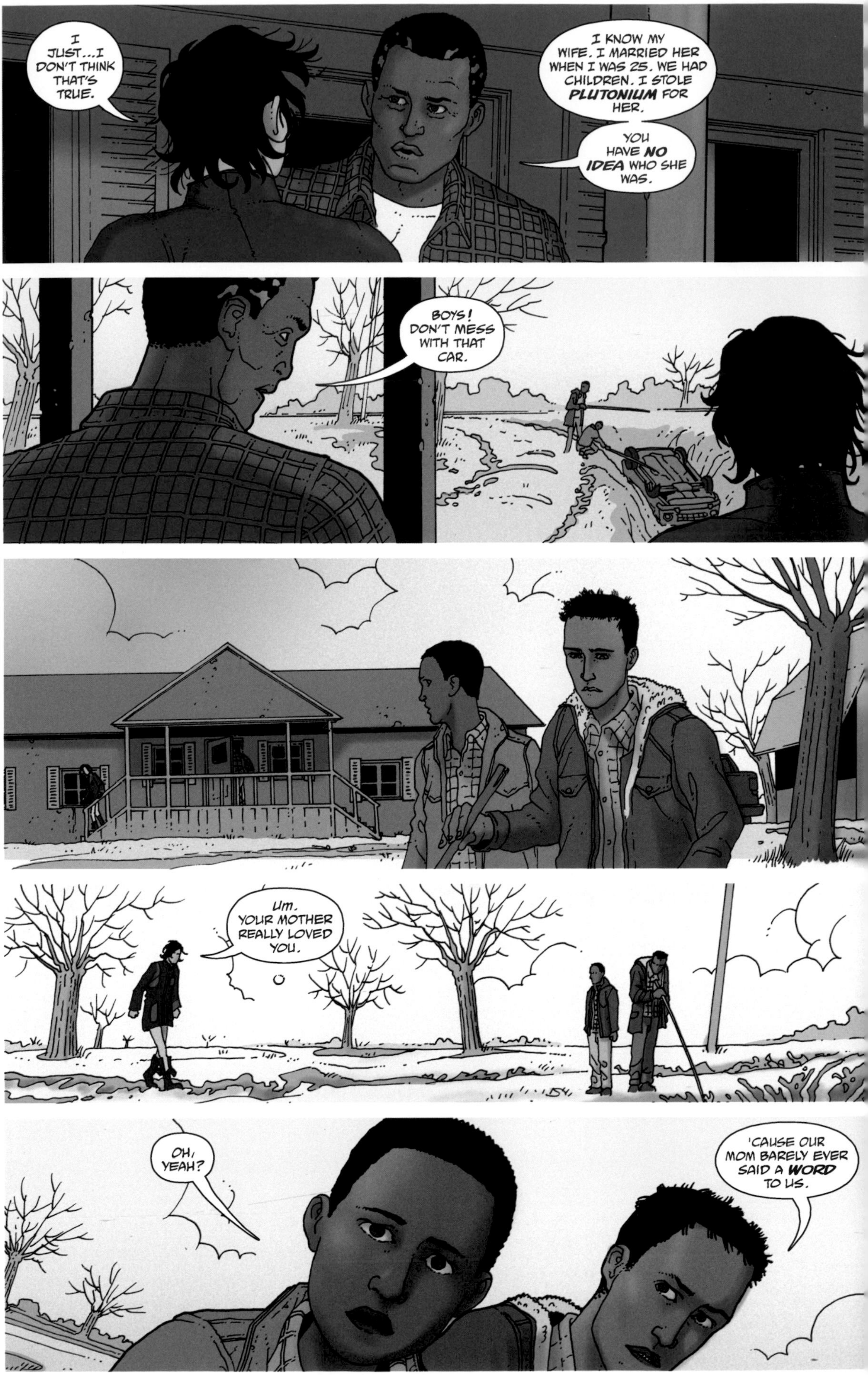
I JUST...I DON'T THINK THAT'S TRUE.
I KNOW MY WIFE. I MARRIED HER WHEN I WAS 25. WE HAD CHILDREN. I STOLE PLUTONIUM FOR HER.
YOU HAVE NO IDEA WHO SHE WAS.
BOYS! DON'T MESS WITH THAT CAR.
Um. YOUR MOTHER REALLY LOVED YOU.
OH, YEAH?
'CAUSE OUR MOM BARELY EVER SAID A WORD TO US.

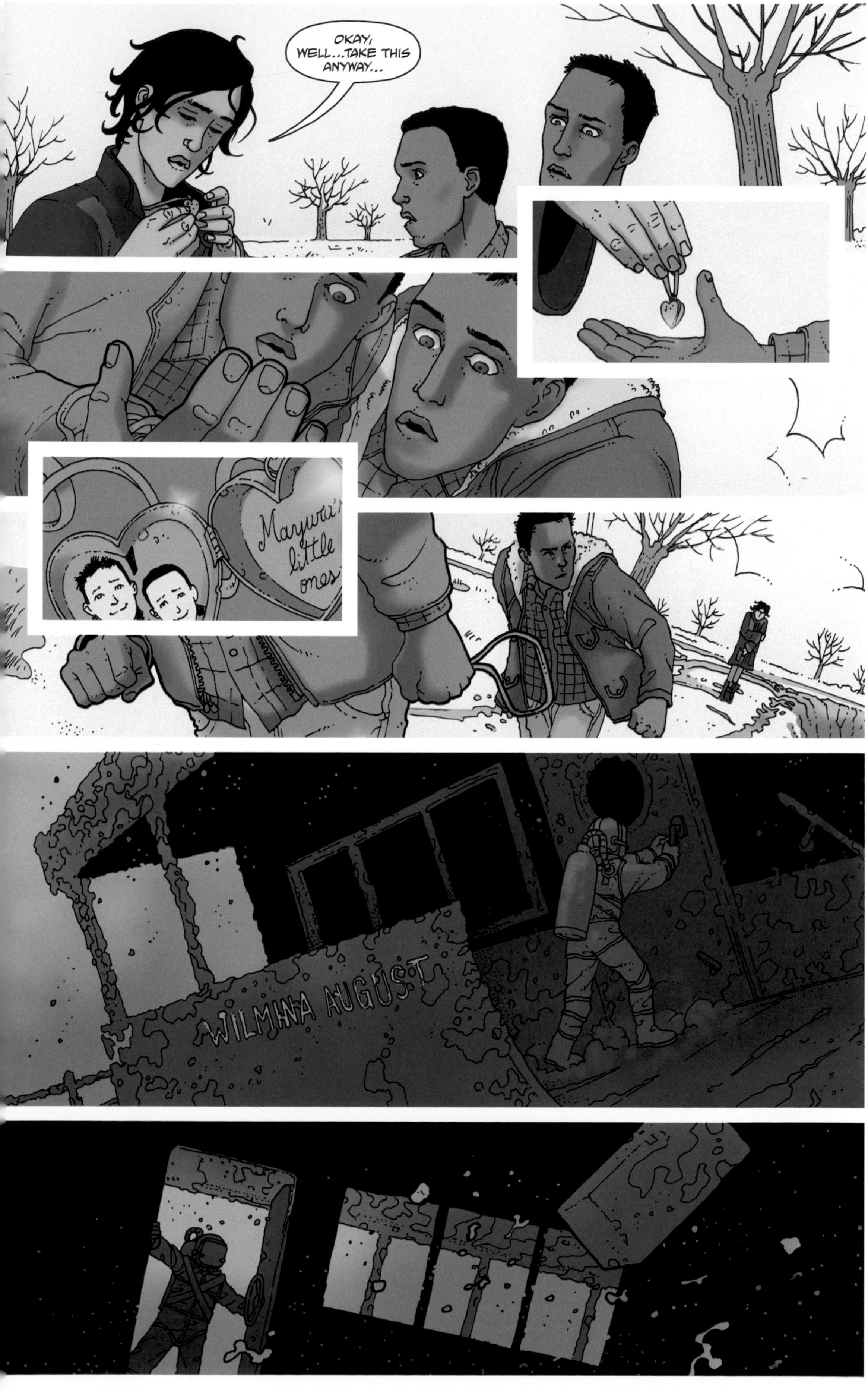
OKAY, WELL...TAKE THIS ANYWAY...
Maywa's little ones
WILMINA AUGUST

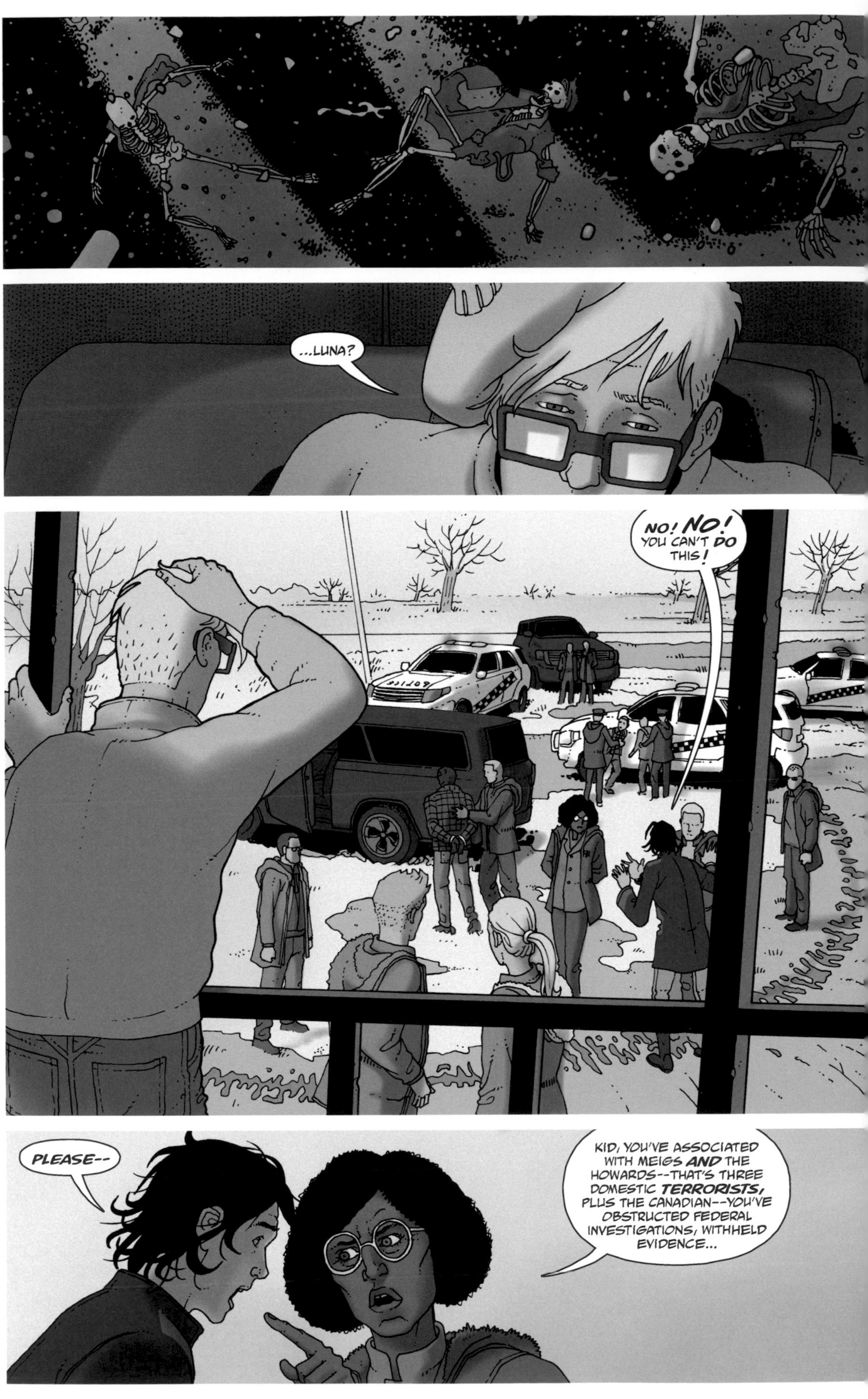
...LUNA?
NO! NO! YOU CAN'T DO THIS!
PLEASE--
KID, YOU'VE ASSOCIATED WITH MEIGS AND THE HOWARDS--THAT'S THREE DOMESTIC TERRORISTS, PLUS THE CANADIAN--YOU'VE OBSTRUCTED FEDERAL INVESTIGATIONS, WITHHELD EVIDENCE...

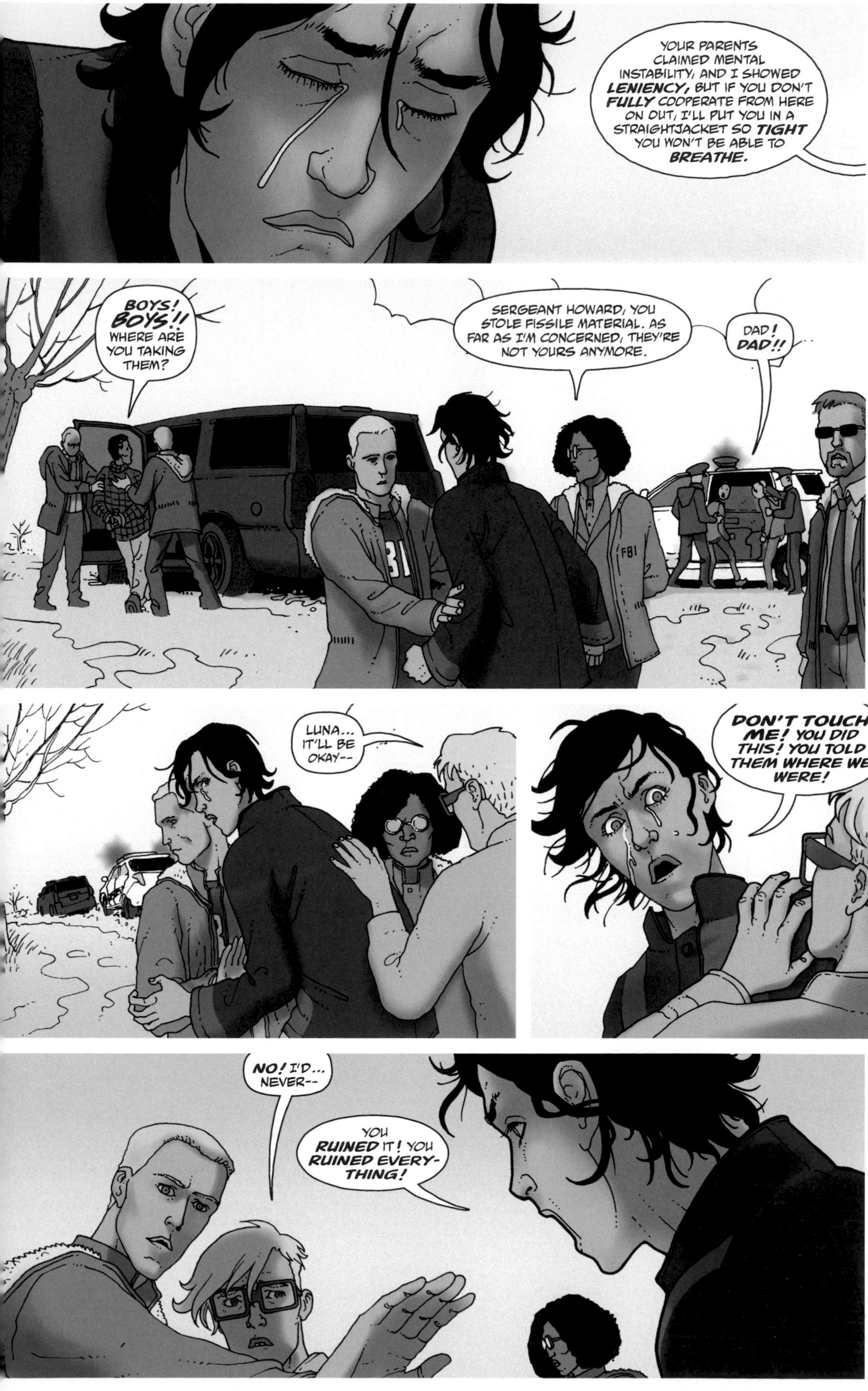
YOUR PARENTS CLAIMED MENTAL INSTABILITY, AND I SHOWED LENIENCY, BUT IF YOU DON'T FULLY COOPERATE FROM HERE ON OUT, I'LL PUT YOU IN A STRAIGHTJACKET SO TIGHT YOU WON'T BE ABLE TO BREATHE.
BOYS! BOYS!! WHERE ARE YOU TAKING THEM?
SERGEANT HOWARD, YOU STOLE FISSILE MATERIAL. AS FAR AS I'M CONCERNED, THEY'RE NOT YOURS ANYMORE.
DAD! DAD!!
FBI
LUNA... IT'LL BE OKAY--
DON'T TOUCH ME! YOU DID THIS! YOU TOLD THEM WHERE WE WERE!
NO! I'D... NEVER--
YOU RUINED IT! YOU RUINED EVERYTHING!

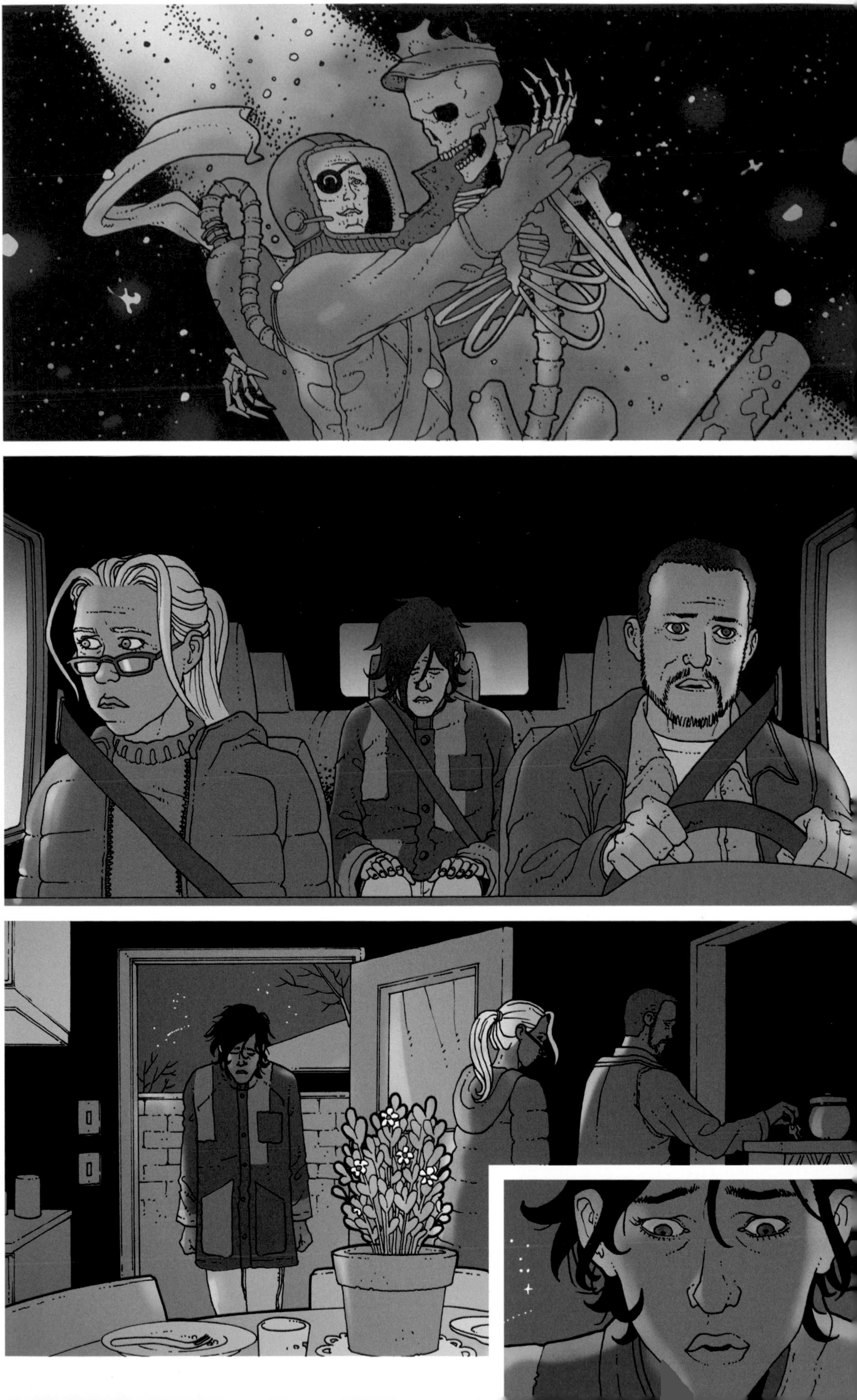

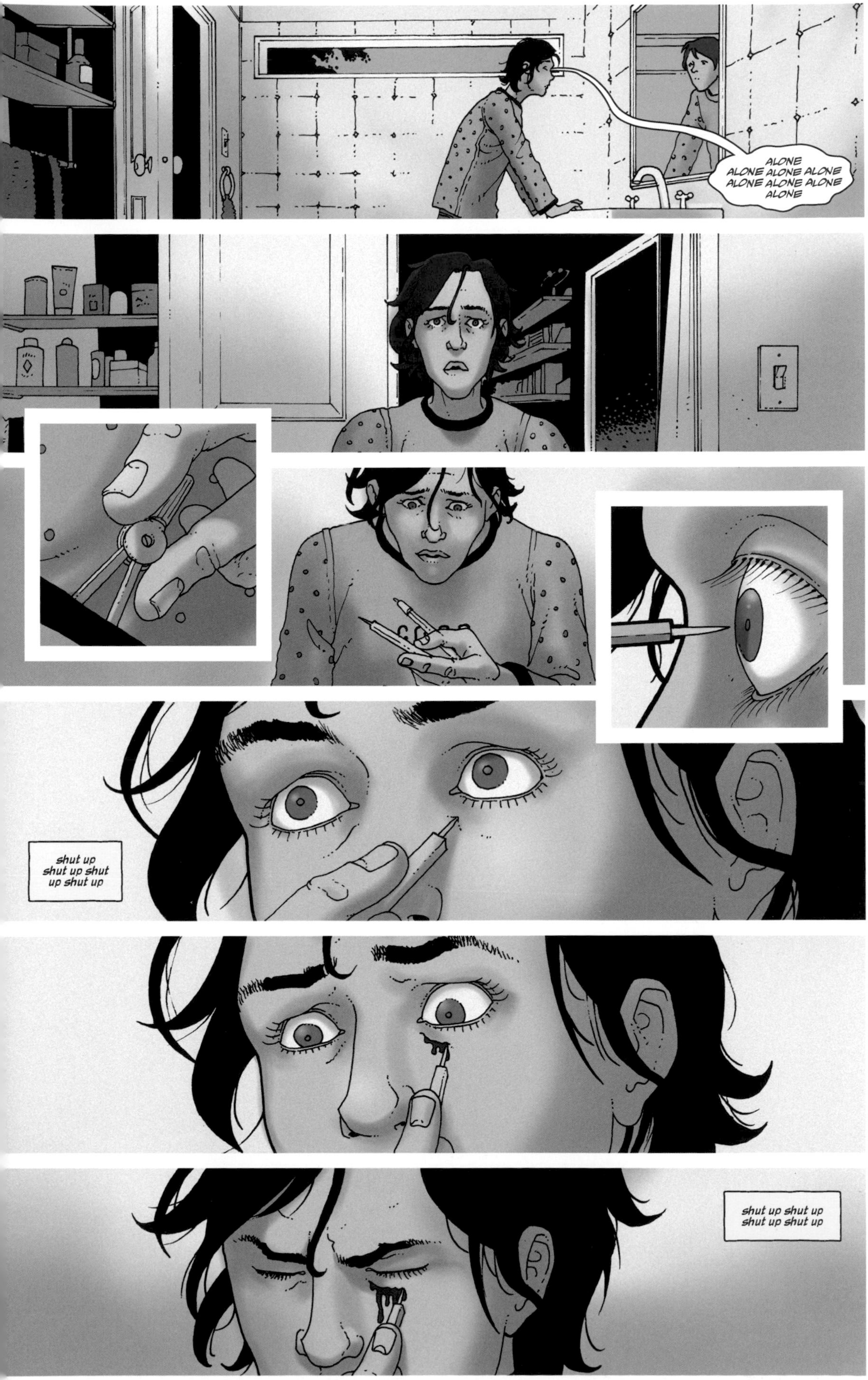
ALONE ALONE ALONE ALONE ALONE ALONE ALONE ALONE
shut up shut up shut up shut up
shut up shut up shut up shut up

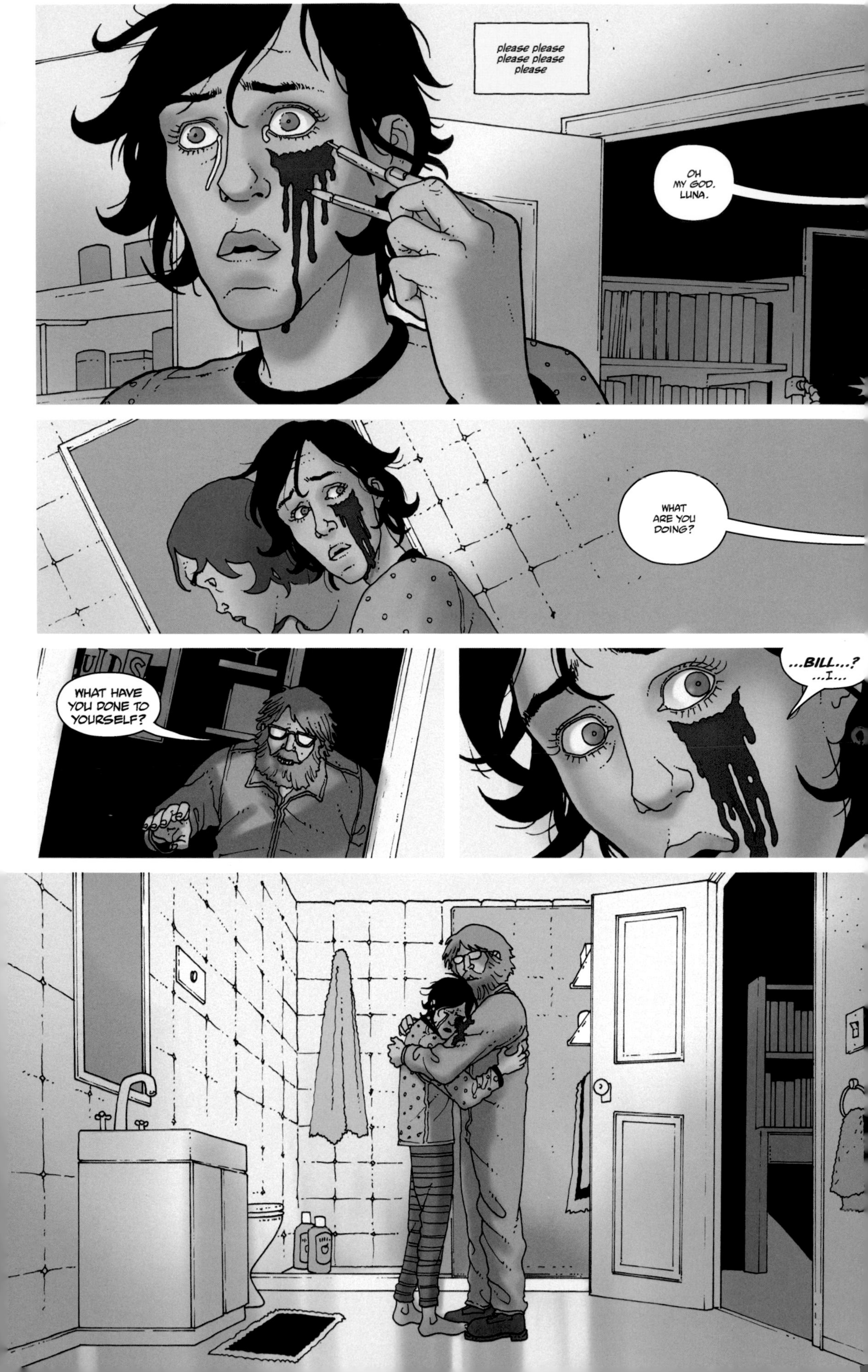
please please please please please
OH MY GOD. LUNA.
WHAT ARE YOU DOING?
WHAT HAVE YOU DONE TO YOURSELF?
...BILL...? ...I...

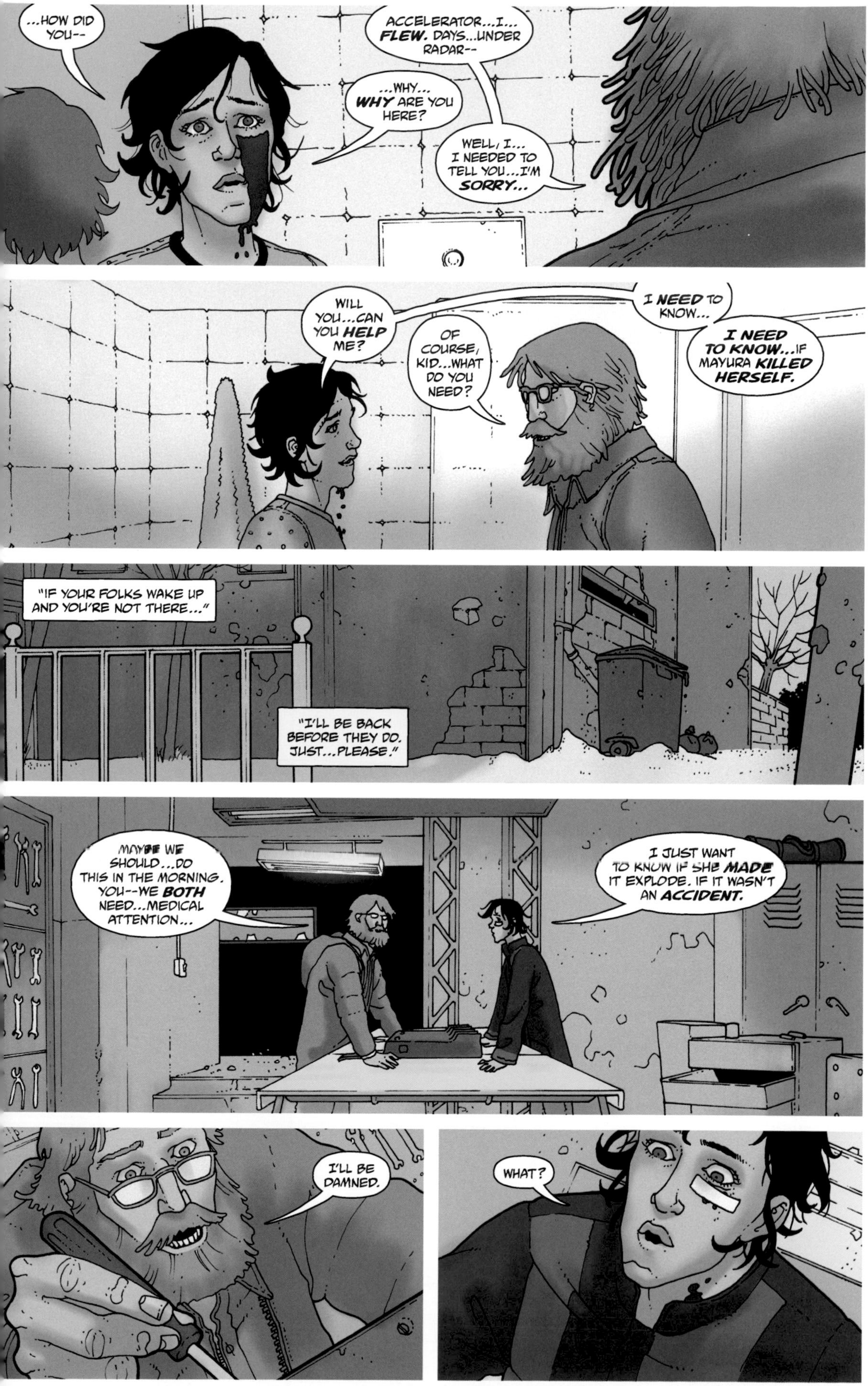
...HOW DID YOU--
ACCELERATOR...I... FLEW. DAYS...UNDER RADAR--
...WHY... WHY ARE YOU HERE?
WELL, I... I NEEDED TO TELL YOU...I'M SORRY...
WILL YOU...CAN YOU HELP ME?
OF COURSE, KID...WHAT DO YOU NEED?
I NEED TO KNOW...
I NEED TO KNOW...IF MAYURA KILLED HERSELF.
"IF YOUR FOLKS WAKE UP AND YOU'RE NOT THERE..."
"I'LL BE BACK BEFORE THEY DO. JUST...PLEASE."
MAYBE WE SHOULD...DO THIS IN THE MORNING. YOU--WE BOTH NEED...MEDICAL ATTENTION...
I JUST WANT TO KNOW IF SHE MADE IT EXPLODE. IF IT WASN'T AN ACCIDENT.
I'LL BE DAMNED.
WHAT?

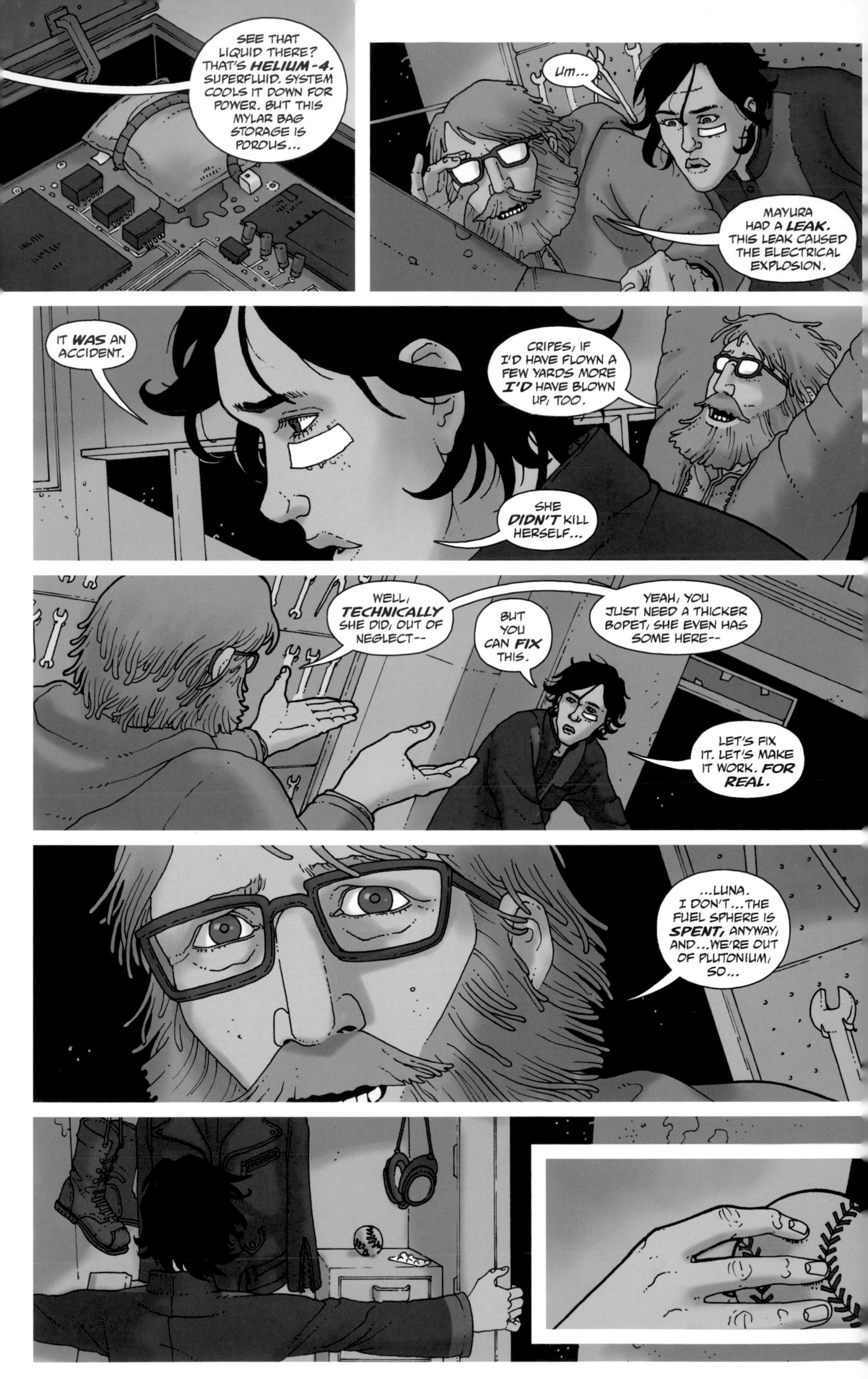
SEE THAT LIQUID THERE? THAT'S HELIUM-4. SUPERFLUID. SYSTEM COOLS IT DOWN FOR POWER. BUT THIS MYLAR BAG STORAGE IS POROUS...
UM...
MAYURA HAD A LEAK. THIS LEAK CAUSED THE ELECTRICAL EXPLOSION.
IT WAS AN ACCIDENT.
CRIPES, IF I'D HAVE FLOWN A FEW YARDS MORE I'D HAVE BLOWN UP, TOO.
SHE DIDN'T KILL HERSELF...
WELL, TECHNICALLY SHE DID, OUT OF NEGLECT--
BUT YOU CAN FIX THIS.
YEAH, YOU JUST NEED A THICKER BOPET, SHE EVEN HAS SOME HERE--
LET'S FIX IT. LET'S MAKE IT WORK. FOR REAL.
...LUNA. I DON'T... THE FUEL SPHERE IS SPENT, ANYWAY, AND... WE'RE OUT OF PLUTONIUM, SO...

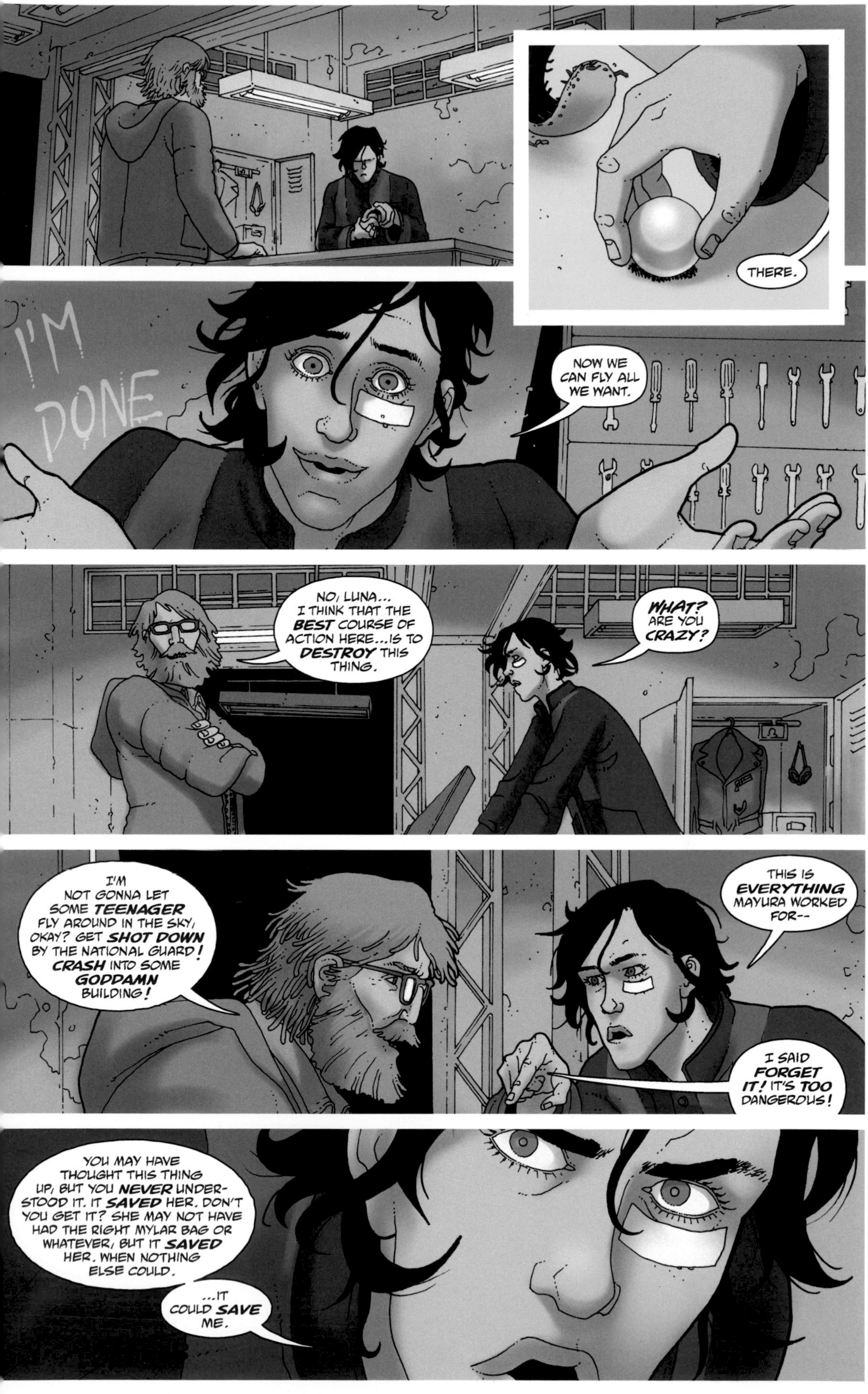
THERE.
I'M DONE
NOW WE CAN FLY ALL WE WANT.
NO, LUNA... I THINK THAT THE BEST COURSE OF ACTION HERE...IS TO DESTROY THIS THING.
WHAT? ARE YOU CRAZY?
THIS IS EVERYTHING MAYURA WORKED FOR--
I'M NOT GONNA LET SOME TEENAGER FLY AROUND IN THE SKY, OKAY? GET SHOT DOWN BY THE NATIONAL GUARD! CRASH INTO SOME GODDAMN BUILDING!
I SAID FORGET IT! IT'S TOO DANGEROUS!
YOU MAY HAVE THOUGHT THIS THING UP, BUT YOU NEVER UNDERSTOOD IT. IT SAVED HER. DON'T YOU GET IT? SHE MAY NOT HAVE HAD THE RIGHT MYLAR BAG OR WHATEVER, BUT IT SAVED HER. WHEN NOTHING ELSE COULD.
...IT COULD SAVE ME.

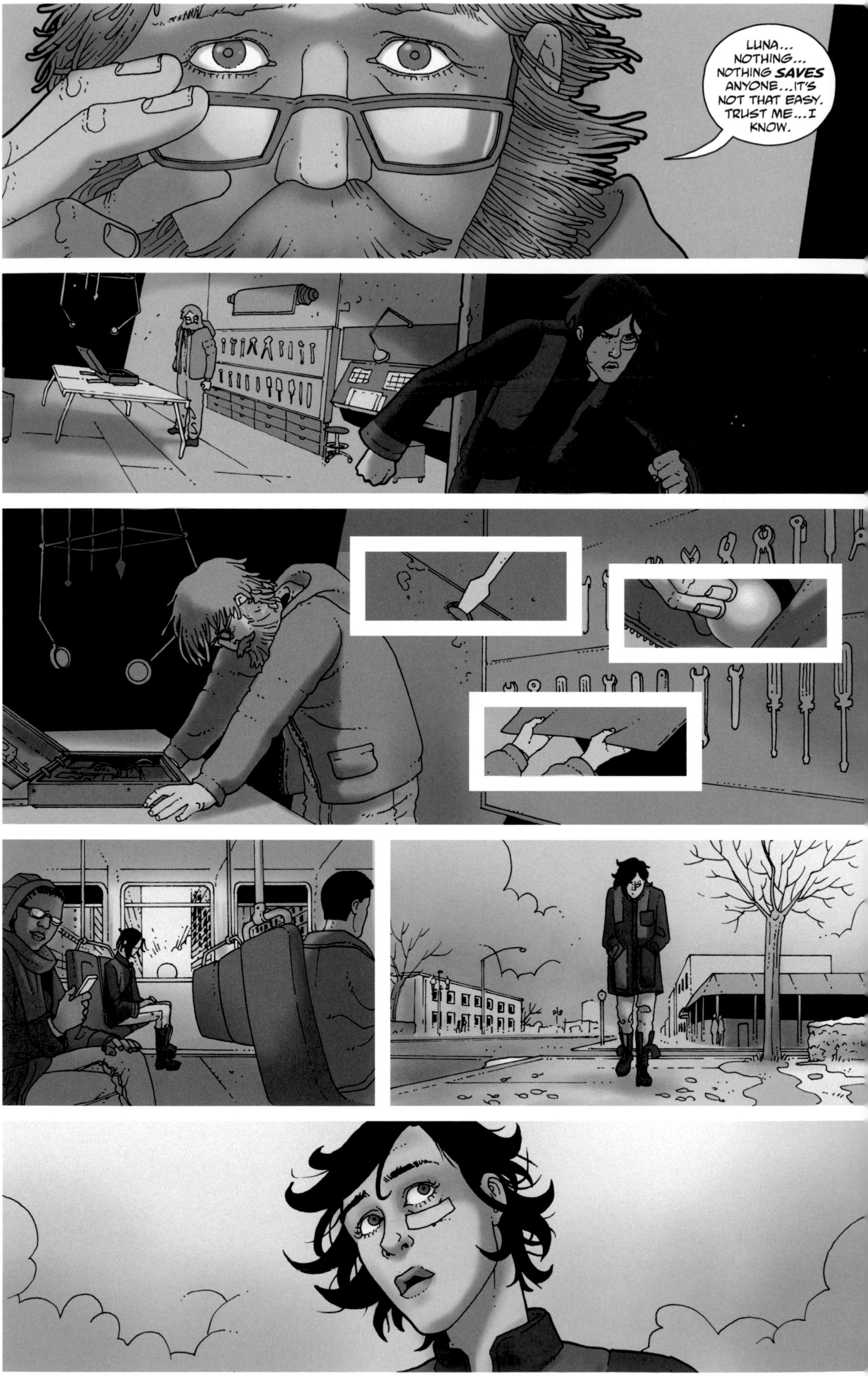
LUNA... NOTHING... NOTHING SAVES ANYONE...IT'S NOT THAT EASY. TRUST ME...I KNOW.

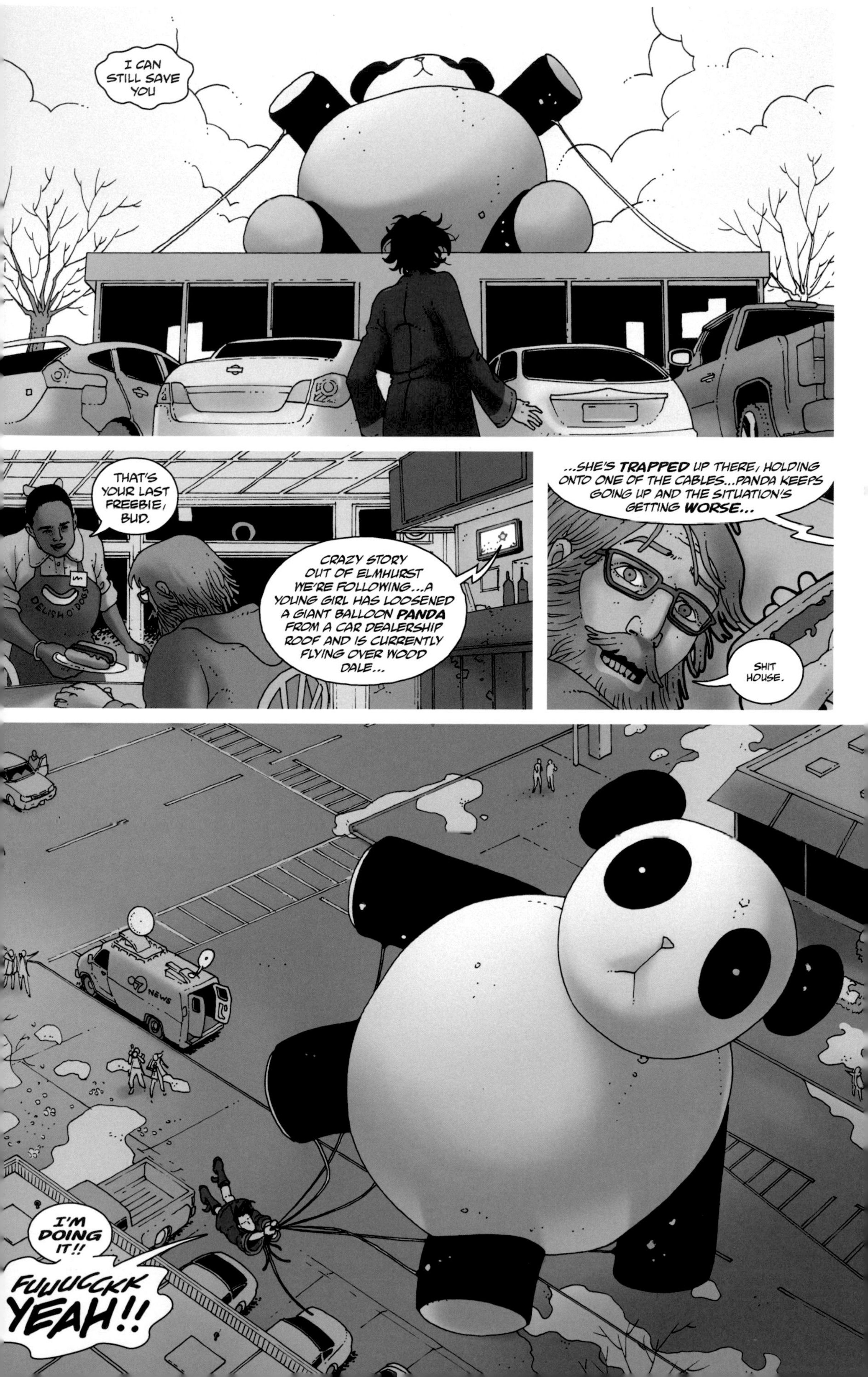
I CAN STILL SAVE YOU
THAT'S YOUR LAST FREEBIE, BUD.
DELISH O' DOGS
CRAZY STORY OUT OF ELMHURST WE'RE FOLLOWING...A YOUNG GIRL HAS LOOSENED A GIANT BALLOON PANDA FROM A CAR DEALERSHIP ROOF AND IS CURRENTLY FLYING OVER WOOD DALE...
...SHE'S TRAPPED UP THERE, HOLDING ONTO ONE OF THE CABLES...PANDA KEEPS GOING UP AND THE SITUATION'S GETTING WORSE...
SHIT HOUSE.
NEWS
I'M DOING IT!!
FUWUCCKK YEAH!!

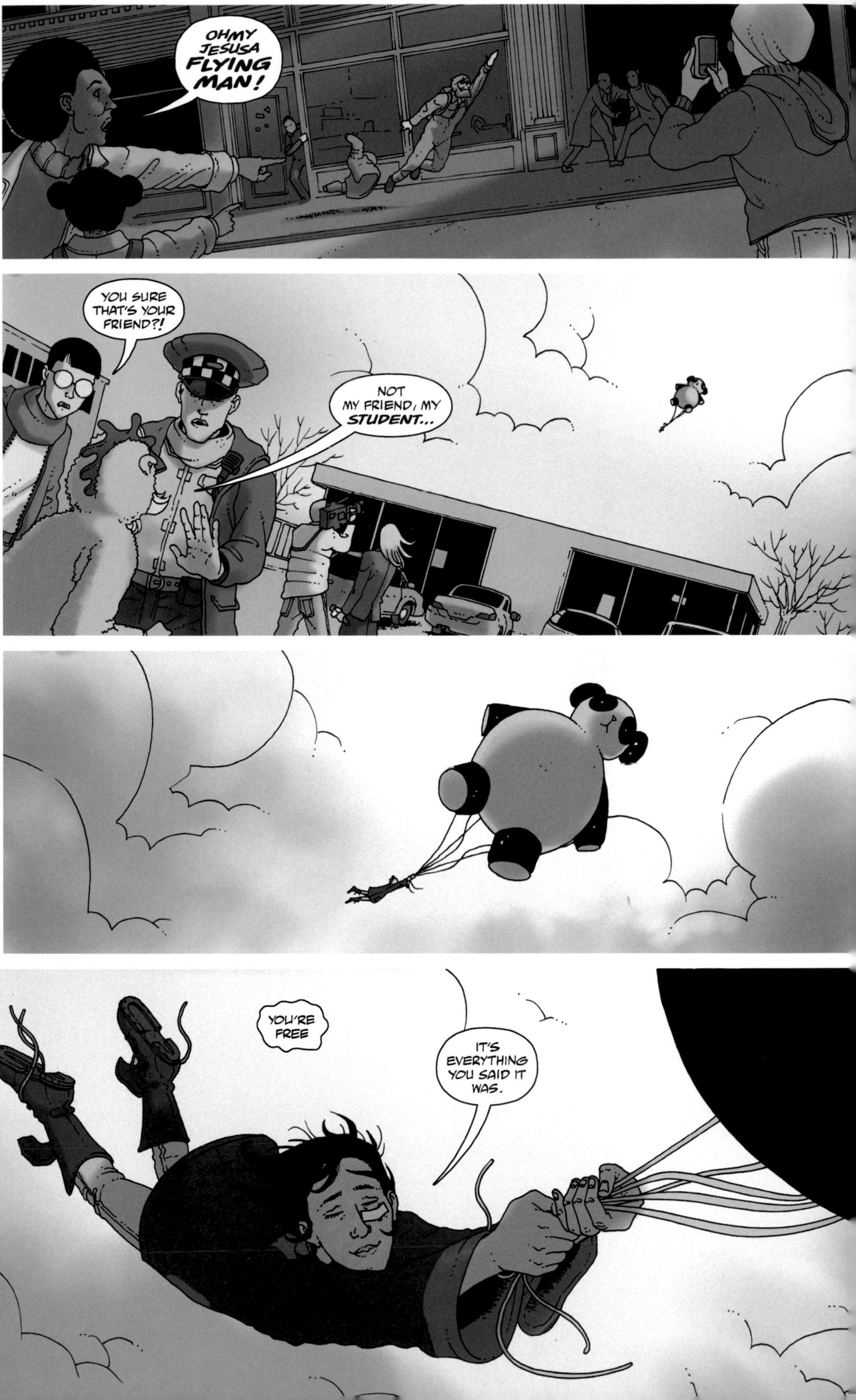
OHMY JESUSA FLYING MAN!
YOU SURE THAT'S YOUR FRIEND?!
NOT MY FRIEND, MY **STUDENT...**
YOU'RE FREE
IT'S EVERYTHING YOU SAID IT WAS.

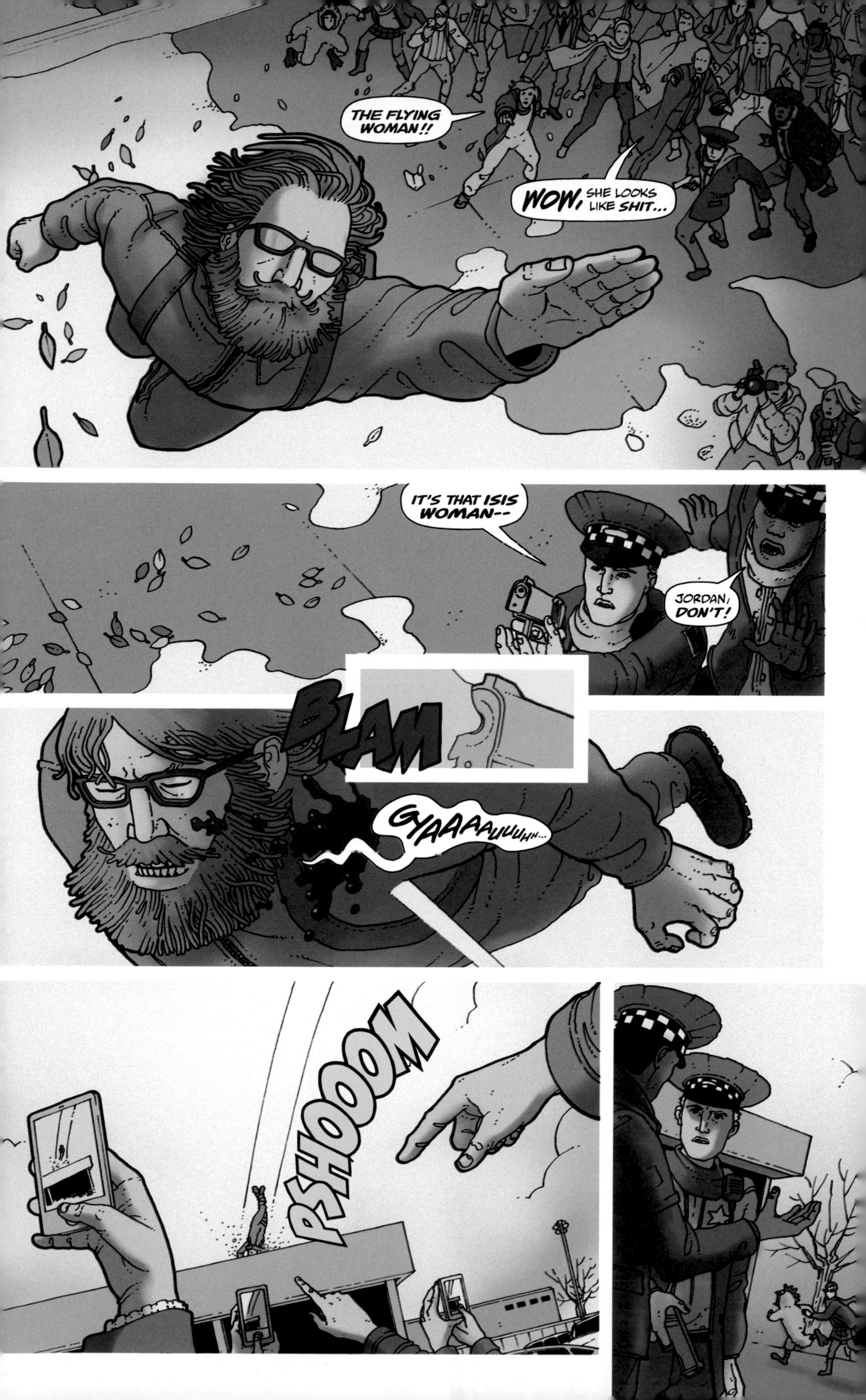
THE FLYING WOMAN!!
WOW, SHE LOOKS LIKE SHIT...
IT'S THAT ISIS WOMAN--
JORDAN, DON'T!
BLAM
GYAAAAUUUHH...
PSHOOOM

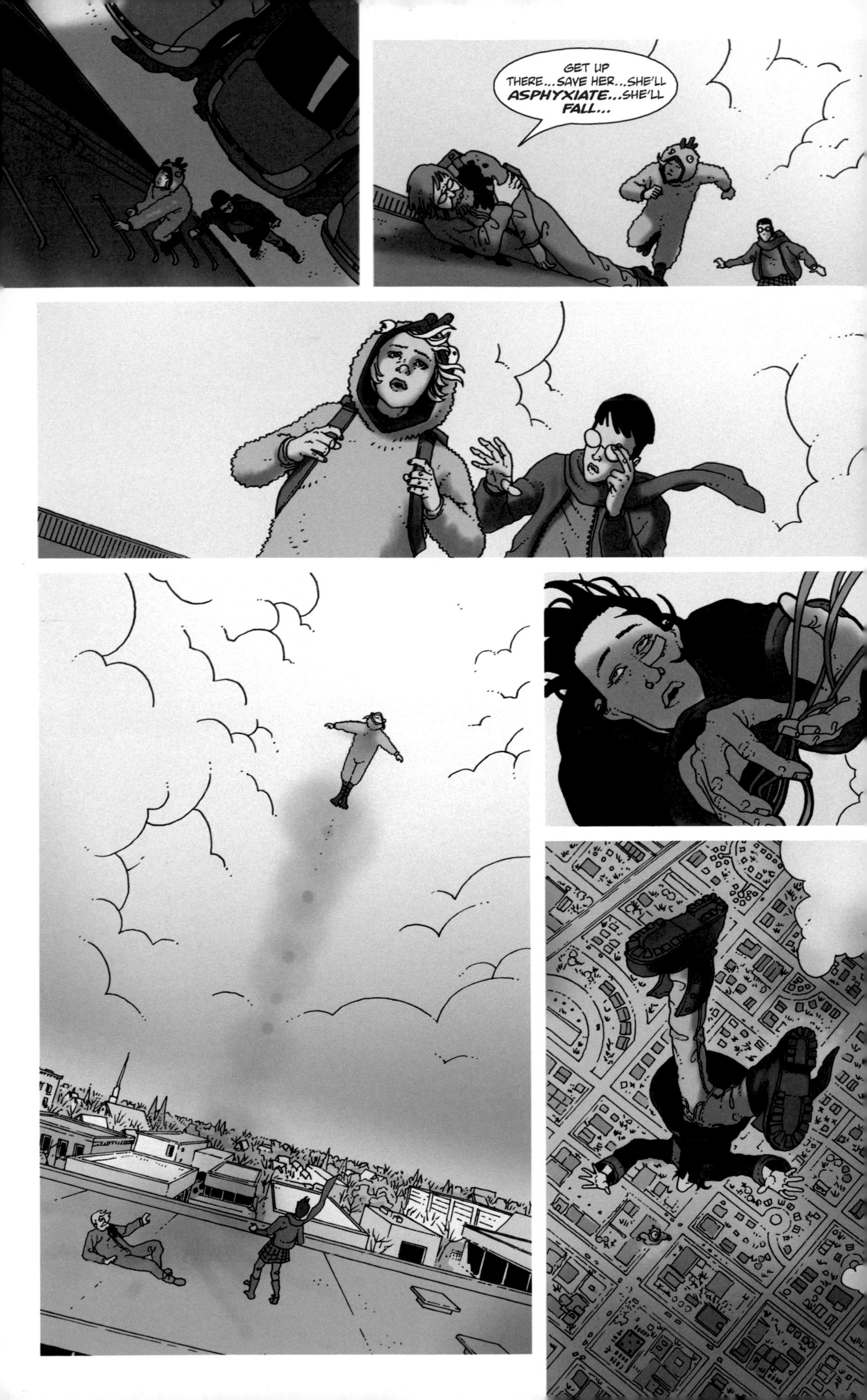
GET UP THERE...SAVE HER...SHE'LL ASPHYXIATE...SHE'LL FALL...

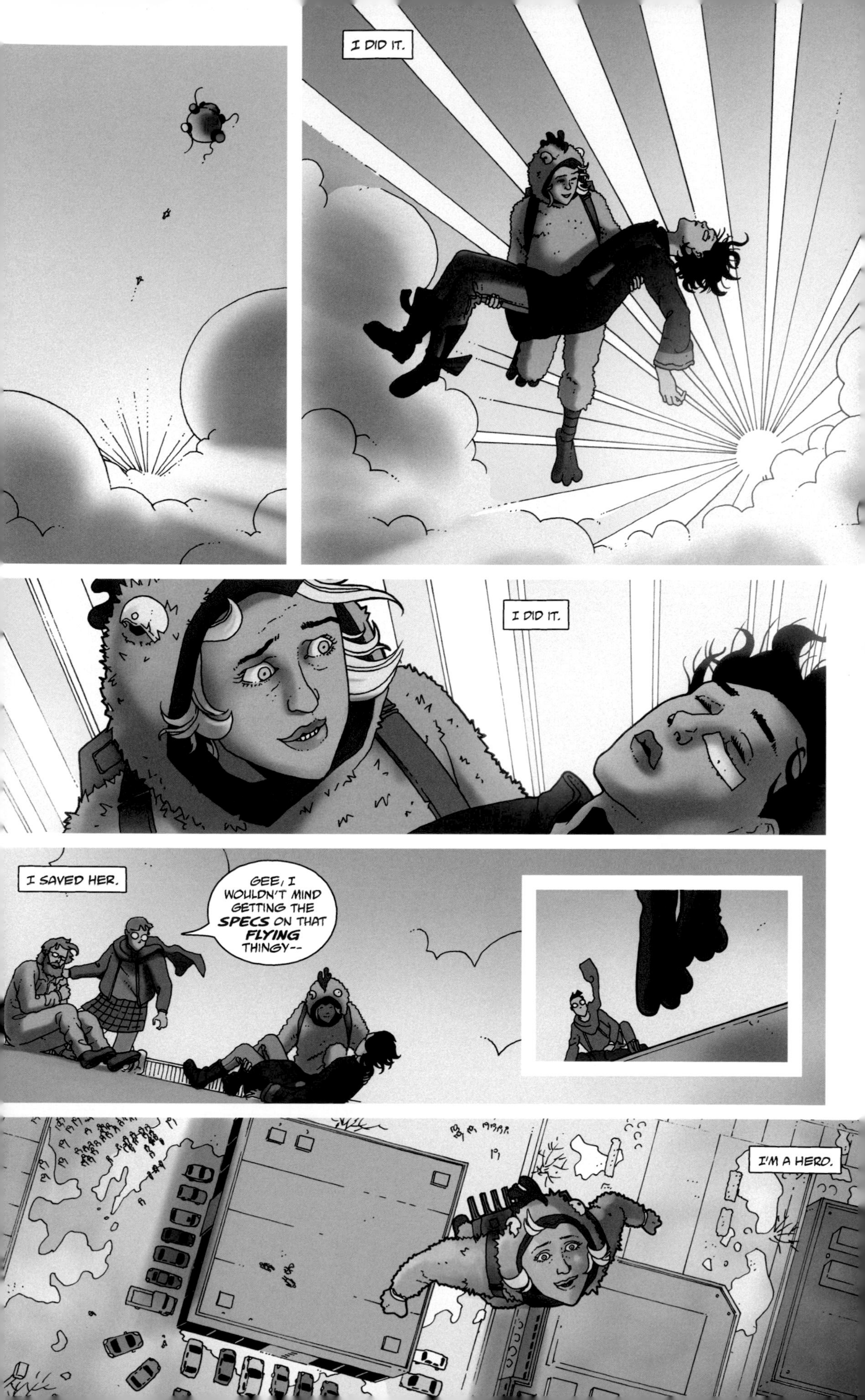
I DID IT.
I DID IT.
I SAVED HER.
GEE, I WOULDN'T MIND GETTING THE SPECS ON THAT FLYING THINGY--
I'M A HERO.

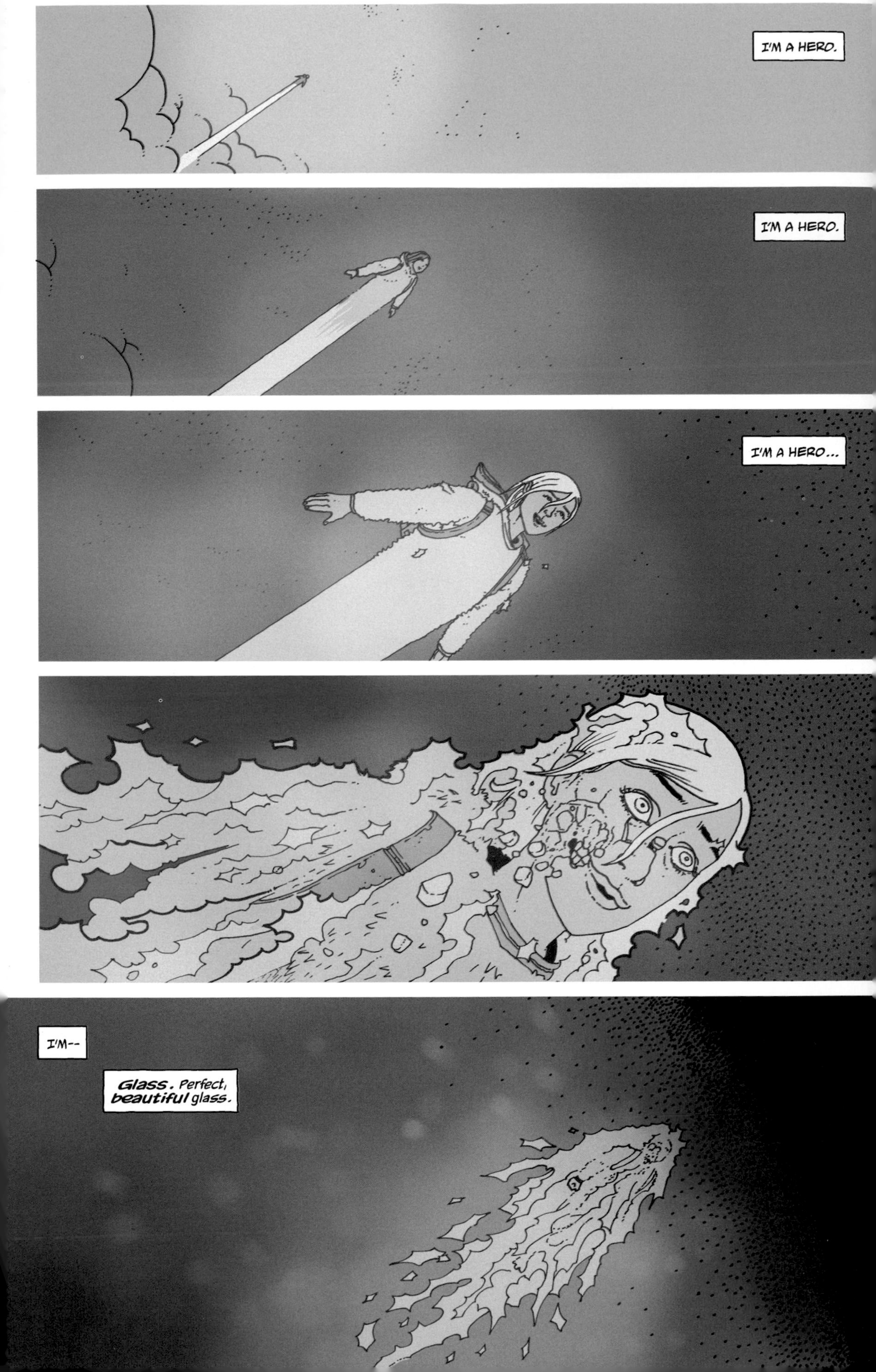

I'M A HERO.
I'M A HERO.
I'M A HERO...
I'M--
Glass. Perfect, beautiful glass.

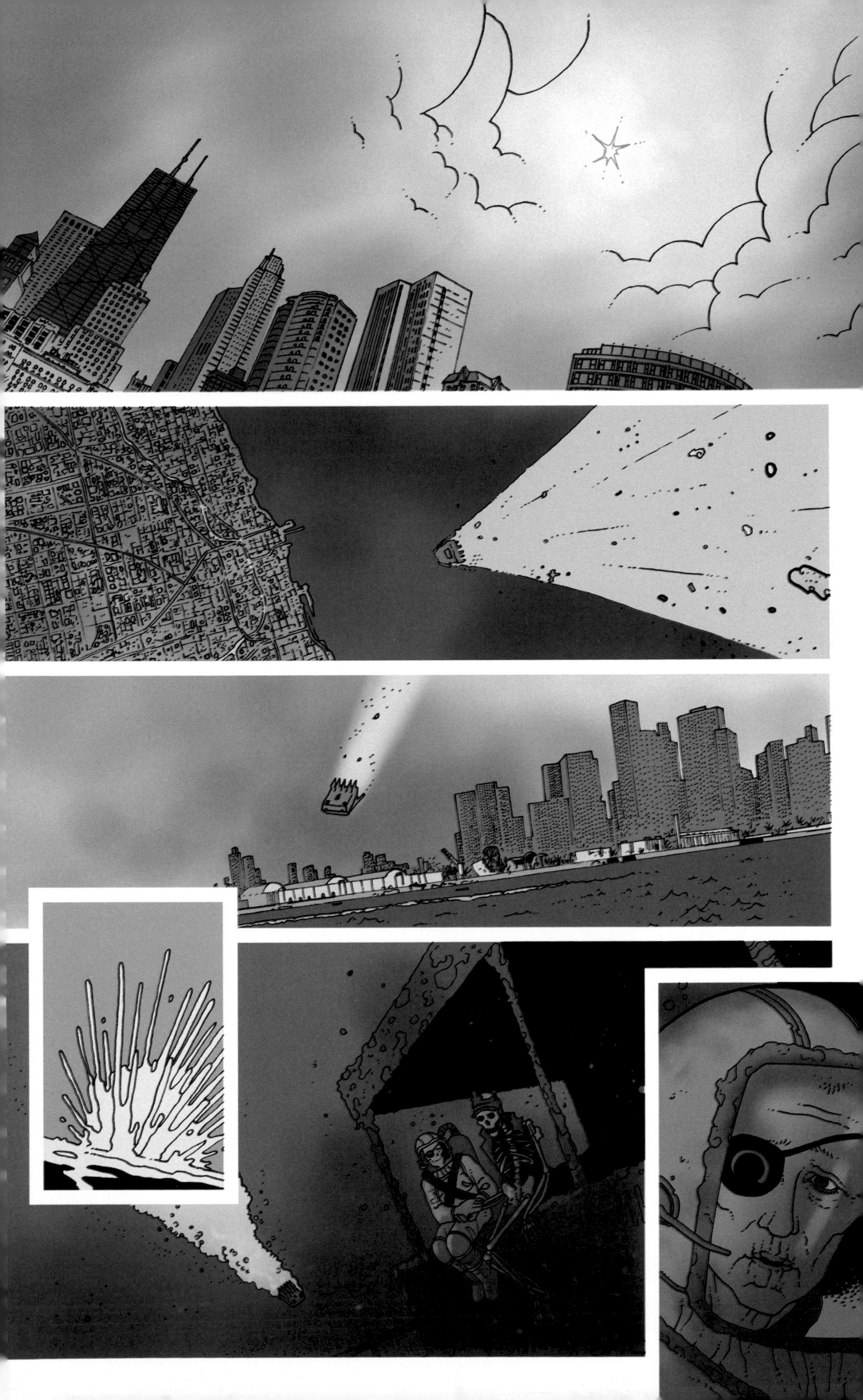

FIVE MONTHS LATER.

BZZZZ

rubberball rubberball rubberball help me god-god...

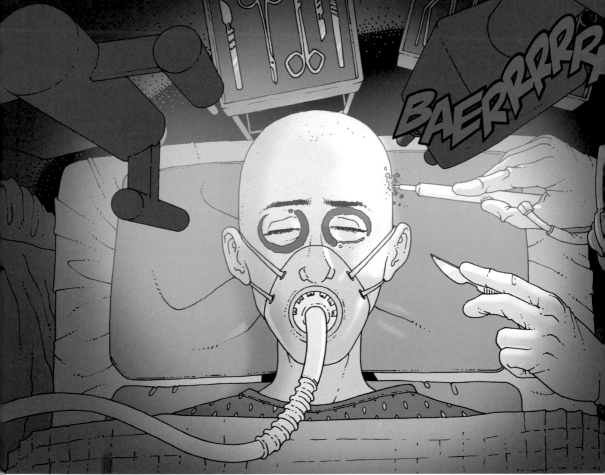

BAERRRRR

...MA?

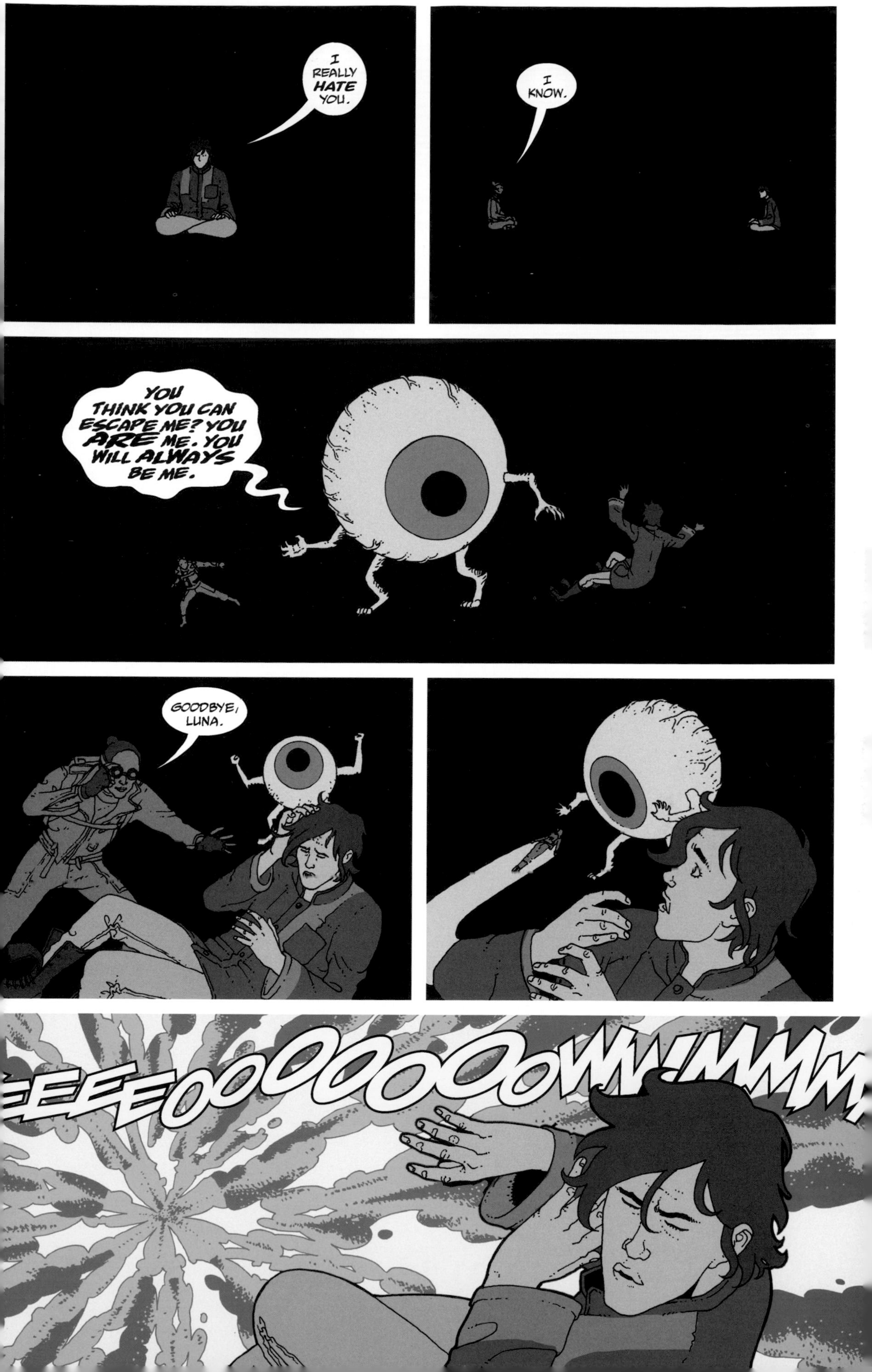
I REALLY HATE YOU.
I KNOW.
YOU THINK YOU CAN ESCAPE ME? YOU ARE ME. YOU WILL ALWAYS BE ME.
GOODBYE, LUNA.
EEEEOOOOOOOOWWMMM

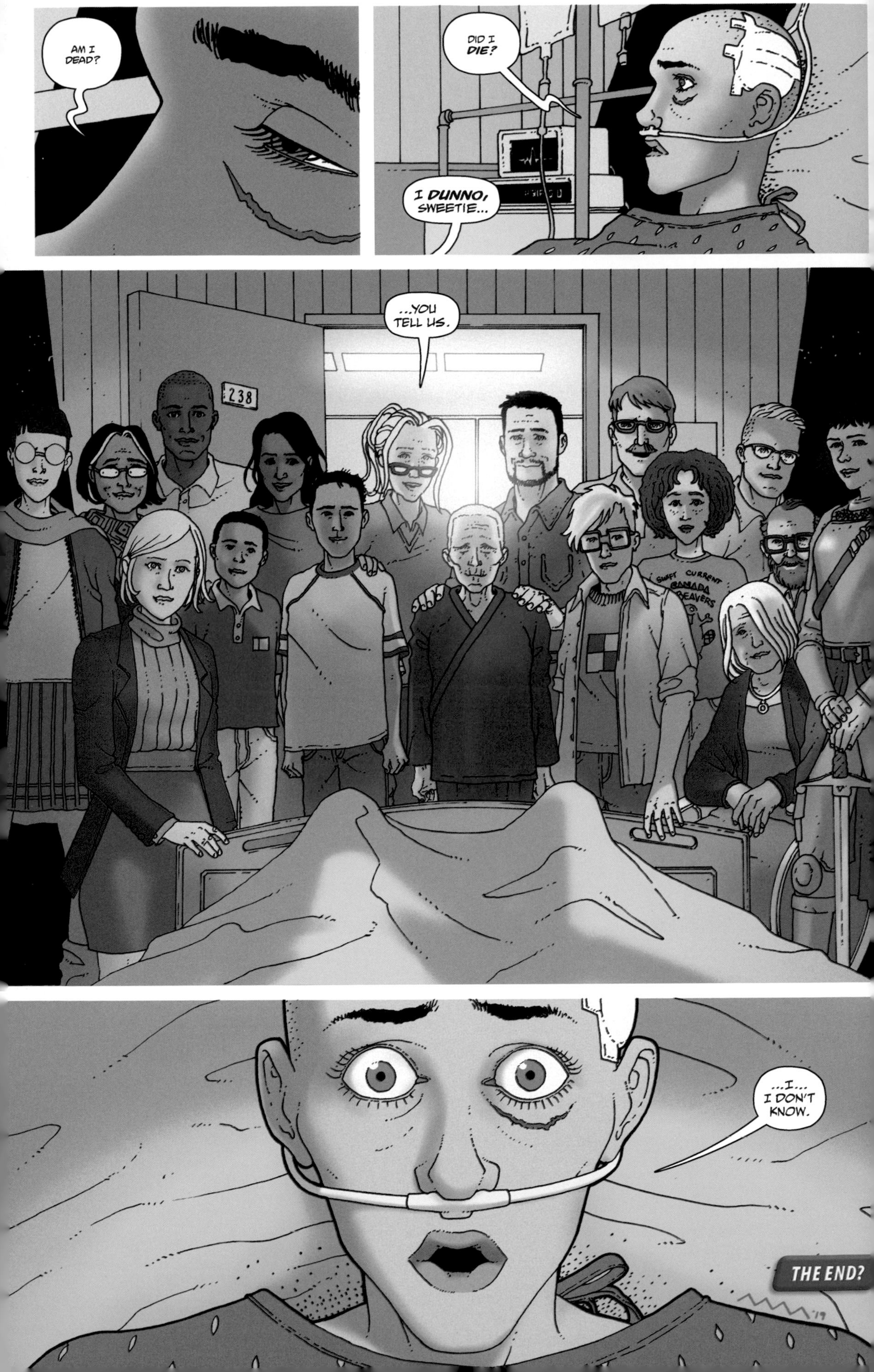
AM I DEAD?
DID I DIE?
I DUNNO, SWEETIE...
238
...YOU TELL US.
...I... I DON'T KNOW.
THE END?

What's it like
when the summer
gets covered in snow,

when the light of enlightenment proves to be just an illusion of clarity that dissipates with the chill of wind frosting your mind?

I think Luna finds out in this volume.

I was born in Chicago, and my parents grew up there. We moved to Texas before I was a year old (but I spent those first few months in Elmhurst, where Luna lives). My dad described going back to Chicago for work, years later, during the winter. He said he crossed Michigan Avenue Bridge, and the wind that came off the water of Lake Michigan was so cold, he felt as if his bones had immediately frozen. He had trouble even moving off the bridge to the other side of the street, to the shelter of the Tribune and Wrigley Buildings. And he grew up there.

What we think we know—even about ourselves—is perhaps nothing at all.

This is where we meet Luna in *The Lost Pilot*. The floor of her life gave out at the end of the last story arc, and she fell to a wooden landing deeper inside the belfry of her mind. But now that landing is about to give way. And there are bats everywhere. Is there ever really a foundation to stand on? The deeper Luna goes, the less she knows—about Mayura Howard, and herself.

In issue #2 of *She Could Fly*, Kido believed that she saw Bodhidharma in an alley. The famous story is that Bodhidharma stood before Emperor Wu after coming to China from India in the 6th century. After Bodhidharma told Emperor Wu that the ruler had gained no merit for building abundant temples across his lands, Wu, upset and incredulous, asked "Who is this that stands before me?" Bodhidharma merely answered "I know not."

Of course, Kido didn't even really see Bodhidharma. It was just a nameless, dead homeless man.

And who has Kido become in this story? Dementia and a gunshot wound to the brain do wonders for removing the sense of one's ego and identity.

Likewise, this story arc takes its title, *The Lost Pilot*, from a James Tate poem about his father, who died in World War II before James was born. He never knew his father, and some of that unknowingness transmuted to James in terms of his own self-knowledge. Father and son became specters orbiting each other, ciphers elusive to each other and themselves.

In this arc, Benji is a version of himself he would not recognize in a mirror in earlier issues. The same is true with Dana—once buttoned up, calm, and in control, but now homeless, at loose ends, and completely lost. We'll also finally get to see glimpses of Mayura's life before she took flight, and these snapshots will provide Luna—and us—with more questions than answers.

This chapter of *She Could Fly* is a story about not knowing where one is headed. Luna really has no idea throughout these issues, I believe. She's groping in the dark—for meaning, for sanity, for love. Who knows if she'll find it? (And that's why I hope we get to keep telling this story for a long, long time.)

And look, I don't know if this comic is anywhere near as deep as this stuff I'm writing here. After all, it's got C-4, Russian mercenaries, and flying devices. But it's also got loss, senseless acts of violence that blindside people, and struggles to process emotion and identity. Who are we? What makes us? Our brains? Our families? Our creations? Our quests? Or none of it?

Truth has a tendency to bubble up inside our bodies when we deny it. The funny thing is, we end up living through our own worst case scenarios. They don't destroy us; they force us through crucibles and temper us into something else, more pure.

Perfect, beautiful glass. Temples of sacred damage.

I often tell my son that happiness is just one color in his box of emotional crayons. He's got a bunch of others that he can use. Happiness doesn't need to get worn down to a nub. The other ones that we're born with are just as vivid, and part of the human experience. It's painful to color with these other crayons. But we should.

This doesn't make our story a sad one.

It makes it one that bleeds with the hues of everything.

— *Christopher Cantwell*

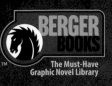

BERGER BOOKS™

The Must-Have Graphic Novel Library

INVISIBLE KINGDOM
Vol. One: Walking the Path

Deluxe Softcover, 136 Pages
$19.99 ◊ ISBN 978-1-50671-227-7

In a distant galaxy, a young religious acolyte and an antagonistic freighter pilot join forces when they uncover an unconceivable conspiracy between the world's dominant religion and the mega-corporation that controls society.

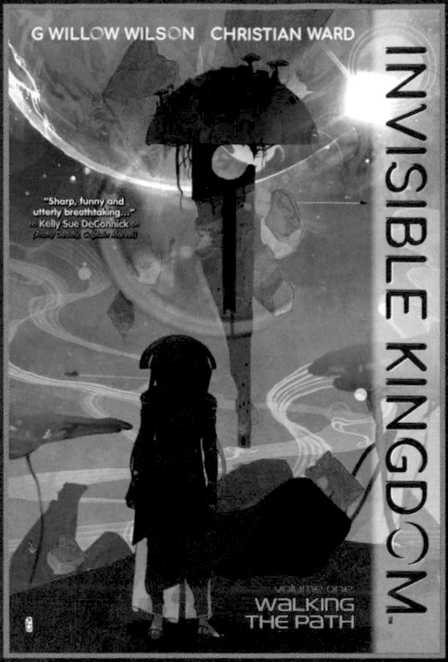
G WILLOW WILSON CHRISTIAN WARD
INVISIBLE KINGDOM
"Sharp, funny and utterly breathtaking..."
— Kelly Sue DeConnick
volume one:
WALKING THE PATH

LAGUARDIA

Deluxe Softcover, 136 Pages
$19.99 ◊ ISBN 978-1-50671-075-4

In an alien-integrated world, a very pregnant doctor named Future Nwafor Chukwuebuka smuggles an illegal, sentient plant through LaGuardia International and Interstellar Airport, and their arrival to New York marks the abrupt start of a an amazing new life—for everyone!

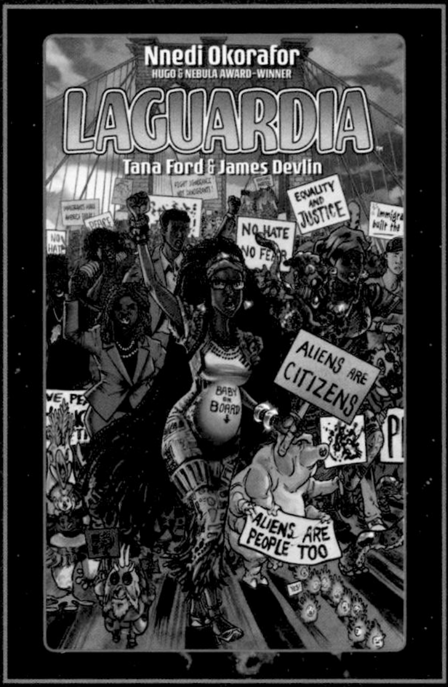
Nnedi Okorafor
HUGO & NEBULA AWARD-WINNER
LAGUARDIA
Tana Ford & James Devlin
EQUALITY AND JUSTICE
NO HATE NO FEAR
ALIENS ARE CITIZENS
BABY on BOARD
ALIENS ARE PEOPLE TOO

ANTHONY BOURDAIN'S HUNGRY GHOSTS

Hardcover, 128 Pages
$14.99 ◊ ISBN 978-1-50670-669-6

Inspired by the Japanese game 100 Candles, a circle of chefs gather to outscare each other with modern tales of fear and food from around the world—and pray that they survive the night.

Includes original recipes by Bourdain.

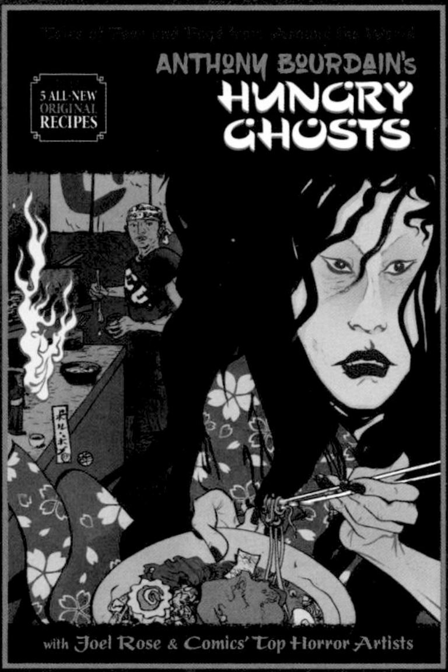
5 ALL-NEW ORIGINAL RECIPES
ANTHONY BOURDAIN'S
HUNGRY GHOSTS
with Joel Rose & Comics' Top Horror Artists

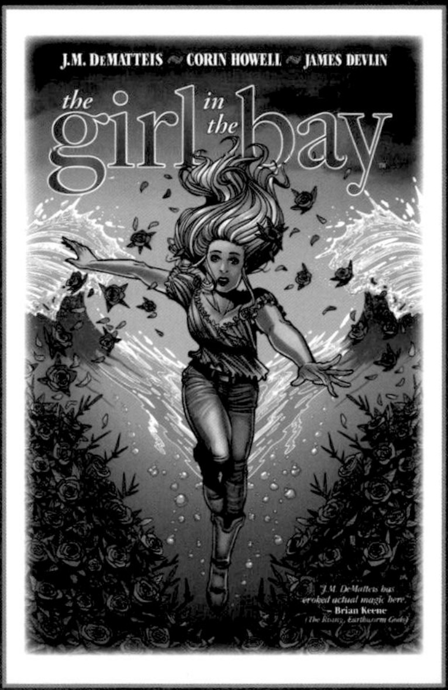
J.M. DeMATTEIS CORIN HOWELL JAMES DEVLIN
the girl in the bay
"J.M. DeMatteis has evoked actual magic here."
— Brian Keene

THE GIRL IN THE BAY

Deluxe Softcover, 112 Pages
$17.99 ◊ ISBN 978-1-50671-228-4

A supernatural coming-of-age mystery begins in 1969, when Kathy Sartori is murdered—only to reawaken in 2019, where another version of herself has lived a full life. And her "killer" is about to strike again.

OLIVIA TWIST:
Honor Among Thieves

Deluxe Softcover, 136 Pages
$19.99 ◊ ISBN 978-1-50670-948-2

In dystopian future London, teenage orphan Olivia Twist joins a girl gang of thieves to save a new friend.

But Olivia has more power than she knows... and it comes at a great cost.

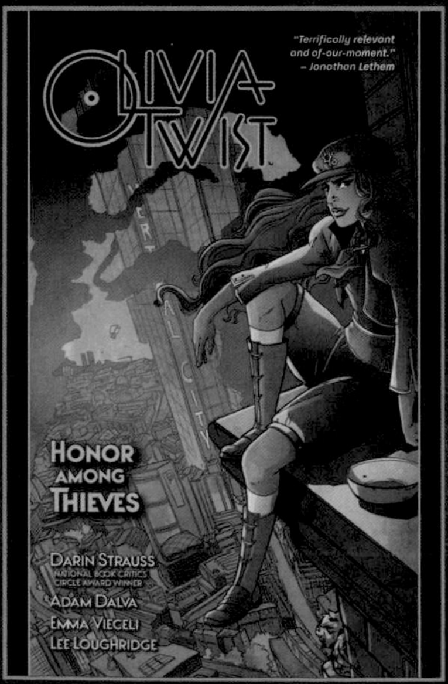
"Terrifically relevant and of-our-moment."
– Jonothon Lethem
OLIVIA TWIST
HONOR AMONG THIEVES
DARIN STRAUSS
NATIONAL BOOK CRITICS CIRCLE AWARD WINNER
ADAM DALVA
EMMA VIECELI
LEE LOUGHRIDGE

BERGER BOOKS
The Must-Have Graphic Novel Library

INCOGNEGRO: A GRAPHIC MYSTERY

Hardcover, 144 Pages
$19.99 ◊ ISBN 978-1-50670-564-4

Reporter Zane Pinchback goes "incognegro," traveling from Harlem to the deep south to investigate the arrest of his brother.

A fast-paced mystery and riveting exploration of race and identity.

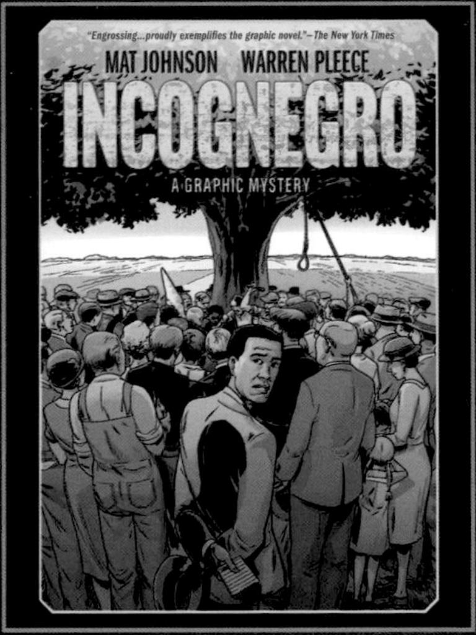

"Engrossing...proudly exemplifies the graphic novel."—The New York Times
MAT JOHNSON WARREN PLEECE
INCOGNEGRO
A GRAPHIC MYSTERY

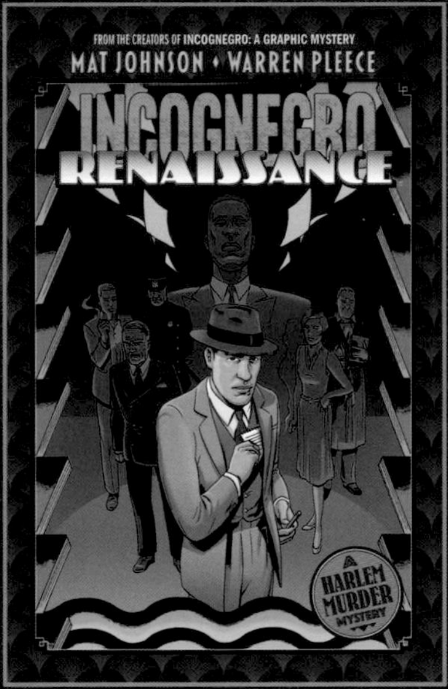

FROM THE CREATORS OF INCOGNEGRO: A GRAPHIC MYSTERY
MAT JOHNSON • WARREN PLEECE
INCOGNEGRO
RENAISSANCE
A HARLEM MURDER MYSTERY

INCOGNEGRO: RENAISSANCE

Hardcover, 128 Pages
$19.99 ◊ ISBN 978-1-50670-563-7

A page-turning thriller of racial divide, this story explores segregation, secrets, and self-image as our race-bending protagonist penetrates a world where he feels stranger than ever before.

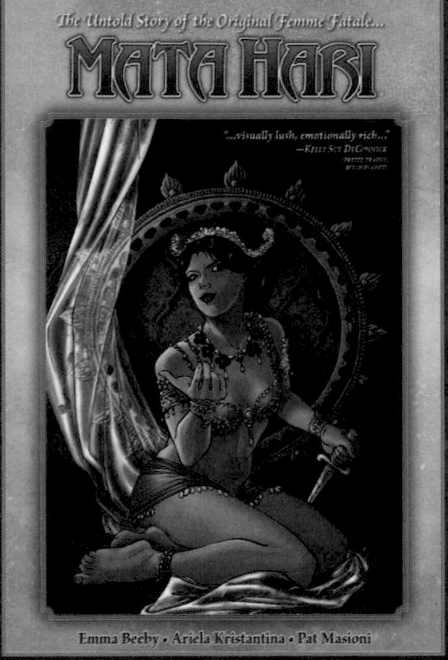

The Untold Story of the Original Femme Fatale...
MATA HARI
"...visually lush, emotionally rich..." —Kelly Sue DeConnick
Emma Beeby • Ariela Kristantina • Pat Masioni

MATA HARI

Deluxe Softcover, 128 Pages
$19.99 ◊ ISBN 978-1-50670-561-3

The unseen side of the notorious exotic dancer and convicted double agent who was executed by a French firing squad in 1917 is explored in this haunting and gripping telling.

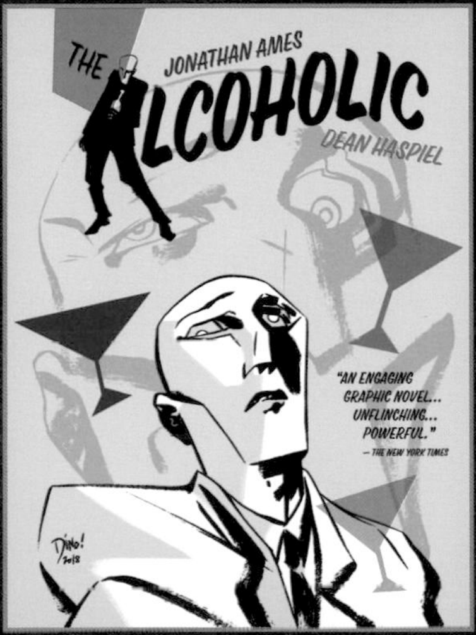

JONATHAN AMES
THE ALCOHOLIC
DEAN HASPIEL
"AN ENGAGING GRAPHIC NOVEL... UNFLINCHING... POWERFUL."
—THE NEW YORK TIMES

THE ALCOHOLIC: 10th Anniversary Expanded Edition

Deluxe Softcover, 144 Pages
$19.99 ◊ ISBN 978-1-50670-808-9

The heartbreaking yet hilarious tale of a boozed-up, sexually confused, hopelessly romantic writer who careens from one off-kilter encounter to another in a mad search for himself.

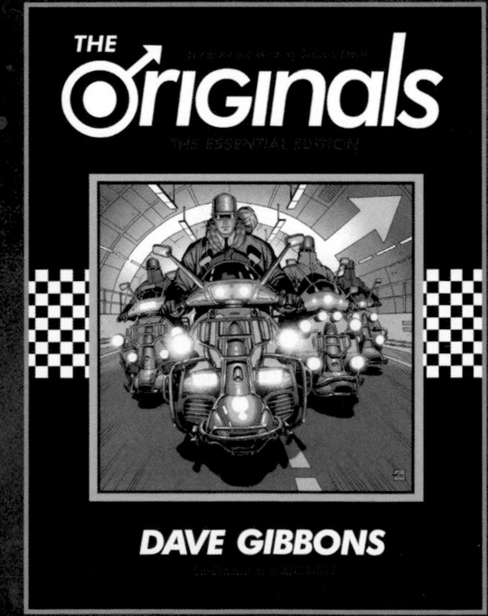

THE Originals
DAVE GIBBONS

THE ORIGINALS: The Essential Edition

Hardcover, 192 Pages
$29.99 ◊ ISBN 978-1-50670-562-0

An oversized new edition of this Eisner Award–winning story, now with additional material including a large sketchbook section.

In a retro-futuristic city, two childhood friends join the toughest, most stylish gang around—but their dreams are dashed when deadly violence changes their lives.

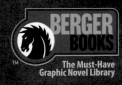

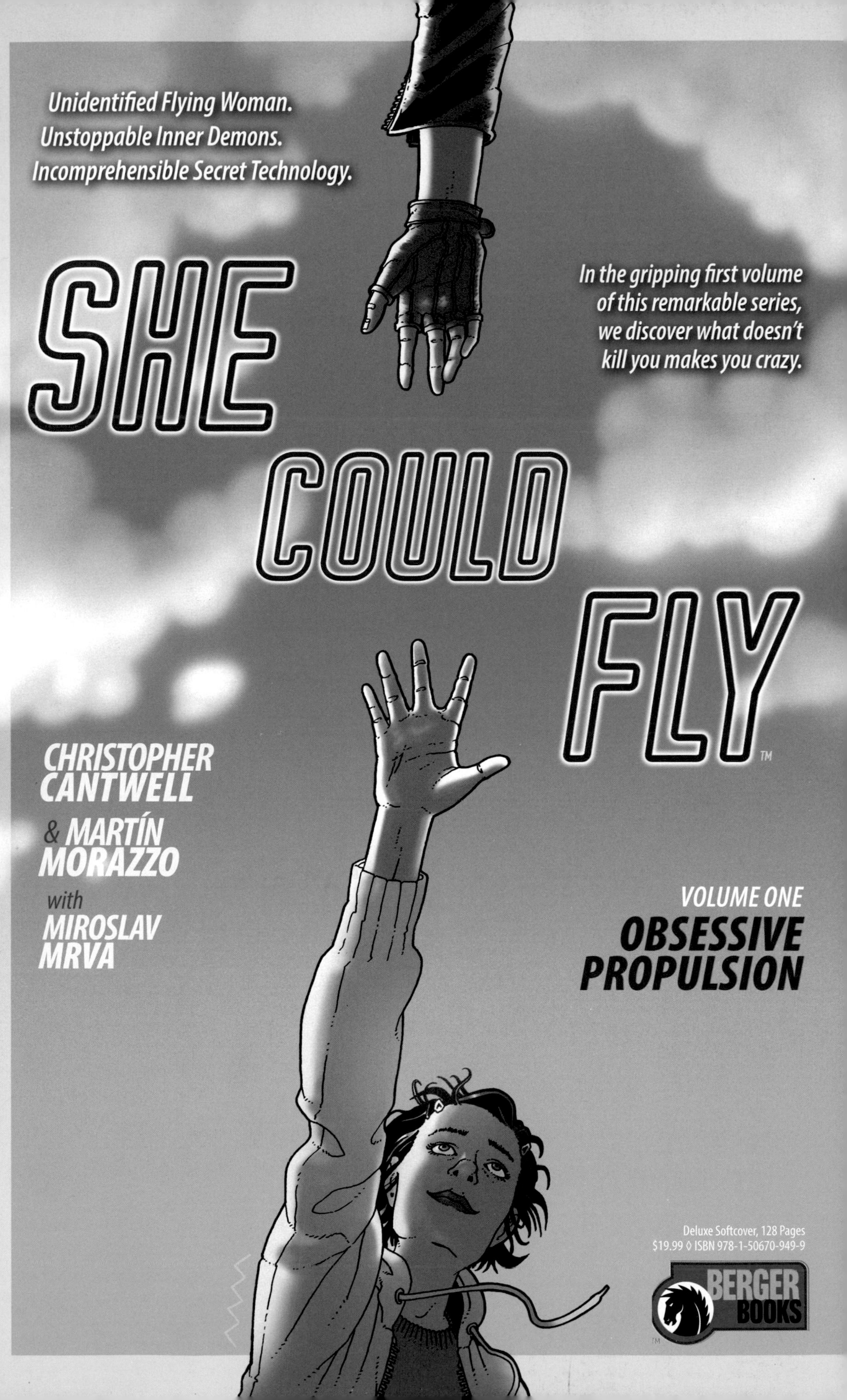

Unidentified Flying Woman.
Unstoppable Inner Demons.
Incomprehensible Secret Technology.
SHE COULD FLY™
In the gripping first volume of this remarkable series, we discover what doesn't kill you makes you crazy.
CHRISTOPHER CANTWELL & MARTÍN MORAZZO with MIROSLAV MRVA
VOLUME ONE
OBSESSIVE PROPULSION
Deluxe Softcover, 128 Pages
$19.99 ◊ ISBN 978-1-50670-949-9
BERGER BOOKS